AT THE ALTAR OF WALL STREET

At the Altar of Wall Street

*The Rituals, Myths, Theologies, Sacraments,
and Mission of the Religion Known
as the Modern Global Economy*

Scott W. Gustafson

WILLIAM B. EERDMANS PUBLISHING COMPANY
GRAND RAPIDS, MICHIGAN / CAMBRIDGE, U.K.

OCT 14 2015

PROPERTY OF
SENECA COLLEGE
LIBRARIES
NEWNHAM CAMPUS

© 2015 Scott W. Gustafson
All rights reserved

Published 2015 by
Wm. B. Eerdmans Publishing Co.
2140 Oak Industrial Drive N.E., Grand Rapids, Michigan 49505 /
P.O. Box 163, Cambridge CB3 9PU U.K.

Printed in the United States of America

21 20 19 18 17 16 15   7 6 5 4 3 2 1

Library of Congress Cataloging-in-Publication Data

Gustafson, Scott W.
At the altar of Wall Street: the rituals, myths, theologies, sacraments, and mission
of the religion known as the modern global economy / Scott W. Gustafson.
    pages   cm
Includes bibliographical references and index.
ISBN 978-0-8028-7280-7 (pbk.: alk. paper)
1. Economics — Religious aspects.   I. Title.

HB72.G873   2015
330.9 — dc23

2015013108

www.eerdmans.com

To
Brenda Lange-Gustafson,
whose presence
enriches life

Contents

Contents

Preface

After years of studying religion, teaching theology, and leading Christian congregations, I opened an online trading account using what little money I had available at the time. I won't say that I was the first to trade online, but I often tell people that my account number was 87. In any case, because of the priming of my theological education, I began to see the religious aspects of Wall Street and The Economy.

My first insight came through the act of investing itself. I found that I was reasonably good at selecting stocks to buy, but I was not so good when it came to selling them. Either I would sell too soon, losing out on tremendous gains to the upside (an early investment in Apple comes to mind here), or I would hang onto a stock while it rose and then fell, selling it only when I had lost much of my original investment. In short, I was subject to the emotions of fear and greed that they say move The Market. I realized that good investors develop virtues that enable them to resist these emotions, and these virtues are remarkably similar to the cardinal virtues of prudence, courage, and temperance described by Aristotle and practiced in medieval monasteries. To paraphrase Aristotle, virtues are actions or attitudes necessary to achieve a desired goal. I clearly saw that the goals of investors and the goals of monks are quite different. But the virtues necessary to achieve their respective goals are remarkably similar, if not the same.

I began watching CNBC business news nearly every day, and I noticed a recurring dialog around the words and actions of the Federal Reserve (FED) Chair. In the early days, CNBC would film FED Chair Alan Greenspan as he walked from his office to the bi-monthly Federal Reserve Board meeting held in a building across the street. (If I am not mistaken,

CNBC often played the song "Mister Big Stuff" as he walked.) Mark Haines (d. 2011), the anchor of *Squawk Box,* CNBC's morning show, began to look for what he called "The Briefcase Indicator." Through this predicting device, based on the thickness of Greenspan's briefcase, he tried to divine if the Federal Reserve Board would raise or lower interest rates.

I suspect this was a little tongue-in-cheek, but it reflects the continued penchant of economic "experts" to parse the words and actions of the Federal Reserve Chair in their efforts to divine the mysteries of our economic future. Most recently this effort involves "serious" discussions centering on "vital" economic questions such as these: When will the Federal Reserve start (or stop) "tapering"? Will the word "patience" be removed from the FED's minutes? (and, at this moment) When will the FED finally raise interest rates? Whatever the topic of the moment, however, these experts always bemoan that fact that the FED is not "transparent" enough, and, as a consequence, there is "uncertainty" about our economic future. There always seems to be an underlying suspicion that our economic officials actually know more than they are letting on, and we unenlightened ones are left in the unfortunate position of scrutinizing their pronouncements as if they were religious oracles or densely reasoned papal encyclicals.

Through investing I also achieved "spiritual" ecstasies of the sort that I never quite felt through more traditional religious experiences. The events that occasioned this euphoria happened on three occasions when I actually made more money than my yearly salary in the first fifteen minutes of trading. Now, in saying this, I know I may have upset those who think that such matters should not be discussed. It's simply not good form to discuss money in public. (It's almost like I've broken a religious taboo, isn't it?) So in repentance I'll also say that I lost all or most of these gains. Sometimes losses happened over time, but on occasion they occurred in the blink of an eye. I once lost a huge sum of money when a stock in which I was heavily invested dropped 70 percent before the market opened. "What The Market giveth, The Market taketh away" (see Job 1:21). Nonetheless, even staggering losses did not diminish the feeling of religious ecstasy I felt when — through The Market's goodness, grace, and bounty — I received great riches. Even in traditional religions such ecstasy does not last. But it is remembered, and many religious adherents spend a lifetime trying to re-create such experiences.

A prejudice of my particular brand of theological education was that the rational ought to take precedence over the emotional or ecstatic. As a consequence I was primed to view these matters more rationally. This I did with the help of many profound thinkers. An article by Harvey Cox, "The Market as God," helped me see that we grant The Market the same qualities — omniscience, benevolence, and omnipotence — that Christians attribute to the biblical God. Another article by Buddhist David Loy expressed the view that economics provides the same function in our culture that religions provide in others, a theme I develop in this book. Economist Robert Nelson's book titled *Economics as Religion* demonstrated that the debates among modern capitalist economists greatly resemble the debates among Christian theologians. These scholars, and others, helped me unravel the all-encompassing religious worldview expressed by our global market economy.

One personal by-product of my fascination with Wall Street and the Economy is the fact that my oldest son, Matthew, developed an interest in economics and finance as well. While he was in business school studying for his doctorate in finance, I noticed (prompted by Nelson's writing) the remarkable similarities between business schools and Christian seminaries — at least those I attended and in which I taught. I will discuss these observations in the text that follows, but what I wanted to point out here is that Matthew now teaches finance in a well-known business school, and he has read this manuscript and offered some important and helpful comments. He doesn't agree with everything I've written, but I'm surprised by some of the things with which he does agree.

Mark Shoepfle and Ron Rude read the entire manuscript in its early stages, and they will never know the magnitude of their service to this project. Mark prompted me to improve the end, and Ron did the same for the beginning. Without their help, readers would have had to work much harder trying to discover the focus and the implications of this book. As usual, my wife, Brenda Lange-Gustafson, contributed mightily to the project. Her editorial advice and demand for clarity set a high standard. If you approach her standards, you have written well. Gregory Gustafson provided technical assistance whenever I needed it. Whenever I have a problem involving technology, he just fixes it.

This book simply would not have been published without the help and encouragement of Norman Hjelm, who read the manuscript and graciously brought it to the attention of Bill Eerdmans, whom I also thank for agreeing to publish it. I also want to thank my editors, David Cottingham, Mary Hietbrink, and Linda Bieze, as well as David Bratt, who, in consultation with Mary, recommended the book's main title: *At the Altar of Wall Street.*

Introduction

*A god is that to which we look for all good and in which we find
refuge in every time of need. . . . That to which your heart clings
and entrusts itself is, I say, really your God.*

Martin Luther, Large Catechism

Socrates was wrong. He thought a person must first correctly define "The
Good" before he or she could actually be good. Before someone can act
justly, Socrates believed it necessary to articulate what justice is. Socrates
believed this about all things. He would argue that religion or economics
must first be defined before they can be known.

This book takes the opposite approach. People engage in practices
like religion and economics long before the words for these practices are
even invented, much less defined. We did not first define religion and then
act religiously. We acted religiously and then rationalized our behavior.
The same is true of economics. We produced, distributed, and consumed
goods and services long before we specifically defined such practices as
economic. Engagement always has historical priority over definition, and
our spoken definitions and rules never completely convey the practice.
Expert practitioners will always "know more than they can tell."[1] Articulated, philosophical knowledge will never take precedence over any
human practice. This is true from carpentry to science to economics to

---

1. Michael Polanyi, *Personal Knowledge: Towards a Post-Critical Philosophy* (Chicago: University of Chicago Press, 1962, 1974), particularly pp. 69-243.

1

religion. *Those intimately engaged in any human practice will always have unspoken knowledge about the practice that cannot completely be conveyed in spoken form.* This is why a chef's recipe will not turn out in the same, succulent way if someone else does the cooking. There is something unspoken in the chef's art. Our definitions and rules will always depend on the unarticulated, lived-in knowledge of practitioners.

This observation about human knowledge allows me to dispense with the common practice of defining economics and religion before discussing their similarities. In fact, I will assume that we generally know what religious and economic practices are. Perhaps on occasion we might be wrong, but generally speaking we know what religion is and what economics is because we first engage in them. Moreover, when we describe religious and economic practices some curious patterns emerge. Much to our surprise, we find that Economics[2] functions in our culture as religions have functioned in other cultures. The reader must determine if this fact is enough to make Economics a full-blown religion. I think it does. Like all religions, Economics has its rituals, sacred places, and pilgrimage sites (Ch. 1); myths (Ch. 2); theologians, prophets, reformers, extremists, terrorists, and priests (Ch. 3); worship centers (Ch. 4); sacraments (Ch. 5); and, like Christianity and Islam, Economics even has a global mission (Ch. 6).[3]

---

2. I will capitalize words like Economics, The Economy, Capitalism, Socialism, and Economists when I am referring to them as a religion; otherwise, they will not be capitalized.

3. This is hardly the first time the religious aspects of Economics have been observed. Economists have done so in the past, but they tend to identify their opponents as religious and count themselves scientists. See Karl Marx, *The Poverty of Philosophy* (1847), ch. 2.1, Marxist.org; Joseph A. Schumpeter, *Capitalism, Socialism and Democracy* (New York: Harper, 1942, 1992), pp. 5ff. Likewise, religious thinkers have observed the similarities between Economics and religion. (Christian) Harvey Cox, "The Market as God," *The Atlantic Monthly,* March 1999; and (Buddhist) David Loy, "Religion and the Market," in *The Religious Consultation on Population, Reproductive Health and Ethics* (1997), www.religiousconsultation.org/loy.htm, are illustrative. Contemporary economists Robert Nelson, *Economics as Religion: From Samuelson to Chicago and Beyond* (University Park: Penn State Press, 2001, 2006), takes this observation further still, and his insightful book contributes mightily to this project. He goes beyond most in recognizing the religious aspects of all economic debates, but his extremely valuable considerations, for the most part, pertain to Economic theology, the Economic priesthood, and Economic myths. Religions also involve rituals, places of worship, pilgrimage sites, sacraments, and religious missions. These will also be included in this study with respect to the religion called Economics.

> Economics is our religion because it functions in our culture as religions have functioned in other cultures.

Since we engage in religion and economics long before we develop our theories, rituals and myths are more fundamental than our doctrines. In fact these rituals and myths give religious and Economic doctrines their content.[4] Contrary to conventional wisdom, our rituals and myths are extremely influential *precisely because* they are pre-rational. We "live-in" our myths and rituals long before we are critical of them. Often they are not recognized as ritual or myth at all. We simply believe these practices are the only possible way to act and live. But when we fail to note that Economics is a religion, these pre-rational rituals and myths undermine our knowledge of economic matters. Their unexamined sacred status prevents their careful scrutiny, and has had some disastrous political and social consequences. As religious fanatics confuse their theological propositions with the mind of God itself, our modern politicians and policymakers often cling to competing Economic theories as if they also expressed the absolute mind of God. When this happens, our politicians and policymakers resemble religious terrorists who stand ready to kill and destroy rather than abandon principles they falsely believe are divinely ordained.[5] Understanding how Economics functions as a religion and how The Economy functions as a God is the

4. George Lindbeck, *The Nature of Doctrine: Religion and Theology in a Postliberal Age* (Philadelphia: Westminster Press, 1984).

5. Mark Juergensmeyer, *Terror in the Mind of God: The Global Rise of Religious Violence* (Berkeley: University of California Press, 2000), demonstrates this phenomenon. From Buddhism to Christianity to Judaism to Islam, those who believe that theological doctrines spring from the mind of God equate faithfulness to these doctrines with religious faithfulness. As a consequence, these doctrines often cause or justify acts of carnage in the name of their deity. By the same token, those who believe that Economic doctrines are straight from the mind of God or, perhaps more often, a reflection of nature itself, sometimes commit atrocities in the name of Economic theories. The death-dealing dynamics of such radical Economic thought and practice will be discussed in Chapter 4. For now the Cold War might be used as an example of the potential threat of the "religious extremism" of Economic theory. During the Cold War, two "denominations" of the religion we are calling Economics, Communism and Capitalism, stood ready to destroy the world largely in the service of their Economic theologies.

first step in addressing many of the political and social problems we currently face.

The Intimate Relationship between Religion and Economics

The agricultural revolution began an intimate relationship between religion and economics that has persisted throughout civilization.[6] To understand this relationship, one must recognize that the agricultural revolution was not just about farming. Of almost equal importance, the agricultural revolution was also a revolution in the way we think about food. For the first time, food became a commodity. It was owned. It was "bought and sold."[7] Before the agricultural revolution, food was no more bought and sold than the air we breathe. In the hunter-gatherer bands that preceded the agricultural revolution, food may have been given by one person to another in the hope and trust that the action might one day be reciprocated. Food may also have been given to enhance the giver's prestige, but the giving of food was seldom a quick *quid pro quo* market exchange. Since food was not yet a commodity, such reciprocity always took time. Civilization's intimate relationship between religion and economics is a consequence of food — a universal necessity for life — becoming a commodity.

Because food became a commodity long before the existence of money, the "owners" of food had to establish criteria to determine who merits food and who does not. These criteria differed from one place to the next because those in control of the food supply valued different things. What we now call morality emerged as a consequence. As it now stands, the universal function of morality is to draw the line between good and evil.[8] Morality — drawing the moral divide between good and evil — began when those in control of the food supply developed crite-

---

6. Civilization is neither an unqualified good nor an evil. In this book it refers to one way humans have ordered their cultures. Today it is the dominant way, but *Homo sapiens* lived in social configurations other than civilization for at least 150,000 years.

7. Daniel Quinn, *Beyond Civilization: Humanity's Next Great Adventure* (New York: Three Rivers Press, 1999), pp. 29-54, is the source of the extremely important idea of the agricultural revolution's centrality in civilization's formation. He examines the implications of the agricultural revolution in three philosophical novels: *Ishmael* (New York: Bantam/Turner, 1992), *My Ishmael* (New York: Bantam, 1997), and *The Story of B* (New York: Bantam, 1996).

8. Enrique Dussel, *Ethics and Community* (Maryknoll, NY: Orbis Books, 1984), pp. 49, 50.

ria establishing who merits food and who does not. If people knew that this divide was of human design, they might have disregarded these moral standards and abandoned agricultural societies. Religious leaders largely prevented this. Through rituals and myths, religious leaders sanctified the arbitrary moral criteria and served emerging civilization by convincing most of the population that the standards designed for food distribution were not arbitrary human standards. Instead, these moral standards were of divine origin and synonymous with reality itself. As such, resistance became unthinkable.[9]

> **Economics concerns all things related to the production, distribution, and consumption of goods and services. Until very recently, religions, not the market, sanctioned and justified the distribution of goods and services.**

To complete this sketch of the intimate relationship between economics and religion, all one needs to note is that the production and distribution of goods and services is the fundamental concern of economics. While people differed on *how* these goods and services should be produced and distributed, all economic *theories* concern the "proper" production and distribution of goods and services. And, until very recently, religions sanctioned and justified the production, distribution, and consumption of goods and services within a given civilization.

Eventually two sorts of people emerged from the agricultural revolution. The smaller group controlled the food supply and used its control of the food supply to subject the larger group who depended on them for their food. Today we would probably call the dominant smaller group "creditors" and the larger subordinate group "debtors." Religions sanctified and interpreted this new social relationship. Using religious myths and rituals, religious leaders claimed that both the well-fed creditors and the hungry debtors owed their status to a divine decree. Revolt was almost unthinkable, and in the rare instances where revolt or desertion came to mind, it was often deemed impossible because rejection of the social order meant the rejection of the divine order.

---

9. Scott W. Gustafson, *Behind Good and Evil: How to Overcome the Death-dealing Character of Morality* (West Conshohocken, PA: Infinity Press, 2009), pp. 30-62.

Even though our modern religions — Buddhism, Judaism, Christianity, and Islam — all tried to lessen in some way the crushing severity of debt, they continue to equate salvation with the elimination of debt.[10] Jesus himself prayed, "Forgive us our debts as we forgive our debtors" in the Lord's Prayer. Buddhists uncritically adopted the Hindu notion of *karma,* which is no more or less than an accounting ledger that follows a particular self or soul from one life to the next. Christians have a doctrine of original sin, which maintains that we are somehow in debt to God from birth — a debt we are incapable of repaying. Chapter 7 argues that the major world religions all uncritically adopt the centrality of the creditor/debtor relationship in their theologies and practices, and each offers its own particular version of salvation based upon its own particular version of debt. In other words, all post-agricultural religions presuppose some version of the creditor/debtor relationship. Since this relationship is central to Economics, the intimate relationship between Economics and religion is disclosed once again.

But this intimate relationship is now changing. To put it a bit too anthropomorphically, Economics wants to divorce religion. Indeed, Economics now needs no religious justification, and the historical relationship between Economics and other religions is almost completely severed. Economics now stands alone. It no longer needs religious sanction. It no longer needs the support of a religion because Economics is itself a full-blown religion. Economics can justify itself.

The Divorce of Economics and Religion

The 1776 publication of Adam Smith's *Wealth of Nations* began the separation of Economics from its religious underpinnings. Adam Smith (1723-1790) was not concerned with the wealth of individuals. He was concerned with the wealth of nations, and he thought he had discovered the mechanisms whereby a given nation can increase its aggregate wealth. He believed that when each individual is allowed to act in his or her own economic self-interest, unimpaired by restrictions of government, morality, custom, family, or religion, the aggregate wealth of the nation will inevita-

10. David Graeber, *Debt: The First 5000 Years* (Brooklyn, NY: Melville House Publishing, 2011), p. 13.

bly increase.[11] For the first time, economics — that is, all things related to the production, consumption, and distribution of goods and services — was explained apart from religion. As a matter of fact, Smith argued that the religious judgments *undermined* the natural functioning of economics itself. This began Economics' divorce from religion.

Other economists followed with similar "natural" explanations of economic phenomena. In *Essay on Population,* Thomas Malthus (1766-1834) asserted that the vast majority of people will always live in poverty because populations always increase to a subsistence level permitted by the food supply. In like manner, David Ricardo (1772-1823) proposed an "Iron Law of Wages," which stated that labor's wages could only rise to a level that would "subsist and perpetuate their race."[12] Since these dire predictions were deemed facts of nature, Malthus and Ricardo reinforced and extended Adam Smith's effort to understand economics apart from religion. In the past, one god or another justified the manner in which a given society chose to distribute its goods and services. Smith, Malthus, and Ricardo began a process that would free Economics from its need for religious justification.

Like his economic predecessors, Karl Marx (1818-1883) also rejected the religious support for economics, but he kept a Christian template for his theories. Christian theology generally held that sin dominates the world, but, in the end of days, God will restore it to its proper state through an apocalyptic event. Marx removed sin and God from this template. He substituted human alienation for human sin, and he substituted the revolution of the proletariat for the apocalypse. Like Christians, Marx believed that his scenario was inevitable, but Marx's scenario would be accomplished by an inevitable "scientific" unfolding of history rather than the inevitable intervention of a transcendent God.

American economic theory was built upon a different Christian template called the Social Gospel Movement. This movement asserted that evil in the form of poverty could be eliminated on earth because of the perfectibility of human nature. The American Economic Association (AEA) was founded by members of the Christian Social Gospel Movement who saw no conflict between their Christian faith and economics

---

11. Adam Smith, *The Wealth of Nations* (New York: Bantam Books, 2003), p. 572.

12. David Ricardo's October 9, 1820, letter to Thomas Malthus as quoted by John Maynard Keynes, *The General Theory of Employment, Interest and Money* (Lexington, KY: BN Publishing, 2008), p. 4, n. 1.

because both tried to discern the *laws of progress* that God had planned for in creation. Economics merely tries to make use of these laws for the betterment of humanity. But American Economists soon came to understand economic progress apart from God and religion. Like Marx, they removed God from their discussions, but maintained a theological template for their economic theories. Progress, instead of God, became the power behind the unfolding of history.[13] They continued to understand history in the same linear way all Abrahamic religions understand it. History progresses from a humble origin to a glorious consummation, but in Economics human innovation, not God, is history's driving force.

Now many understandably argue that the divorce of economics from religion is indicative of secularism — the process whereby sectors of society and culture are removed from the domination of religious symbols and religious institutions. We observe secularism's effects in arts, philosophy, literature, and the rise of science as autonomous enterprises.[14] But, in fact, secularism has many religious qualities. Like all religions, secularism affects the totality of culture. The arts, philosophy, literature, and music express a secular worldview. Like any religion, secularism seeks to be a complete way of life. Moreover, secularism is inextricably bound to the modern Global Economy. *It is a historical fact that secularism is always the by-product of an expanding industrial economy.* Wherever the industrial economy expands, secularism is never far behind.[15] And, in a day and age where calling something religious diminishes its status, secularism may only be a convenient word we use to hide the religious status of Economics while granting Economics the authority a dominant religion once had over its civilization. Finally, it is precisely because secularism is in fact an all-encompassing religious worldview, that dominant religions from Christianity to Islam to Buddhism to Taoism have always opposed secularism whenever the expanding industrial Economy led to its creation. *Whereas Economics and secularism may not understand themselves to be a religion, all other religions have recognized secularism and Economics to be a religious rival.* In fact, most religions treat secularism and Economics as a religious threat until Economics becomes the dominant religion. When this happens, these once-dominant religions either become culturally in-

---

13. Nelson, *Economics as Religion,* pp. 41, 42.

14. Peter L. Berger, *The Sacred Canopy: Elements of a Sociological Theory of Religion* (New York: Random House, 1967, 1990), p. 107.

15. Berger, *Sacred Canopy,* p. 109.

consequential or accommodate themselves to Economics and its versions of art, literature, philosophy, rationality, and life.

Economics functions in our current global culture as religions have functioned in other cultures. It has rituals and pilgrimage sites (Ch. 1). It has myths and narratives that give meaning to human life (Ch. 2). It has priests, theologians, reformers, extremists, and terrorists (Ch. 3). It perpetuates a worldview that, like every religious worldview, seems synonymous with reason itself. Economics has places like churches and mosques where people gather to serve their God and receive benefits from their God (Ch. 4). Economics has sacraments (Ch. 5), and it even has a global mission — we call it globalization — that like Christianity and Islam seeks to "evangelize" the world (Ch. 6). Some may hesitate to call Economics a religion because it does not believe in a transcendent deity, but Buddhism and Hinduism may not have a transcendent deity either. Indeed, many Buddhists say that Buddhism does not have a god at all. This is why it is worth returning to the quotation from Martin Luther with which we began these introductory remarks. There Luther described a god subjectively, saying, "a god is that to which we look for all good and in which we find refuge in every time of need. . . . That to which your heart clings and entrusts itself is, I say, really your God."[16] For many, the benefits we receive from The Economy *truly are* "that to which we look for all good and in which we find refuge in every time of need." This being so, The Economy is our God and Economics is a religion. It is the goal of this book to describe how Economics functions as a religion in our emerging global culture.

16. Martin Luther, *Large Catechism*, in *The Book of Concord: The Confessions of the Evangelical Lutheran Church,* trans. and ed. Theodore G. Tappert (Philadelphia: Fortress Press, 1959), p. 365.

CHAPTER 1

Economic Rituals

*Each day on Wall Street begins with a simple liturgy. A presider
. . . stands at a podium and rings a bell. For the next eight hours
exchanges occur that determine the well-being of the market for
that day that bring either hope or despair to the participants
in the ritual. This experience of a bull-market "heaven" or a
bear-market "hell" is indistinguishable in effect from revivalist
experiences of being "saved" or "damned." A simple economic
exchange becomes something "more" than that within the ritual
parameters of the Wall Street market. The day ends, of course,
exactly as it began: with a ritual ringing of a bell. The stock
market is the soul of capitalism, and capitalism is the soul of the
nation.*

Jon Pahl, *Shopping Malls and Other Sacred Places*[1]

The Power and Function of Ritual

Human life is replete with rituals. We don't think about them much. We
just participate. We uncritically believe our rituals are synonymous with
reality itself. Our Economic rituals hold such power over us. We rarely
think about them, we seldom see an alternative to them. As such they
have a strong hold over our lives.

---

1. Jon Pahl, *Shopping Malls and Other Sacred Places: Putting God in Place* (Eugene,
OR: Wipf & Stock, 2008), p. 68.

> Rituals are the social grammar that provides each person with a defined place and status within family, community, and public life.

Confucius (551-479 BCE) was the first person to understand the power of ritual *(li)*. Over two thousand years before modern sociologists began to discuss ritual, Confucius described ritual *(li)* as objective prescriptions of human behavior that bind human beings together. Rituals are meaning-invested roles, activities, relationships, and institutions that foster communication and create a sense of community between diverse people. Rituals include all formal conduct from table manners to greeting employers or employees. Weddings and funerals are obviously rituals. Others, like public transactions between strangers, are less obvious but they are rituals nevertheless. Rituals are the social grammar that provides each person with a defined place and status within family, community, and public life. Rituals help transmit meaning from one generation to the next. They help the values of a culture persist through time.[2]

One of Confucius' most important observations is that rituals modify human behavior in ways far more powerful than direct commands or written rules because commands and rules always bring to mind the possibility of doing otherwise. There is no obvious alternative to a ritual. A person either participates or refrains from participation. Participation creates harmony. But, for the individual, refusing to participate often has severe social consequences. For example, it is risky for a person to remain seated during the National Anthem when it is played at a sporting event. Threats and violence could be directed at such a person because such public refusal to engage in any ritual creates disharmony. But, once engaged in a ritual, doing is believing, and, quite often, we perform our rituals without conscious reflection.[3]

The power inherent in ritual is most obvious when we feel uncertain, anxious, or impotent. At such times rituals provide "patterns of predictability" that create an illusion of control over the uncontrollable

---

2. Roger Ames and Henry Rosemont, Jr., "Introduction to the Analects of Confucius," *The Analects of Confucius* (New York: Random House, 1998), p. 51.

3. Peter Winn, "Legal Ritual," in *Readings in Ritual Studies,* ed. Ronald L. Grimes (Upper Saddle River, NJ: Prentice Hall, 1996), p. 559.

powers that confront us.[4] In his classic novel *The Sleepwalkers,* Hermann Broch artfully describes ritual's power in his account of a funeral's ability to transform the horror of death into the mundane.

> . . . he went slowly over and touched the black-draped wall, felt under the gloomy hangings the picture-frames and the frame of the case where the Iron Cross hung, and this refound fragment of actuality transformed death in a novel and almost exciting way into a matter of drapery, accommodating almost cheerfully the fact that Helmuth in his coffin, decked with all his flowers, had been introduced into this room like a new piece of furniture, thus once more reducing the incomprehensible so radically to the comprehensible, the certain and the assured that the experience of these few minutes — or had they been seconds? — passed over into a soothing feeling of quiet confidence.[5]

Economic rituals provide this same transformative function. The Economy threatens us with uncertainty, disorder, abject poverty, and death. What will we do if the stock market collapses? How will we survive hyperinflation? Will our children be better off than we are? How can I put food on the table? Will I have a job tomorrow? In times of crisis as well as normalcy, our economic rituals transform the incomprehensible and uncertain into the comprehensible and certain.

When an Economic crisis ensues, the President appears before the American flag and other symbols of state in the ritual attire we call a business suit. If the crisis is great, he will also be surrounded by other appropriately clad men and (some) women we believe to be experts. These experts function as Priests of the Economy whose religious sanction is always needed by political rulers. These men and women stand behind the President to assure us that the President is not "shooting from the hip." Experts are in control. Order will soon arise from the chaos of the moment. We are told that we need not be anxious. The crisis is under control. As a matter of fact, we are told that some of the people on the stage actually predicted and expected this disaster and are "ahead of the curve" in protecting us because, in their wisdom, they "saw it coming."

---

4. Barbara G. Meyerhoff, "Death in Due Time: Construction of Self and Culture in Ritual Drama," in *Readings in Ritual Studies,* p. 395.

5. Hermann Broch, *The Sleepwalkers,* trans. Willa and Edwin Muir (New York: Random House, 1996), p. 42.

The ritual of words, postures, and symbols turns the uncertain into the certain, the unpredictable into the predictable, and the incomprehensible into the comprehensible.

The media also provides us ritualistic certainty during difficult times. The wild drop in the stock market is "explained" by Hungary's skyrocketing interest rates or online shopping. Media experts tell us to remain calm. They say that this drop is a "necessary correction" to a market that "got ahead of itself." The more intrepid tell us that we should use this as a "buying opportunity" because we will never see prices this low again! The closing bell rings (not the only liturgy in which a bell or a gong rings). The traders applaud. They go in peace to serve their God. The Market rituals have conveyed the certainty that this extraordinary and frightening event is actually normal and that everything is under control and explainable. It doesn't really matter what the explanations are. It does not matter if the explanations are consistent with reality. It does not matter if they make sense. All that matters is that there is an explanation.

Explanation rituals operate even if there is nothing to be explained. Sometimes we hear of the Dow Jones Industrial Average dropping by .02 percent on a volume of 1 billion shares. Our experts (or are they really our priests?) even offer their explanations for this non-event by citing something like a lukewarm consumer report or a rise in Latvian interest rates. Such obviously ridiculous pronouncements are important rituals because they create the belief that someone understands even the minutest details behind the millions of decisions surrounding the stock market each day. Explanations of non-events are very important economic rituals. They are conducted so that when a crisis does occur, we will be primed to believe in and perhaps even be comforted by the explanations that once more transform the incomprehensible into the comprehensible, the certain, and the assured.

Rituals have the unique ability to convince us of the unbelievable.[6] Their ordered and repetitive characteristics suggest that order and meaning triumph over disorder and meaninglessness. Since many believe that the Market stands between us and the unbridled forces of scarcity, disorder, poverty, and death, we have developed economic rituals to protect us from these threats. We do so by introducing the regularity of ritual into the irregularity of market transactions, and we strive to "save ourselves" by so doing. If one reflects on the unspoken assumptions behind our ritu-

6. Meyerhoff, "Death in Due Time," p. 395.

als, the unspoken claims our rituals make may appear quite dubious; however, we normally do not reflect on our rituals. We participate in them long before we reflect upon them. Such unreflecting participation is the source of ritual's power.

Economic Rituals That Revive Our God, The Economy

The ancient Babylonians had an interesting creation myth. They believed that before the earth and Babylonia were created, there were many gods. There were male gods and female gods. There were older gods and younger gods. The older gods had a problem. The younger gods were rambunctious. They were making too much noise. Tiamat, the mother of all the gods, decided that the only way to achieve peace and quiet was to kill all the young gods. The young gods heard of the plan and were terrified, but Marduk saw this as an opportunity. He told his siblings that he would kill Tiamat, but, in exchange, the surviving gods had to recognize him as supreme. Marduk's siblings agreed, and Marduk killed Tiamat. From her body he formed the earth, and he created the Babylonian people to serve Marduk and the rest of the gods.

The Babylonians understood that they owed their lives and their great empire to Marduk, but they never quite believed that Tiamat had been completely dispatched. This posed some rather difficult problems because the earth had been fashioned out of Tiamat's body. If Tiamat were somehow alive, chaos was a threat to the world's order. Moreover, each year life became dormant. Crops did not grow. The soil did not seem to work as it did during the last growing season. The Babylonians attributed this to the reemergence of Tiamat's chaotic presence. To make matters worse, Marduk did not seem to be paying attention! Maybe he was asleep!

The Babylonians held a yearly, five-day-long religious ritual in response to their dire situation. Its purpose was to revive Marduk so he could dispatch Tiamat once again. Evidently this annual ritual worked. Shortly after the five-day ritual, crops started growing, and the Babylonian people thought they were secure for another year. Tiamat's threat remained, but the Babylonians continued to meet the threat with another annual religious festival. The purpose of this yearly ritual was simple. It was performed to *revive(!)* their God Marduk.

Now we moderns are obviously more sophisticated than those superstitious Babylonians. We firmly believe that we do not need such rituals; for we do not have any gods to revive. Nonetheless, we unwittingly participate in a similar yearly ritual. Every year on the day after Thanksgiving, rotund, bearded men dressed in red snowsuits descend on every shopping mall in the United States inaugurating the thirty-day buying frenzy we call the Holiday Shopping Season. Throughout this month, a curious narrative always develops. Economists will calculate and journalists will report statistics like the amount of money the average shopper will spend during the holiday season. They predict whether the average consumer will spend more or less this year than last year, and they will ask if the holiday bargains offered by the retail industry will ultimately hurt profits. One question dominates. "Will this year's buying activity be enough to *revive* The Economy?" Like the Babylonian rituals attempted to *revive* their God Marduk, our Economic Christmas rituals are performed to *revive* The Economy.

The more money that is spent in this holiday ritual, the greater is the revival of The Economy. No one is commanded to participate in this buying frenzy, but the social consequences of nonparticipation are immense. Perhaps a family man might survive if he refused to buy gifts for his wife and children, but the holiday season is not simply about giving gifts. It also involves receiving gifts. This same man's business or job would be undermined if he refused to accept gifts. Since a Christmas party is actually a gift from the one giving the party, absolute nonparticipation means refusing party invitations as well. Once again such nonparticipation would undermine a person's business, social status, and employment. It borders on the antisocial. As a consequence, we comply, and The Economy benefits from our compliance whether we like it or not. This is the strength and power of The Economy's social ritual we call the Holiday Shopping Season, and it is done to revive The Economy. Its purpose is the same as that of the ancient Babylonian ritual. Both rituals are intended to revive our respective Gods.

Economic Rituals That Transform Citizens into Consumers

Not only do Economic rituals seek, with some success, to revive The Economy, certain rituals seek to shape us into the sort of beings that serve The Economy.

Advertisements are such rituals. Like many rituals, they are repetitive. As is the case with any liturgy, we know what to expect. As a lapsed

Catholic remembers the *Kyrie,* we remember "Ford has a better idea," "Winston tastes good like a cigarette should," and the embarrassment surrounding "ring around the collar." Advertising teaches us Economic hymns like the McDonald's hymn, "You deserve a break today; . . . so get up and get away; . . . to McDonald's." Since we know our advertisements by heart, we underestimate their hold on us. We think we can avoid them. During an ad, we go to the refrigerator or perhaps channel surf. Few people believe they are influenced by advertising. They are wrong.

Advertising tells young men that they will be magically irresistible to women if they use a particular body wash. Women are told that they can hold back the ravages of time if they use certain cosmetics. Energy drinks promise us more vitality and more efficient minds. Automobile ads promise to transform people from the middle class to upper class, and other ads promise that some vehicles will enable middle-aged men to attract younger women. Oil companies use advertising to transform themselves from polluters into environmental advocates. The list can be extended to pharmaceutical companies that pledge to give old men the sex drive of a nineteen-year-old and footwear companies suggesting that the answer to the plight of poor adolescents is an expensive pair of basketball shoes. We buy because we actually believe these magical claims. We believe with our bodies. We believe by doing. We believe when we buy. The question is, "Are we *really* transformed by these rituals?"

The answer depends on the nature of our transformation. Certainly very few young men are made irresistible to women by a body wash, and advertising's magic cannot transform an oil company into the Sierra Club. But advertising has transformed us into the type of person The Economy needs if It is to thrive. Advertising transforms us into consumers. Americans, in particular, have been changed from citizens into consumers.

> Advertising transforms us into consumers, the very sort of person The Economy needs if It is to thrive.

To even begin to understand advertising's power to transform, you must remember that advertisers are not engaged in a zero sum game. One company, like Coca-Cola, does not compete with a rival, like Pepsi, in a fixed, stable market where the growth of one company diminishes the other. Both companies benefit from market expansion. If Coke has a

50 percent market share, and the market doubles in size, Coke will sell 60 percent more product even if it only has 40 percent of the larger market.[7] The advertising of both Coke and Pepsi cooperate to promote such market expansion, and market expansion depends on increased consumer participation in the market.

To expand their markets, advertisers seldom employ direct, rational arguments. In the late 1950s Vance Packard coined the phrase "The Depth Approach" to describe how advertising works.[8] In general, advertisers do not want you to make a rational choice when you purchase a product. As is the case with all good rituals, advertisements seldom command. They merely suggest, and many of these suggestions are subliminal.[9]

Subliminal techniques work because human beings are only conscious of a small percentage of what is happening around them. But this does not mean that we are not influenced by the things of which we are unconscious. In fact, our subconscious mind greatly influences our behavior, emotions, and dispositions. The following example, unrelated to advertising, demonstrates the influence of the subconscious on our thoughts, feelings, and actions.

Throughout her life, a young woman has heard her loving parents say, "Honey, let me help you with that." They said this when she obviously needed help, and they said it when she did not need their help. They helped her with everything from making her bed to her school projects. In fact, all her parents ever wanted to do was help her, but the young woman's subconscious mind had a different interpretation. Her subconscious mind asked her why her parents thought she needed all this help. Did her parents think she was incapable of performing the most routine tasks on her own? This subconscious message began to dominate her life. Her unspoken interpretation of her parents' desire to help led to some very serious self-esteem issues. Her subconscious was in control, and alternatives to her belief that she was not good enough or competent enough to

7. This is simple arithmetic. If the market is one hundred units and Coke's share of the market is 50 percent, then Coke sells fifty units. If the market expands to two hundred units, and Coke's market share declines to 40 percent, Coke's 40 percent share of two hundred units is eighty instead of fifty. This means that Coke sold 60 percent more product in the expanded market (eighty units as opposed to fifty units) even though its market share decreased.

8. Vance Packard, *The Hidden Persuaders* (New York: Simon & Schuster, 1957, 1972), pp. 1-7.

9. Wilson Bryan Key, *Subliminal Seduction* (New York: Signet Paperback, 1974).

do anything could not be addressed until she could consciously express alternative interpretations for her parents' need to help her with everything. Advertising techniques *intentionally* try to influence our behavior in similar ways.

Advertisers encounter an important obstacle at this point. Returning to our young woman once again, many people do not develop self-esteem issues when their parents try to help them with everything. They might refuse the offered assistance. Others might accept it and quickly move on. Some might even try to get their parents to do all their work and have no self-esteem issues as a consequence. This is because individuals respond to subliminal stimuli in different ways.

Advertisers know this. Their approach is not random. They target a particular demographic or a personality type. For example, before Tiger Woods made golf popular among the masses, I wondered how golf could possibly be on TV. The ratings for golf tournaments were minuscule; yet, a network devotes seven to ten hours of programming to golf tournaments each weekend. The logic that escaped me is obvious to almost everyone now. Golf is a sport of rich men. Televised golf tournaments gather a demographic that can afford expensive cars, life insurance, or stock brokerage services. Few venues could attract such a demographic, so the companies promoting such products made sure golf tournaments remained on the air.

Advertisers discover a target group. They identify characteristics the group holds in common, and they develop their advertisements to influence the subconscious desires of the group in question. Wilson Key narrates how this is done with respect to the advertising of hard liquor. The target group is a relatively small group of people who drink at least two fifths of hard liquor each week. These people are directly responsible for the consumption of around 80 percent of the retail sales and indirectly responsible for another 10 percent of the sales (indirect sales are a consequence of the brands of heavy drinkers being purchased by their friends). Once the group is identified, advertisers discover certain psychological traits held by members of this group. As strange as it might appear, the advertisers think that heavy drinkers have a death wish, so hard liquor ads subliminally promise death.[10]

Promising death sounds absurd on a conscious level, but advertisers

10. Wilson Bryan Key, *The Clam-Plate Orgy and Other Subliminal Techniques for Manipulating Your Behavior* (New York: Signet Paperback, 1980), pp. 33-35.

operate on a subconscious level. On this level it is quite rational to assume that those directly responsible for the consumption of 80 percent of the retail sales in hard liquor may subconsciously desire death. It is quite likely that a large proportion of heavy drinkers consume alcohol "to escape from life's everyday pressures." Once you realize that the ultimate escape from life is death, the logic behind subliminally promising death to people who consume large quantities of hard liquor becomes clear. This subliminal promise of death is not a random, shotgun approach aimed at the entire population. It is a very specific "smart bomb" approach targeting a defined demographic with a specific psychological profile.

Advertisers define a target group. This group can be anything from children to heavy drinkers. They construct psychological profiles for the target group, and they design advertising campaigns to attack a group's psychological vulnerabilities. These techniques are rarely aimed at the conscious, rational minds of these groups. Indeed, the actual *appearance* of rationality in an advertisement is used to divert our attention so that we are less likely to notice the subliminal nature of the advertisement. Like an illusionist distracts his or her audience by directing its focus away from the trick, so advertising uses sex appeal or the appearance of rationality to misdirect attention from its subliminal message. These techniques sell everything from breakfast cereals to computers. They are responsible for creating our desires and turning our desires into perceived needs. In many ways advertising techniques have magically transformed nearly all Americans into the consumers we are. When we participate in advertising rituals, we are transformed into better specimens of our "true nature" — our "true nature" as The Economy understands it to be.

Our advertisements are so mundane and repetitive that they are boring, and this is also characteristic of a religious liturgy. But this is not the case all the time. Just as religious festivals make ordinary liturgy meaningful and exciting for believers, The Economy has its special times when advertising becomes the exciting focal point. There are the high festivals like Thanksgiving (a celebration of abundance), Christmas, and New Year. There are minor festivals like Valentine's Day, Mother's Day and Father's Day, and Halloween. But as far as advertising is concerned, one day stands out above all the rest. It is the High Holy Day of advertising. It is a day much more anticipated and with more national parties than any other day with the possible exception of New Year's Eve. The day is called Super Bowl Sunday! The other religions do not even bother trying to compete on this Sunday. Churches often close down their programs.

Weddings can only happen at half-time.[11] Super Bowl Sunday is the most important ritual in the United States. It unites everyone. Few people refrain from participation.

There is a very curious thing about Super Bowl Sunday. Not everyone who participates in the festivities is a football fan. Some could care less about the game itself, but nearly everyone wants to see the commercials. The boring advertisements that prompt our leaving the room or changing the channel during normal TV viewing now become our focus. We truly want to see the new ways that companies plan to sell us their products. The next day, sports news shows discuss the game. Everyone else discusses the company that created the best advertisement.

Someone once observed that before 1965 Americans were called citizens. After this date we were called consumers. This comment was not uttered in the context of the national ritual surrounding Super Bowl Sunday, but the date is significant. The first Super Bowl happened following the 1966 season. It may be that the Super Bowl ritual began our transformation from citizens into consumers. This transformation, largely created by our advertising rituals, is not without its consequences.

Religious rituals orient believers toward their respective deities by creating patterned behaviors that benefit the perpetuation of the religion in question. In her book *The Overworked American,* economist Juliet Schor notes that one such patterned behavior is the work-spend-work cycle. This cycle is created by consumers' insatiable desire for consumer goods which advertising rituals try to keep unsatisfied. The cycle begins when we work to buy goods we do not necessarily need, but desire, because of advertising.[12] Personal credit further augments the cycle because it allows us to spend quite a bit more money than we earn. The debt that is incurred handcuffs us to our jobs; for, no matter how boring, demanding, risky, or death-defying our job might be, it is very difficult to quit a job if the next six months of our salary has already been spent.[13]

---

11. A pastor friend of mine was in the home of a man when he died on Super Bowl Sunday. The family called the morgue to come and pick up the body at around 5:30 p.m. They said they would be "right over." Much to the chagrin of the man's family, they came five hours later and one-half hour after the Super Bowl concluded. In America, very little is allowed to interfere with the religious rituals surrounding the Super Bowl.

12. Juliet Schor, *The Overworked American: The Unexpected Decline of Leisure* (New York: HarperCollins, 1992), p. 117.

13. The only book in the Bible that talks about totally undeserved and incredibly severe suffering is spelled J-O-B.

Advertising perpetuates the work-spend-work cycle, and the work-spend-work cycle orients us to The Economy. The consumers that advertising creates — particularly in North America — are essential to the world's Economic growth. Without these consumers, America's Economy would surely suffer and stagnate, but people in the rest of the world would suffer even more because they would not have a place to sell their products. Our advertising rituals keep the word-spend-work cycle going so that The Economy remains robust. Our advertising rituals also orient us toward the performance of actions, such as work and shopping, that benefit Economic growth, and growth is absolutely essential to the religion we call Economics.

The Home as the Icon of Economic Salvation

The home is a sacred space that also orients us toward The Economy and motivates us to Its service. It is an icon of Economic salvation. All religions promise salvation of some kind, and the God we call The Economy is not different. Whereas Christianity promises the Kingdom of God; Islam promises paradise; and Buddhism promises Nirvana; The Economy promises success. "Millions who practice no organized religion (and millions who do) call themselves to regular internal judgments on the basis of their standards for success. Have they done well in school, in their careers, in their families? Have they made good use of their gifts? To conclude that one has succeeded in life offers the only consolation in facing death that many will accept."[14]

An icon is a religious object through which we look in order to illuminate divine mysteries. The home is an Economic icon because the success of the homeowner can be viewed through the home. The United States government clearly understands the iconic status of the individually owned home. In its support of The Economy, the government supports the sacred status of home ownership through tax deductions on mortgage interest, tax credits for first-time home buyers, institutions like Fannie Mae and Freddie Mac, as well as many other government laws and policies. Historically, this effort has been very successful. For example, in 1940, 44 percent of American families owned their own homes. By

---

14. Peter Gardella, *Domestic Religion: Work, Food, Sex and Other Commitments* (Cleveland: Pilgrim Press, 1998), p. 9.

1950, that percentage increased to 55 percent, and by 1989 64 percent of American families owned their own homes.[15] Moreover, according to oft-repeated statistics, this percentage increased to 69 percent by 2008.

Two additional factors make the growth in home ownership even more staggering. First, the population of the United States more than doubled from 1940 to 2008. If home ownership had remained at the 44 percent level of 1940, the number of people who owned homes would have doubled. But homeownership's increase from 44 to 69 percent combined with the doubling of the population suggests that the *actual number* of homeowners tripled from 1940 to 2008. Second, the average physical size of our houses has nearly tripled since 1950. This means that there are now three times the number of homeowners and their houses are almost three times the size.[16]

Obviously, tripling the number and size of homes greatly stimulates The Economy. A large number of consumer items adorn a modern abode. There is furniture, appliances, electronic gadgets, carpets, hardwood floors, lumber, siding, bricks, copper pipes, heating, air-conditioning equipment, wiring, and roofing materials. Everything purchased for the home serves The Economy. Normally, the home is a family's largest contribution to the Gross Domestic Product (GDP). The home's status as a sacred place within the religion of the Economy makes sense when the home's considerable contribution to economic growth is understood.

Not only does the home function as an icon through which others can view our Economic success, the American home *orients* its owners toward serving The Economy. For example, all homeowners risk the chastisement of their neighbors if the house's condition deteriorates. One dilapidated house undermines the perceived success of all who live in the neighborhood. The responsibility of the home's interior falls to women who are accountable for the home's cleanliness. This fact appears to be slightly less true than it was thirty years ago. Today men are more likely to help with cleaning. Indeed, on rare occasions some men may do the majority of cleaning even if a woman lives in the house; yet, even in these rare circumstances, it still will be the woman of the house who faces social embarrassment if the home's interior is not deemed clean enough.

What a clean interior is to a woman, a well-manicured lawn is to a man. In an article written for *Life* magazine in 1969, William Zinsser

15. Schor, *The Overworked American*, p. 111.
16. Schor, *The Overworked American*, pp. 111, 112

describes a man's role in lawn maintenance in a quite humorous, if not slightly dated manner. "Let a man drink or default on his taxes or cheat on his wife, and the community will find forgiveness in its heart. But let him fail to keep his front lawn mowed and to be seen doing it, and those hearts will turn to stone. For the American front lawn is a holy place, constantly worshiped but never used. Only its high priest, the American husband, may set foot on it, and then only to perform the sacred rites: mowing with a mower, edging with an edger, sprinkling with a hose, and rooting with a rooter to purify the temple of profane weeds."[17]

Both lawn care and housecleaning are prime examples of how homeownership orients us to serve the needs of our God The Economy; for, the work around the home is remarkably similar in structure to the work-spend-work treadmill described above. Homeownership provides us with perpetual tasks, and these tasks are impossible to complete! No matter how clean you make the house, imperfections in the form of grime, dirt, and dust immediately reemerge. Likewise, no matter how perfect you cut the grass or pull the weeds, the grass grows again. The weeds reemerge. Writing in the *Chicago Tribune*, Dennis Rodkin connects the perpetual tasks of housecleaning and lawn care with an ancient Greek myth. "The ancient Greeks told the story of a mortal who so angered the gods that he was sentenced to spend eternity performing a futile hopeless chore. Sisyphus spent each day pushing an enormous boulder uphill, only to watch it roll back down each night. No matter how hard Sisyphus worked on any day, he still had the very same job ahead of him the next day. This, to the Greeks, was hell. Modern Americans who do the same kind of never-finished perpetually frustrating work, call it lawn care. The difference between Sisyphus and us is that upon reaching the top of the mountain each afternoon, Sisyphus didn't shove the boulder back down the slope. It wasn't his fault that the job was never complete. We, on the other hand, keep the endless cycle going on our own."[18] The perpetual character of both lawn care and housecleaning not only mimics the Myth of Sisyphus, but, once again, it exposes us to the perpetual work-spend-work cycle demanded by The Economy's need for constant growth. Since this perpetual work

17. William Zinsser, "Electronic Coup de Grass: The Mowing Ethic," *Life,* August 22, 1969, as quoted in Pahl, *Shopping Malls,* p. 115.

18. Dennis Rodkin, "Lawning of America: Our Quest for a Perfect Patch of Earth Is Harming the Earth," *The Chicago Tribune,* July, 2, 1995, as quoted in Pahl, *Shopping Malls,* p. 115.

cycle is essential to a robust Economy, it can also now be said that the home is a sacred space.

The only disagreement I have with the insightful quotation immediately above is its contention that we keep this cycle going on our own. The cycle is perpetuated by The Economy in much the same manner as the Myth of Sisyphus says the offended Greek gods perpetuated Sisyphus' everlasting work. Our cycles — be they expressed as work-spend-work or through the perpetual character of housecleaning and lawn care — are fueled by our adherence to and worship of The Economy. Indeed, explanations for our extreme housecleaning and lawn care are augmented if it is recognized that our homes are sacred space, and one thing sacred space does in a religion is *orient* religious adherents toward their deity. In other words, *sacred space is the place where we reproduce the actions of our God and take part in our God's salvific actions.*[19] Once we remember that The Economy's version of salvation is success, we can see how the home orients us toward this God. In our participation in the perpetual cycles just discussed, we reproduce the actions of our God and receive the benefits The Economy bestows.

The work-spend-work cycle is essential to Economic growth, and growth is essential to the Economy. If The Economy does not grow — if it contracts — nearly all people experience The Economy's wrath. Growth is measured by the amount of money spent. It does not matter what is purchased. It only matters that money is spent on something. The GDP measures the amount of money spent. If more money is spent in the current year than the previous year, The Economy is said to grow. This is deemed "good." If less money circulates in the current year than the previous year, The Economy is in recession or depression. This is deemed "bad" or may be even "evil." If only 10 or 15 percent of the people thought their needs were essentially met and removed themselves from the work-spend-work cycle, The Economy would suffer disastrous consequences. Advertising and homeownership prevent such an Economic tragedy. Advertising induces us to buy things we do not even need or use. The constant movement into better houses, or refinancing to remove some money from our current houses, also keeps us in the work-spend-work cycle that supports our God The Economy. But our homes give The Economy even more support than this.

The iconic status of the home induces us, in the first place, to "pur-

---

19. Mircea Eliade, *The Sacred and the Profane: The Nature of Religion,* trans. Willard R. Trask (New York: Harcourt, Brace & World, 1959), p. 23.

chase" a home. Most of us do not actually purchase the home, because, technically, most of us cannot afford a home. We borrow money — a lot of money — in order to do this. The debt we accrue often changes our lives because it places us on the work-spend-work treadmill, and this debt is often enough to keep us on this treadmill for life. To be sure, we did not think the home trapped us until recently. Before the Great Recession of 2008-2009, the value of our homes increased substantially. Just as we believed The Economy would grow indefinitely, so we thought the value of our homes would increase forever. Our certainty was almost universal.

Inflated home prices allowed The Economy to grant homeowners its version of salvation by allowing them to appear to be even more successful. When the value of homes magically increased, homeowners borrowed more money based on the increased "equity" their homes had graciously conferred. Increased debt (both in amount of the debt and sometimes the length of time now necessary to retire the new loan) guaranteed that many homeowners would be on the work-spend-work cycles all the longer. The plan, of course, was for the homes to continue to increase in value. This would allow the homeowner to retire and cash out of the home investments and purchase, without debt, smaller houses where they chose to retire. If the homeowner was lucky, the difference between the amount for which the old house sold and the smaller cost of the retirement home would also help finance retirement. The plan, of course, would only work if home prices continued to rise. They did not. For some, this meant losing the home in foreclosure. For most, it meant delaying retirement and continuing on the work-spend-work-spend treadmill indefinitely. How much the sacred status of our homes played into the sequence of events that led to the Great Recession of 2008-2009 is debatable, but everyone involved in this economic debacle — from Congress to government agencies to lenders to mortgage brokers to real estate speculators to borrowers — all had some belief in the home's iconic status whether or not they articulated it.

Shopping Malls as Sacred Space

Shopping malls demonstrate another function of sacred space. Our homes *orient* us toward The Economy. Our shopping malls *disorient* us from our more traditional religions and *reorient* us toward The Economy.[20] This

20. Pahl, *Shopping Malls*, p. 265, n. 17.

disorientation and reorientation process is subtle and often goes unnoticed. For the most part, it is a subconscious process.

I personally became consciously aware of this process of disorientation and reorientation while Christmas shopping a few years ago. I was standing in line waiting to buy some presents for my kids while Christmas carols were being played. It was then that I realized that a woman in front of me in line was buying a G.I. Joe doll to the tune of the Christmas carol I know as "What Child Is This?" This Christmas carol begins, "What Child is this, who laid to rest, on Mary's lap is sleeping" (William C. Dix, 1837-1898). Cognizant of these words, I, being Christian, had cognitive dissonance to say the least.

My experience is only a small instance of the intentional disorientation our shopping malls provide. A traditional religious symbol, in this case a Christmas carol, is used to sell things.[21] What we normally expect to hear in the context of a Christian worship service is now experienced in the context of a shopping experience. As is the case with most ritual, the uncritical participants are not conscious of the process. Our unconsciousness increases rather than decreases our disorientation.

The process of disorientation and reorientation is most effective in the architectural design of our shopping malls. Just as advertisers are extremely mindful of each second of an advertisement's sacred time, so are the architects of shopping malls extremely mindful of each square foot of a shopping mall's sacred space. The sacred character of such mindfulness is revealed when one notes that there may be less difference between the designs of our indoor shopping malls and the architecture of individual Roman Catholic churches. In both spaces, everything has its place. Shopping malls all have strategically located water fountains, sources of natural light, and trees. Light, water, trees, and other natural phenomena are used in a symbolic way by all religions, and the shopping mall employs these symbols to disorient and then reorient those who visit. For example, water symbolizes purification, refreshment, and rebirth in many of the world's religions. In Christianity, water is the element used in baptism, which is Christianity's initiation rite that cleanses the neophyte from his or her sins. This same sort of cleansing ritual may also be operative in our malls. Jon Pahl suggests that this might be cleansing the shopper from worrying about the "filthiness" of what actually goes into the things we

---

21. The Economy may well have already so disoriented us that we are no longer consciously aware of the fact that Christmas carols were written to be sacred music for Christians.

purchase (i.e., Asian sweatshops and other forms of labor exploitation), or perhaps it is an initiation rite into consumerism itself. Like the Tree of Life alleged to be at the center of the Garden of Eden, trees and other vegetation are present at crucial places in our enclosed shopping malls. These trees, however, never shed their leaves, and they never die. They represent the abundant life made possible by the Economy and its markets. "It is the Garden of Eden without the Fall; the resurrection without the cross; spring and summer without fall and winter."[22]

After *disorienting* us the mall uses these reconfigured symbols to *reorient* us. This reorientation, of course, points us toward The Economy and its values. It is a subtle shift from the "spiritual" to the "material" in the sense that The Economy values economic exchanges, and these take place in "this material world" instead of a world to come. There is no transcendent value here. The Economic exchange is ultimate because the exchange alone helps The Economy grow. Our more traditional religions never believe in the *ultimate* status of anything that happens in the material world. The material world may be important, but it is never of *ultimate* importance.[23] The shopping mall's reorientation, therefore, shifts our attention from our needs of nurture, companionship, food, and safety to material desires. In its use of traditional symbols, it shifts the religious focus from a hope of a good world *to come* to *this* world of goods. Because we usually engage in shopping rituals as uncritical participants, we seldom realize this transition has occurred; yet, our frequent visits to the shopping mall further reinforce our transition.

According to James Rouse, the architect who designed and built over sixty of our earliest enclosed malls, the shopping mall has the same goals as a church building. It is the place where "all people come together — rich and poor, old and young, black and white. It is the democratic unifying, universal place which gives spirit and personality to the city."[24] Our shopping malls promote service to the God we call The Economy.

---

22. Pahl, *Shopping Malls*, p. 73.

23. The major religions of the world have different understandings of "this world." Some think "this world" is only a source of suffering. Others understand there to be much to value in the things of this world. Nonetheless, it is probably correct to say that none of the major religions of the world think the products of this world are of ultimate value. They are always penultimate in some sense. This is not the case with the religion called Economics. In this religion, the exchange of the products of the world is ultimate, and a clear sign of The Economy's version of salvation.

24. Pahl, *Shopping Malls*, p. 70.

They disorient us and then they reorient us. They disorient by placing our religious symbols in a different context. Then they reorient us by providing new meanings for these deconstructed religious symbols. Since this is ritual, most people notice neither the disorientation nor the reorientation that happens in all shopping malls. It is a pre-rational or subconscious process that would be far less effective if it were an activity of which we were aware.

Walt Disney World as Pilgrimage Site

Most religions have pilgrimage sites. Jerusalem, the Vatican, and Mecca are examples. Walt Disney World functions as The Economy's pilgrimage site. It is the most visited place on earth. The number of "pilgrims" who visit Disney World is quite staggering. In 2007 the Magic Kingdom alone received 17 million visitors. This compares to 2.3 million Muslims who made their Hajj to Mecca in 2008.[25] Of course, Disney World is called a tourist attraction rather than a pilgrimage site, but, like all pilgrimage sites, Disney World reinforces the values of its God, The Economy, and helps convey these values from one generation to the next.

The ride on Disney's monorail begins the Disney experience. As we pull away from the station, the view opens before us. "Immediately on the left, beyond the manicured grass . . . is Seven Seas Lagoon. Across it are the Polynesian Village and the Grand Florida Resorts. Ahead in the distance we can see the spire of Cinderella's Castle and the top of Space Mountain. Soon, to the right, Bay Lake comes into view. Our transition into Disney World is marked by water, and our passage through the womb-like lobby of the Contemporary Hotel . . . symbolizes rebirth."[26] Our rebirth begins a process of disorientation and reorientation that happens to all serious religious converts who abandon their old values as they are indoctrinated into the values of their new religion.

Disney World disorients us in many ways. On *The Jungle Cruise,* the Amazon River connects to the Congo and the Nile. *The World Showcase* places the Norway pavilion beside China and Mexico. Minnie Mouse

25. Cara Drover, "Disney as Religion," http://religion31812.webs.com, 2010.
26. Stephen M. Fjellman, *Vinyl Leaves: Walt Disney World and America* (Boulder, CO: Westview Press, 1992), p. 188.

wears a kimono while wandering through the Japanese pavilion, and Leonardo da Vinci becomes AT&T's favorite Renaissance man.[27]

Disney also disorients our relationship to nature. Disney requires a sort of order and cleanliness never found in nature. The lakes of central Florida are not that blue. Not all islands have sandy beaches, and the birds do not sing as sweetly or as predictably as they do in Disney World. It is Disney's specialty to fix nature. Nothing in nature is beyond Disney's ability to be refined in the name of entertainment. No place is safe. "Imagine promoting a universe in which raw Nature doesn't fit because it doesn't measure up; isn't safe enough, accessible enough, predictable enough, even beautiful enough for company standards. Disney is not in the business of exploiting Nature so much as striving to improve upon it, constantly fine-tuning God's work."[28]

The process of disorientation and reorientation dominates Disney's presentation of American history. In *The American Adventure,* robot images of Ben Franklin and Mark Twain guide us through American history.[29] Ben Franklin's robot summarizes this optimism, saying, "Hope and fear created this land. We built America and the process made us Americans — a new breed, rooted in all races, stained and tinted with all colors . . . a streaming ethnic anarchy. Then, in a bit of time, we became more alike than we were different . . . a new society . . . fitted by our very thoughts for greatness."[30] Sure there have been bumps on the way — small, barely mentioned "inconveniences" like slavery, the attempted genocide of the indigenous population, the oppression of workers, child labor, the exploitation of women, and Japanese internment camps — but Americans are good, hard-working people who have overcome these minor obstacles. We march into a future that can only improve.

27. Fjellman, *Vinyl Leaves,* p. 400.

28. Carl Hiaasen, *Team Rodent: How Disney Devours the World* (New York: Random House, 1998), p. 18.

29. Using Mark Twain as a guide through American history is itself a disorientation and reorientation; for, late in his life, Mark Twain was deeply critical — almost to the point of despair — of the imperialistic policies of the United States. He thought the Spanish-American War was an imperialist war, but what really depressed him was our war of aggression against the Philippines — a war that has basically been expunged from the annals of American history. Twain put his "Comments on the Killing of 600 Moros" in his posthumous autobiography; see Richard Drinnon, *Facing West: The Metaphysics of Indian-Hating and Empire Building* (Norman: University of Oklahoma Press, 1980, 1997), pp. 346, 347. In any case, to use Twain as an unqualified, optimistic supporter of the American enterprise is quite a reorientation.

30. Fjellman, *Vinyl Leaves,* p. 100.

Disney cannot simply deny the racism, sexism, and imperialism that have been perpetuated by America. Its audience now knows a little too much for such omissions to go unnoticed. As a consequence, Disney employs the robots of Frederick Douglass and Susan B. Anthony to mention the uncomfortable issues of slavery, racism, and sexism. Few people, however, are capable of contrasting the speeches of these robots with what Frederick Douglass and Susan B. Anthony actually said.

Fortunately Richard Robbins has made such a contrast. He compared the speech of Nez Perce Chief Joseph's (1841-1904) Disney speech with his actual recorded words. After leading a brilliant military campaign against the United States, Chief Joseph was forced to surrender. These words are spoken by his Disney robot to mark this occasion. "Enough, enough of your words. Let your new dawn lead to the final sunset on my people's suffering. When I think of our condition, my heart is sick. I see men of my own race treated as outlaws, or shot down like animals. I pray that all of us may be brothers, with one country around us, and one government for all. From where the sun now stands, I will fight no more forever."[31]

Citing Merrill Beal's book, *"I Will Fight No More Forever,"* Robbins proceeds to quote what Chief Joseph was actually recorded to have said on the day of his surrender.

> Tell General Howard I know his heart. What he told me before I have in my heart. I am tired of fighting. Our chiefs are killed. Looking Glass is dead. The old men are all killed. It is the young men who say yes or no. He who led the young men is dead. It is cold and we have no blankets. The little children are freezing to death. My people some of them have run away to the hills and have no blankets, no food; no one knows where they are, perhaps freezing to death. I want time to look for my children and see how many of them I can find. Maybe I will find them among the dead. Hear me my chiefs. I am tired; my heart is sick and sad. From where the sun now stands, I will fight no more forever.[32]

The Disney speech and the recorded battlefield speech are different. In Disney's hands, Chief Joseph gives positive testimony to the very thing

---

31. Richard Robbins, *Global Problems and the Culture of Capitalism* (New York: Pearson Education, 2008), p. 35.

32. Merrill D. Beal, *"I Will Fight No More Forever": Chief Joseph and the Nez Perce War* (Seattle: University of Washington Press, 1963), p. 229, as quoted in Robbins, *Global Problems and the Culture of Capitalism*, p. 35.

he opposed, namely, an all-encompassing nation state. "I pray that all of us may be brothers, with one country around us, and one government for all." This is history as Disney thinks it should be. The speech justifies the death and destruction that happened in pursuit of American victory.[33] Chief Joseph's people may have suffered. Many may have died, but the outcome justifies the exploitation and warfare because now we can live "with one country around us, and one government for all."

Every version of history has a point of view, and Disney is no exception. The point is that Disney's view is remarkably consistent with the religious values of The Economy. Moreover, Disney promotes this perspective in a playful, entertaining manner. "Sometimes the playfulness is clear, but sometimes the stories are pedagogically wrapped in seriousness. The problem comes in remembering that however dramatic, the stories are part of a purposeful pastiche — *history as commercial for optimistic individual consumerism and corporate management.* What Disney does, perhaps, is kill the idea of history by presenting it as entertainment. If the truth value of parts of the past is indistinguishable from the truth value of fantasy and futurology, then what is history but crafted amusement?"[34]

Disney World does not distinguish between fantasy and reality. Some say that this is only entertainment, and Disney is in the entertainment business. As is the case with advertising, however, entertainment is a distraction that prevents us from focusing on the themes that are really operating in Disney World. Behind the entertainment is the promotion of optimism about consumerism, corporate management, and productivity. In fact, there is no scientific reason to be optimistic about such things, and there is some evidence (sexism, environmental damage, exploitation of labor, etc.) that these Economic values have certain death-dealing consequences. Nonetheless, Disney World reinforces these optimistic beliefs of The Economy. It does so in a way that is pre-rational. For many children this is an entertaining introduction to the myths and foundation narratives of the religion that worships the Economy, and their entertainment begins long before they will develop the intellectual capacities to challenge the content of these stories. Some may never develop such critical capacities, and if they never do, they will remain uncritical participants in the Economy's rituals — rituals that can easily be described as religious.

---

33. Robbins, *Global Problems and the Crisis of Capitalism,* p. 35.
34. Fjellman, *Vinyl Leaves,* p. 60. Emphasis mine.

CHAPTER 2

Economic Myths, Metaphors, and Rhetoric

No time can exist before the appearance of reality narrated in the myth.

Mircea Eliade, *The Sacred and the Profane*[1]

A myth is a story that happens outside common time which explains phenomena inside common time. The story of Adam and Eve illustrates this. God forms Adam out of the mud and breathes into his nostrils the breath of life. God plants a garden called Eden around Adam and commissions him to work tending this garden. Two trees — The Tree of Life and the Tree of the Knowledge of Good and Evil — are in the middle of this garden, and, under penalty of death, God forbids Adam to eat fruit from the Tree of the Knowledge of Good and Evil.

God recognizes that it is "not good" for Adam to live alone and attempts to find him a suitable companion. God creates all sorts of animals. Adam names them, but finds no suitable companion. In near desperation, God causes Adam to fall asleep and surgically removes one of Adam's ribs. God creates a woman from Adam's rib. When Adam awakens, God presents the woman. Adam is delighted. He names her Eve, and God is satisfied that Eve is the partner Adam needed.

Eve encounters a serpent in the garden, and the serpent asks her if they can eat fruit from any tree growing in the garden. Eve responds that

1. Mircea Eliade, *The Sacred and the Profane: The Nature of Religion*, trans. Willard R. Trask (New York: Harcourt, Brace & World, 1959), p. 72.

they can eat of any tree except the Tree of the Knowledge of Good and Evil. If they eat from that tree, they will die. The serpent tells her that she will not die if she eats and goes on to say that God told them this because God knew that when they ate that fruit, both Adam and Eve would be like the gods themselves — knowing good and evil. She ate the fruit and gave some to Adam, and he ate some too. Immediately, their eyes were opened, and they realized they were naked. God discovered their disobedience and cursed the woman saying she would always be subordinate to the man; she would have pain in childbirth; she would, despite the pain of childbirth, always desire her husband; and she would always hate and fear serpents. God also cursed Adam saying that Adam would always toil to achieve the fruits of his labor from the ground, and the fruits of Adam's labor would never be as great as the amount of toil Adam exerted. God then clothed Adam and Eve, banished them from the garden, and placed angels at the entrance of the garden to prevent Adam and Eve from ever entering the garden again.

A myth is a story that happens outside common time which explains phenomena inside common time.

As previously stated, a myth is a story that happens outside of our common time. In the case of Adam and Eve, they can never go back to the Garden of Eden. Since the life they live after being expelled from the garden has nothing in common with the one they once lived in the garden, the story happens outside common time. They enter common time when they are banished from the garden. The second feature of a myth is that a myth uses its narration of events that happened outside common time to explain the human situation inside common time. In Adam and Eve's case, this story explains phenomena like: the origin of human and animal life, the origin of sexual differentiation, clothing, sexual desire, a woman's pain in childbirth, patriarchy, fear of snakes, why we understand almost everything in terms of good and evil, and why our labor is never as productive as we think it should be. Moreover, as long as the myth remains myth, there is no reason to discuss or study alternative origins to these phenomena. Since they came into being with time itself, no alternatives are possible.

All religions have myths. These stories did not happen in history.

They are not factual, although modern believers often contend they are. The surprising thing is, The Economy has its own myths. Like the Economic rituals discussed in Chapter 1, Economic myths are also pre-rational. We hear these stories long before we have the critical capacity to rationally reflect upon them. Lacking this critical capacity, religious people often take their myths to be factual, historical truths. This happens to some Christians who believe that the Adam and Eve myth is as historically factual as the Reagan administration. In Economics, the barter myth functions in a similar manner. It accounts for the origin of money by telling a story about a time and place that never existed.[2] In this way the barter myth is similar to all myths. It happens outside common time and is used to explain things (like money) that occur inside common time.

The Barter Myth: The Myth of Money's Origin

> Barter is the immediate exchange of one item for another. It should not be confused with credit, which is the promise to pay for an item in the future.

The barter myth says that human beings have always been engaged in some kind of exchange. As the mythological story goes, people exchanged goods and services through barter — the *immediate* exchange of one item for another — before money was invented. If one person had an excess of corn but needed a blanket, that person would seek out someone with an

---

2. Caroline Humphrey, "Barter and Economic Disintegration," *Man* 20 (1985): 48-72, is considered "the definitive work on barter." Her conclusion is, "No example of a barter economy, pure and simple, has ever been described, let alone the emergence from it of money; all available ethnography suggests that there never has been such a thing." Anne Chapman, "Barter as a Universal Mode of Exchange," *L'Homme* 22, no. 3 (1980): 33-83, notes that if barter only concerns swapping objects as economists assert, it is not clear that barter ever existed. Objects were swapped with the express purpose of rearranging social relationships, but this is not barter exchange, which has no purpose other than exchange as a goal. For the best discussion of the barter myth, the source of the articles just mentioned, and from where the idea that there *actually is a barter myth* was first presented to me, see David Graeber, *Debt: The First 5000 Years* (Brooklyn, NY: Melville House Publishing, 2011), pp. 21-41.

excess of blankets and trade corn for the blanket. According to the barter myth, money was invented because barter was inefficient. As Adam Smith says, ". . . when the division of labor first began to take place, this power of exchange must frequently have been very much clogged. . . . One man . . . has more of a certain commodity than he himself has occasion for, while another has less, the former consequently would be glad to dispose of, and the latter to purchase a part of this superfluity."[3] In other words, barter works if people can find trading partners, but it runs into difficulty when no trade can be found.

Given the likelihood of such impediments to trade, Adam Smith thought that prudent people would order their affairs so that they would have a large quantity of a commodity everyone needed. Cattle, salt, shells, tobacco, sugar, leather, nails, or precious metals functioned in this capacity.[4] Smith thought this was an intermediary time frame between a society built on pure barter and one that used precious metals in exchange.

Precious metals, however, had two inconveniences. The first was weighing the metal. For a precious metal like gold or silver, a small miscalculation of the weight could result in a substantial error in the transaction. Determining the quality of the metal was the second difficulty. This assaying process could be the source of even more fraud. "To prevent such abuse, to facilitate exchanges and thereby to encourage all sorts of industry and commerce, it had been found necessary, in all countries that have made any considerable advances toward improvement, to affix a public stamp upon certain quantities of such particular metals, as were in those countries commonly made use of to purchase goods. Hence the origin of coined money and of those public offices called mints."[5] Behind this account lurks a subtle but profound assumption. The barter myth assumes that economic markets exist before governments, and governments do not get involved in economic markets until they are needed to make the market run more efficiently. Governments are needed to guarantee the coins that make economic exchange more efficient by eliminating the need to weigh and assay the metal used for exchange.

Efficiency demands that money continues to get more and more abstract. Paper money is introduced. Paper represents the coin that is composed of the precious metal. Paper money is not the coin. It is not

---

3. Adam Smith, *The Wealth of Nations* (New York: Bantam Books, 2003), p. 33.
4. Smith, *The Wealth of Nations,* pp. 33, 34.
5. Smith, *The Wealth of Nations,* p. 37.

a precious metal. It is a more symbolic and abstract expression of the precious metal that provides the coin's value. Next, checks are introduced, which is an even greater abstraction. A check represents the paper money that represents the coin. According to the barter myth, credit is the next form of money to emerge. It is even more abstract. Credit does not even represent paper money *per se.* It actually represents money that will one day be in possession of the borrower, but is not now in his or her possession.

Adam Smith made the barter myth economic canon, and, as a consequence, the barter myth has been uncritically adopted as a true, factual account of the origin of money. But as anthropologist David Graeber points out in his book, *Debt: The First 5000 Years,* there is little if any evidence that any primitive society ever used barter, and there is quite a bit of evidence that barter was never used in any society not already familiar with money. "For centuries now, explorers have been trying to find this fabled land of barter — none with success. Adam Smith sets his story in aboriginal North America. . . . But by mid-century, Lewis Henry Morgan's descriptions of the Six Nations of the Iroquois, among others, were widely published — and they made clear that the main economic institution among the Iroquois nations were longhouses where most goods were stockpiled and then allocated by women's councils, and no one ever traded arrowheads for slabs of meat. Economists simply ignored this information."[6]

Barter did exist, but it was not employed between people who lived in the same community or tribe. One might barter with strangers or even enemies, but, as far as we know, no *society* ever operated using barter as Smith and modern economists postulate. Indeed, barter — the *immediate exchange* of one item for another — probably would have undermined the social structure of hunter/gatherer societies.

The Bushmen of the Kalahari (Ju/wasi) provide an example. Writing of her experiences living among the Ju/wasi, Elizabeth Marshall Thomas discusses how gift giving was an important way to enrich and maintain the social fabric. In doing so, she makes what the Ju/wasi believe to be an important distinction between barter and gift giving. "There were rules involved, of course. You could never refuse a gift, although it obligated you, and you had to make a gift in return, but not immediately. A return gift made too soon would seem like a trade, not like a gift made from

6. Graeber, *Debt,* p. 29.

the heart, and thus would not strengthen the social bond. . . . This concept was so strong that *the Ju/wasi never traded with one another.* Trading was acceptable but only with different people."[7] Hunter/gatherer bands could not afford to barter because *immediate exchange* undermined the lasting relationships such bands needed to survive. No lasting relationship needs to persist between two parties engaged in barter or any other sort of monetary exchange. After the exchange, the parties are free to go their separate ways. They do not ever need to see each other again. Hunter/gatherer bands were too fragile to live with an exchange-based economy. They depended on relationships that extended over time, and their gift-giving economy supported these long-term relationships.[8]

If primitive societies never used barter in their day-to-day functioning, then the story of barter has one important characteristic of a myth. It is a story that takes place in a setting outside of our common time or outside history. Just as there was no historical Garden of Eden, there was no historical society that functioned along the lines indicated by the barter myth. Money did not arise from barter any more than the fear of snakes came from God's curse on Eve. This is interesting because Economists are supposed to be social scientists, and social scientists are not supposed to uncritically accept myths. Yet, Economists still tell the barter myth as if it were historical fact.

The idea that Economists are like theologians or priests might explain their acceptance of the barter myth, and their disregard for historical facts. Like priests or theologians, Economists also use their myths to account for certain Economic phenomena. The barter myth answered some important questions about life in real time (if real time was eighteenth- and nineteenth-century England). First, it states that human nature itself accounts for the origin of market economies. According to this myth, human beings have a *natural propensity* to engage in exchange. Despite the fact that such exchange was extremely limited during the Middle Ages and nearly nonexistent the numerous millennia hunter-gatherer cultures operated, the barter myth demanded and Adam Smith asserted, "*Every man thus lives by exchanging, or becomes in some measure a merchant, and the society itself grows to be what is properly a commercial society.*"[9]

7. Elizabeth Marshall Thomas, *The Old Way: A Story of the First People* (New York: Picador, 2006), pp. 222, 223, my emphasis.

8. Graeber, *Debt*, pp. 102-7.

9. Smith, *The Wealth of Nations*, p. 33.

Second, since the barter myth asserts that The Market (barter) Economy pre-dates government, adherents of the barter myth deduce that The Market Economy preexists the government, and, as a consequence, The Market Economy should be able to function quite well without government support or intervention.

Third, the barter myth's unexamined assumptions allow Economists to assert that the market exchange economy is "natural" and the government is not natural. In contrast to the near-eternal Markets, governments are deemed mere human creations designed to support the needs of the Market. These ideas about the relationship between the market and government — ideas derived from a nonfactual assumption — also allow Economists to assert that government intervention in the market should be avoided because it is unnatural.

Fourth, the barter myth allows Economists to uncritically assert the near eternality of the Market Exchange Economy. It prejudices important issues such as beliefs about human nature and the relationship between the economy and government. Moreover, the barter myth allows Economists to disregard historical facts like the fact that to our knowledge there has never been a society that employed barter within the confines of society (unless the society already knew about money).

Fifth, the barter myth asserts that the history of money runs from the concrete to the abstract. It says that first there was barter. Then, for efficiency's sake, trade was conducted in commodities like salt, tobacco, metals, or seashells. Next, coins and money emerged. Coins assumed the value of the metal of which they were made or for which they could be exchanged. Finally, credit and virtual money emerged. In fact, this is not the history of money at all! "What we now call virtual money (credit) came first. Coins came much later, and their use spread only unevenly and never completely replaced the credit system. Barter, in turn, appears largely as an accidental by-product of the use of coinage or paper money: historically, it has mainly been what people who are accustomed to cash transactions do when they have no access to money."[10]

While an alternative account of money's origin will be postponed until Chapter 5, it is important to note that much evidence exists to support the claim that money existed as credit long before coins were widely circulated. Most Mesopotamian writing, dated around 3500 BCE, appears to be accounting ciphers that record who owes what to whom. *This is ev-*

10. Graeber, *Debt*, p. 40.

idence of a credit system. It is not a barter system. A barter system involves the *immediate* exchange of one item for another. A credit system does not involve *immediate* exchange. It is based on the trust — backed by religious morality and political force — that a person will repay what is owed, not immediately, but in the future.

You do not have to be an economist to recognize that money is an important component of economics. Economists, therefore, should know as much about money as possible. The barter myth, however, obscures the origins of money. If one uncritically adopts the barter myth as the origin of money, one cannot deal with the facts, and the facts turn out to be that there never was a society that operated on a barter system unless it was already quite aware of the existence of coin and paper money. Moreover, many societies used a credit system long before money circulated widely as coins. This fact has implications for economic history and current policy that, at the very least, call for an adjustment in the conventional wisdom of economics. Failure to acknowledge this fact means Economics will remain religion-like and our policies will be distorted by the barter myth.

The Invisible Hand:
The Capitalist Story of The Economy's Providence

Adam Smith used "The Invisible Hand" to describe an unseen, benevolent, providential power that guides a nation's market towards the greatest possible prosperity. It assumes that a nation is composed of people who are individual, isolated economic units. Each person, *by nature,* engages in economic exchange where he or she attempts to maximize the greatest economic benefit possible. Like divine providence, "The Invisible Hand" guides these diverse acts of pure self-interest so that they result in the maximum benefit for the entire nation. Adam Smith speaks of "The Invisible Hand" in this way:

> . . . the annual revenue of every society is always precisely equal to the exchange value of the whole annual produce of its industry, or rather precisely that same thing with that exchange value. As every individual, therefore, endeavors as much as he can both to employ his capital in support of domestic industry, and so to direct that industry that its produce be of greatest value: every individual *necessarily* labors to render the annual revenue of the society as great as he can.

He generally indeed, neither intends to promote the public interest, nor knows how much he is promoting it. By preferring the support of domestic to that of foreign industry, he intends only his own security; and by directing that industry in such a manner as its produce may be of greatest value, he intends only his own gains, and he is in this, as in many other cases, *led by an invisible hand* to promote an end which was no part of his intention. Nor is it always the worse for the society that was no part of it. *By pursuing his own interest he frequently promotes that of the society more efficiently than when he really intends to promote it.*[11]

In other words, "The Invisible Hand" guides the self-interested behavior of all the isolated individuals that compose society toward the best possible social outcome. This means that the best possible society will exist if self-interest is not restricted or regulated. According to The Invisible Hand, any restriction or regulation of self-interested behavior undermines the best possible outcome for a nation and therefore should be avoided.

Smith apparently assumed that "the annual revenue of every society" is synonymous with the nation's well-being. In Smith's words, the well-being of a nation is "precisely equal to the exchangeable value of the whole annual produce of its industry." Today this measurement is called the Gross Domestic Product (GDP). The GDP measures the total amount of money that is exchanged during the year in a given nation. "The Invisible Hand" promotes the common assumption that the GDP accurately and completely measures *our* well-being. The more money that is spent, the greater is the GDP, and, the greater the GDP, the healthier the nation. The healthier the nation, the greater is the well-being of its citizens. Conversely, well-being suffers when the GDP declines.

But a rising GDP does not always improve our well-being! An automobile accident adds to the GDP because money is exchanged when repairs are made. Any injury further increases the GDP because hospital services must be paid. Clearly, an automobile accident rarely enhances our overall well-being, yet, according to the GDP metric, it does. There are other ways our well-being might be measured. Life expectancy, environmental quality, and the availability of healthy food are possible metrics. Despite such alternative metrics, we do not measure our well-being

11. Smith, *The Wealth of Nations*, p. 572. Emphasis mine.

in this way. We refuse to abandon the GDP metric for religious reasons. Alternative metrics do not disclose the health of our God, The Economy. Only the GDP informs us of the health or robustness of our God.

Robust monetary transactions inform us that our God, The Economy, is doing well. Declining transactions mean The Economy is suffering. The GDP is important because it measures the health of our God. So long as we exchange more money each year, The Economy's well-being will, by definition, increase, and since a religion usually links personal well-being with the well-being of its God, those devoted to The Economy will prosper as well. This is why restriction of Economic exchange imposed by any source whatsoever — the government, morality, environmental considerations, religion, etc. — will be religiously opposed by most Capitalist Economists. The GDP metric is testimony to the fact that we are more concerned with the vitality of our God than we are with the well-being of our society and its people. Only religious faith in The Economy leads us to equate our own well-being with The Economy's well-being.

"The Invisible Hand" appears to be a mysterious, spiritual power that transforms petty acts of self-interest into a social benefit in much the same way some Christians believe that the bread and wine is changed into the actual body and blood of Christ in the sacrament of Holy Communion. Both are divine mysteries before which believers should bow. The inner workings of such mysteries cannot possibly be explained. We must leave such mysteries to our Economists and theologians. But, in fact, "The Invisible Hand" is not a mystery at all. It is an intellectual construct based upon religious definitions we have uncritically adopted.

We should, however, avoid trading one uncritically adopted notion for another. The fact that our well-being cannot *always* be equated with unencumbered expressions of self-interest does not mean that self-interested monetary exchange *never* has social benefit. It often does. A businessman might start a business only motivated by the possibility of his own personal gain. He might be very successful and make a great deal of money. In the process, the businessman supports the lives of hundreds or even thousands of men, women, and children. The social benefit of his self-interested activity cannot be denied. But it also cannot be denied that sometimes such selfish acts undermine social well-being.

The unencumbered self-interested pursuit of profit has been socially damaging on numerous occasions. One need only mention corporate names like Enron, Bear Stearns, Lehman Brothers, or people like Michael Milken and Ivan Boesky to remember the recent, socially damaging consequences of unencumbered self-interest.[12] Economic history contains many disastrous examples of selfishness run amok.

The Dutch Tulip Bulb Debacle of 1636
The South Sea Bubble of 1720
The Mississippi Bubble of 1720
The Stock Market Crash of 1929
The Japanese Bubble in Stocks and Real Estate 1985-1989
The U.S. Savings and Loan Crisis of the Late 1980s
The Asian Stock and Real Estate Bubble 1992-1997
The U.S. Bubble in Over-the-Counter Stocks 1995-2000
The Mortgage and Housing Bubble and Crash 2004-2009

If the unrestricted self-interested pursuit of profit is in any way responsible for these economic debacles, the religious assertion that the pursuit of one's self-interest *always* benefits society is inaccurate.

No economic policy is absolute. Human beings must determine which policy is best at any given moment. Sometimes, the self-interested pursued of profit is a benefit to society. Sometimes, self-interested activity is a detriment to society. Sometimes debt enhances the quality of life, and sometimes it diminishes the quality of life. Sometimes the government should take an active regulatory role. Sometimes it should just leave the markets alone. It depends on the conditions present in the society. There are no economic absolutes, but to the extent we uncritically practice Economics as a religion, we will tend to think in terms of Economic absolutes. Society does not benefit when such absolutes are imposed.

Marxism: Christianity without a Messiah?

Marxism presents a narrative that follows the pattern of the Christian story of the fall and redemption. In the Christian version, sin entered the

12. For an account of the Enron debacle see Bethany McLean and Peter Elkind, *The Smartest Guys in the Room: The Amazing Rise and Scandalous Fall of Enron* (New York: Penguin, 2003); for Bear Stearns see William D. Cohan, *House of Cards: A Tale of Hubris and Wretched Excess on Wall Street* (New York: Random House, 2009); for Lehman Brothers see Andrew Ross Sorkin, *Too Big to Fail: The Inside Story of How Wall Street and Washington Fought to Save the Financial System — and Themselves* (New York: Viking Penguin, 2009); for Michael Milken and Ivan Boesky see James Stewart, *Den of Thieves* (New York: Simon & Schuster, 1991, 1992).

world through the first sin of Adam and Eve, and all humanity has been in the grip of this "original sin" ever since. Jesus, however, redeems us from this sinful state, and ultimately establishes the Kingdom of God where the harmony between God and humanity is restored. Karl Marx has his own version of this story.

He substitutes "alienation" for original sin, and, instead of the Kingdom of God, Marx envisions a classless society. In Christianity, Jesus is the agent of redemption. In Marx, the supreme power of economic and historical law creates his classless society. Just as sin is destroyed in the Kingdom of God, so is alienation eliminated in Marx's future society.[13] "It can scarcely be denied that Marxism has the structure of a messianic religion. It has a doctrine of final things brought about in a certain way via a Savior. . . . It is of course a secular faith. In the retreat that religion in general has been engaged in ever since the Enlightenment and the phenomenally rapid ascension of the scientific point of view, all the longings still rooted in the hearts of millions could still be satisfied only by something in the guise of science."[14]

While disagreeing on what the promised future is, Christians and Marxist Socialists both experience a gap between their understanding of the promised future and the world in which they now live. Each thinks the gap will be overcome, but it will be overcome in different ways. The Christian story uses a three-story picture of the universe (heaven above and hell below) to describe its story of salvation. Marxism uses an interpretation of history based on class struggle that tells its story of alienation and redemption in pseudo-scientific language. Marxism's pattern is clearly Christian, but it is Christianity without God or a Messiah.

The Legend of Efficient (Omniscient) Markets

The Efficient Market theory, or as I call it, the legend of omniscient markets, is derived from the law of supply and demand. In the words of Paul Samuelson's classic economic text:

13. For more on the source and character of Karl Marx's understanding of alienation see Judy Cox, "An Introduction to Marx's Theory of Alienation," *International Socialism* 79 (July 1998), www.littleprints.free-online.co.uk/pubs/isj79/com.htm.

14. Joel Carmichael, *Karl Marx: The Passionate Logician* (New York: Charles Scribner's Sons, 1967), p. 248.

The bare outlines of a competitive profit-and-loss system are simple to describe. Everything has a price — each commodity and each service. Even the different kinds of human labor have prices usually called "wage rates."

Everybody receives money for what he sells and uses this money to buy what he wishes. If more is wanted of any one good, say shoes, a flood of new orders will be given for it. This will cause its price to rise and more to be produced. Similarly, if more is available for a good like tea than people want, its price will be marked down as a result of competition. At the lower price people will drink more tea, and producers will no longer produce so much. Thus equilibrium of supply and demand will be restored.

What is true of the markets for consumers' goods is also true of markets for factors of production such as labor, land and capital inputs.[15]

The Efficient Market theory is, in fact, a theory of Market omniscience. The law of supply and demand means the Market will always know what the correct price should be and will always establish that price according to its all-knowing attribute. True, there will be *external* shocks to the system such as technological innovations, new sources of energy, political unrest, and war. But The Market, in its omniscience, will respond to these external challenges and always achieve optimal equilibrium.

Make no mistake: the law of supply and demand could very well regulate the "Main Street" consumer market. In this market, increased demand for a given product increases the price of that product. In due time, however, these higher prices promote more production which, in turn, increases supply and lowers prices. For example, the price of nails will increase when the supply of nails decreases due to high demand. To "cash in" on the high price of nails, manufacturers will produce more nails. The increased supply of nails will then drive down their price. This is how the law of supply and demand "knows" the "correct" and most optimal price in the "Main Street" consumer market. No external factors are necessary. No one needs to set prices. The "Main Street" market takes care of that and actually can operate in a more or less efficient manner if it is just given the room to operate.

But there are more markets than the "Main Street" consumer mar-

---

15. Paul A. Samuelson, *Economics,* 4th edition (New York: McGraw-Hill, 1958), p. 39. Emphasis mine.

ket, and it is not so clear that the law of supply and demand establishes their prices. In the quotation that began this section, Samuelson merely proclaims that all other markets are subject to supply and demand. He simply declares without argument or proof, "What is true of the markets for consumers' goods is also true of markets for factors of production such as labor, land and capital inputs." Like a preacher, he merely proclaims that labor, land, and capital markets are also efficiently regulated through supply and demand. "This logical trick is pervasive in economic teaching: we are first persuaded that the markets for goods are efficient, and then beguiled into believing this to be a general principle applicable to all markets."[16]

The collateralization of debt, for example, is an internal process that occurs in asset markets like stocks or real estate. It involves lenders lending money against a borrower's assets to secure or collateralize a loan. Some property like a house, car, or stock is used to guarantee that the debtor will repay. If payment is not made, the creditor takes the house, car, or stock. Collateralization of debt is important because it exposes an internal market dynamic that undermines the legend of market efficiency.

When the price of the asset that secured the loan falls, a loan can become under-collateralized. Banks try to remedy this problem by a process known as mark to market. This is the daily reevaluating of the worth of assets used to secure the bank loans. When this process reveals that the debtor's assets no longer are enough to collateralize the loan, the banks demand further payments from the debtor. In the stock market, this is called a margin call.

Almost any shareholder can use the stocks in her possession as collateral to buy other stocks "on the margin." If, for example, I own $1000 in stock, I can use this asset as collateral to purchase $1000 more in stock "on the margin." This means I now own a $2000 asset, but I owe $1000 to my lender. Each day the value of my asset fluctuates. If I am lucky or smart, the value of my asset might increase to $2200 or much more. If I am unfortunate or stupid, the asset value can decrease. In any case, every day my lender will mark my asset to market to determine if the $1000 loan is fully collateralized. My loan will be fully collateralized so long as my assets are worth over $1000. If, however, the stock price drops by over 50 percent, the value of my stocks (once purchased for $2000) would be less

---

16. George Cooper, *The Origin of Financial Crises: Central Banks, Credit Bubbles and the Efficient Market Fallacy* (New York: Random House, 2008), p. 6.

than $1000 (the amount of my loan). In this case, my lender would demand more collateral from me, and I would have to do one of two things. I would either pay the lender the difference between the value of the asset and the $1000 I owe, or I would be forced to sell my stock and lose some of my investment. This is called a forced sale, and it is not based on the laws of supply and demand. Instead, it is largely based on an internal dynamic created by using my stock as collateral.

The existence of margin calls such as the one just described undermines market efficiency — at least with respect to the asset market — because it demonstrates an internal market factor that prompts a sale of stock that is independent of the law of supply and demand. Market efficiency, on the other hand, requires the market to be moved only by external forces.

In this example the stakes are pretty low, and I might be the only one affected by the scenario. If, however, the value of collateralized assets increases to trillions, we have another matter. Such a reduction in asset prices could lead to disaster for the asset market itself. This may have recently happened in the housing market when housing prices dropped precipitously and the entire housing market found itself in jeopardy. Homeowners were walking away from their loans because they owed thousands of dollars more than their houses were worth. Since the whole banking system depended on the repayment of debt and since a large percentage of people merely walked away from their homes, the entire system was in jeopardy. In other words, forces internal to the market itself played a huge role in the crisis.[17] Those who believe in market efficiency cannot even consider such possibilities. For them, The Legend of Efficient Markets functions as all myths and legends do. It prevents people from seeing reality. In this case, it blinds them to studying the internal dynamics of markets because, according to their unexamined legend, the internal dynamics of the market do not cause market fluctuation.

Economists are as divided on the legend of market efficiency as Christians are on the facticity of the Garden of Eden story. For example, John Maynard Keynes's theory is that the market is not efficient and the government itself should make adjustments to this inefficient market. In bad times, the government should stimulate the market by increasing the money supply. In good times, the government should decrease the money supply through taxation and other measures in order that the market does

17. Cooper, *The Origin of Financial Crises*, p. 105.

not get overstimulated.[18] Despite such formidable opposition to the myth of efficient markets within Capitalism itself, the legend of omniscient markets remains the guiding narrative of the *laissez-faire* school of thought.

Just as the Western Christian Church once defended the geocentric understanding of the cosmos despite all evidence to the contrary, those who believe in efficient markets do the same. One rather interesting example of this "defense" is a 2006 article from the *Journal of Financial Economics* titled "Was There a Nasdaq Bubble in the Late 1990s?" In the early days of the Internet speculation, the stock prices of these and other technology companies were so high that even Federal Reserve Chairman Alan Greenspan called the run-up in stock prices "irrational exuberance." In early 2000 this speculation ran the Nasdaq Stock Exchange to a high of 5048 before plunging to 1660. People who lack religious belief in Market omniscience can simply answer, "Yes, there was a Nasdaq bubble in the late 1990s" and move on with their lives. It would not even occur to them to write an article asking if there was a Nasdaq bubble. But these authors had to defend their religious belief; hence, they argued "not necessarily" because a firm's value increases with *uncertainty* about average future profitability, and, clearly, there was a lot of uncertainty in the late 1990s. In the unlikely case that this is a cogent argument, this argument implies that companies are more valuable the less that is known of them. If this is so, the dubious belief that The Market grants us the information necessary to make rational decisions is undermined.[19] In any case, those who maintain the legend of market efficiency in all markets do so despite overwhelming evidence to the contrary. Their position is similar to that of a religious fanatic who equates faithfulness to his or her God with faithfulness to his or her doctrines about that God.

Scientific Rhetoric in Economics

Religious myths, rituals, and sacred stories circumvent our critical faculties. They enclose us in a worldview long before we are ever conscious of

---

18. This is important. According to Keynes the government should stimulate the market *only when it is in recession or depression!* Today we stimulate preemptively! This was not Keynes's intention, and the application of stimulus to prevent the economy from going into recession is a misappropriation of Keynesian theories. Even Keynes would gladly admit that stimulus, improperly administered, creates market instability and greater risk. Preemptive stimulation is as much a myth for "liberals" as the efficient market is for "conservatives."

19. Cooper, *The Origin of Financial Crises,* p. 10, n. 4.

it, and they beckon us to understand our worldview as God-given rather than of human design. But this is not the only source of our inability to see certain facts. Today science dominates religion, and we grant exalted status to anything that looks or sounds like science. The simple use of scientific words gives Economics unwarranted authority, and the use of scientific rhetoric in Economic matters also circumvents rational inquiry.[20] The following are a few of these pre-rational Economic contentions that come to us in the guise of science.

Through his study of music, Pythagoras (c. 550 BCE) proposed that number was the foundation of the cosmos. Sir Isaac Newton (1642-1727) applied this insight to physics and astronomy. He discovered that the motion of any physical object in the universe can be calculated, and that mathematical formulae could accurately predict the future motion of these objects.

> **The mere use of scientific language does not make something scientific.**

Economists tried to derive the same sort of laws from economic transactions. While physicists would eventually argue that the random motion of all physical particles produces a stable, potentially intelligible universe capable of supporting life, Economists contend that the random acts of isolated individuals pursuing their own utilitarian self-interest creates a stable, rational, intelligible, and benevolent Market.[21] But even Sir Isaac Newton himself had misgivings about such comparisons. After losing a small fortune in the South Sea Bubble of 1720, he declared, "I can calculate the motions of heavenly bodies, but not the madness of people."[22]

Sir Isaac Newton's dilemma was caused by what economist F. A. Hayek calls scientism. This describes the mechanical application of hab-

20. F. A. Hayek, *The Counter-Revolution of Science: Studies on the Abuse of Reason* (Indianapolis: Free Press, 1952, 1979), pp. 15, 16.

21. Stability, rationality, intelligibility, and benevolence are often deemed divine attributes.

22. As quoted by David Orrell, *Economyths: Ten Ways Economics Gets It Wrong* (Toronto: John Wiley & Sons, 2010), p. 3. Sir Isaac Newton's comments were not the comments of an amateur economist. He spent thirty-one years at the Royal Mint, first as Warden and later as Master of the Royal Mint. In other words, in his time he might have been the equivalent of a voting member of the Federal Reserve.

its of thought to fields other than those in which they were formed.[23] Economic "scientism" emerges when Economists misappropriate useful models from one discipline (in this case, physics) to their own. This enables Economists to operate under the guise of science and conceal their assumptions from everyone including themselves.

Many deductions are made from this unproven comparison between economics and physics. First, this false comparison allows the Economists to deduce that self-interested behavior — described as maximizing one's pleasure and minimizing one's pain — is virtuous behavior because it *always* contributes to the public good.[24] Second, it also follows from this image that The Market is stable and will remain stable and benevolent if only we allow it to function according to its nature. Third, the widely held belief in Market omniscience emerges from this image. The Market determines what we need, how much things should cost, and how much people should earn. Finally, our modern soothsayers employ statistics or personal experience to peer into the mystery of the Market and tell us whether the Market is exuberant or depressed. Discovering these hidden secrets can save us from disaster or create wealth and abundance beyond our wildest dreams. Many ancient and modern gods have allegedly offered the same protection and similar riches.

Now many of the ideas gleaned from these pseudo-scientific models prove helpful, but they are often misleading. They certainly are not universal or absolute truths. As long as these ideas are presented in the guise of science, the high status of science will preclude us from critically examining their pre-rational, religious assumptions, and thereby prevent us from accurately discerning economic reality.

Summary

Chapters 1 and 2 explored the pre-rational in the religion called Economics. We participate in Economic religious rituals long before we are critically aware of this fact. Moreover, such participation allows many to tacitly assume that these rituals are natural or of divine design. Along with many others, modern Americans find it much easier to be critical of the rituals of traditional religions than of our Economic rituals. We know our

23. Hayek, *The Counter-Revolution of Science*, pp. 15, 16.
24. Orrell, *Economyths*, pp. 220-22.

religious rituals are of human design. But when it comes to Economic rituals, we are far more accepting and much less critical.

Our uncritical attitude is reinforced because we seldom understand the religious character of Economics. We rarely acknowledge giving and receiving of presents at Christmas, Mother's Day, Halloween, and Valentine's Day as rituals of the religion we call Economics. We seldom see that these gifts serve The Economy and help it stay robust. We only understand this to be the American way of life — a way of life we are willing to defend by sacrificing the lives of our young warriors. (Human sacrifice has often been a religious practice.) It rarely occurs to us that our shopping centers reorient us toward the Economy. We just think they are nice places to shop and spend money. We do not experience our trips to Disney World as religious pilgrimages. They are just enjoyable vacations. Ironically, the power of these rituals would diminish if we began to think of them as religious rituals; for, in this day and age, one way to reduce the perception of something's importance is by proving it is religious.

Economic myths, foundation narratives, and rhetoric will dominate Economic thought as long as Economics functions as a religion in American culture. Because most Americans simply grow up participating in Economic rituals, believing Economic myths and using the pseudo-scientific language of Economics, our critical thinking about economic matters is undermined. As a consequence, our Economic debates and our Economic policy resemble theological debates. Because of the religious conviction of Economic adversaries, these "debates" end in shouting matches or even violence. In fact, the religious debate between Capitalists and Socialists could have culminated in nuclear war and humanity's destruction! Today, debates between Keynesian Economic theologians and neoconservative Economic theologians threaten to stop the American government from functioning. It is to such theological debates within the religion called Economics that we now turn.

CHAPTER 3

The Economy's Theologians, Prophets, Reformers, Terrorists, and Priests

The ideas of economists and political philosophers, both when they are right and when they are wrong, are more powerful than is commonly understood. Indeed the world is ruled by little else. Practical men, who believe themselves to be quite exempt from any intellectual influences, are usually the slaves of some defunct economist.

John Maynard Keynes,
General Theory of Employment, Interest and Money[1]

A religion is a cultural attempt to interpret known facts in a meaningful way. Often this attempt is pre-rational. We practice religious rituals and hear religious myths long before we develop the critical capacities to question their veracity. The first two chapters, on Economic rituals, myths, metaphors, and rhetoric, discussed these pre-rational components of the religion called Economics. The underlying theme of this discussion was that these pre-rational components of Economics are more fundamental and more basic than the conscious thoughts of Economists themselves.

When we discuss Economic giants like Adam Smith (1723-1790), Thomas Malthus (1766-1834), and David Ricardo (1772-1823), we enter the domain of Economic theology. These are the first rational theologians of The Economy. In one way or another they provide the foundation for

---

1. John Maynard Keynes, *The General Theory of Employment, Interest and Money* (Lexington, KY: BN Publishing, 2008), p. 383.

all subsequent Economic reflection. These men developed Economic understanding of human nature, reality, The Economy's providence, poverty, and even what some might call sin. In addition to these classical economists, Economics also has prophets like Karl Marx (1818-1883) who challenged some of the assumptions of these classical theologians and offered alternative interpretations. All religions have their theological reformers, and Economics is not an exception. Reformers differ from the prophets in this important respect. Like the prophets, they recognize that something has gone wrong, but unlike the prophets, reformers believe that the defects the prophet exposed can be fixed without jettisoning the entire system.

All religions have a violent component that will also be discussed in this chapter. These religious extremists assume that their religious doctrines are straight from the mind of God. Moreover, they firmly believe that their salvation depends on their faithfulness to these doctrines regardless of the consequences. If this means people must die, this is a necessary price to pay for the purity of their faith. Finally, all religions have their priests and holy ones. Economics does too. We call them "economic professionals," and a discussion of the education of our Economic priests, and its consequences, will conclude this chapter.

> The fundamental difference between Capitalists and Socialists is that Capitalists believe the means of production should be privately held, and Socialists believe the means of production should be in the hands of a centralized government committee.

Every religion has "denominations" or "schools of thought." Islam is divided between Shiite and Sunni. Christianity is divided between Eastern and Western Church, and the Western Church is further divided between Catholic and Protestant. In Economics, the most fundamental theological divide is between Capitalists and Socialists. Over the years, our political rhetoric has obscured their actual differences, so the following distinction is extremely important to remember. Capitalists believe that the means of production — which includes property, money, financing, industrial equipment, organization, etc. — should be privately held. Socialists believe that the private ownership of the means of production is the source of inequality and poverty; therefore, they think that the means of production should be in the hands of government experts and officials who, they believe, have the expertise to direct the nation's output toward more socially beneficial ends. This is an important distinction that should not be forgotten when Capitalists and Socialists are mentioned in the following discussion.

Classical Economists: Theologians of Perpetual Poverty

In his book *The Great Transformation*, Karl Polanyi notes that the transition from feudalism to a modern market economy had profound social consequences that included: the removal of peasants from their traditional association with the land; the weakening of traditional social relationships such as religion, family, and village; the influx of population to the cities; and the commodification of labor. While economists eventually realized that these consequences were not totally positive, the first theologians of the market economy did not focus on the social disruption caused by the emergence of Capitalism. They focused on the unprecedented wealth in nations where this new economic system prevailed. Before the emergence of this new system, wealth was intimately associated with force and power. A different situation emerged in the eighteenth century. Political associations were no longer essential to the creation of wealth. A person could now become rich through trade and exchange, and this newfound source of wealth increased the aggregate wealth of the nation. Adam Smith was the first person to account for this new phenomenon.

As the full title of his classic, *An Inquiry into the Nature and Causes of the Wealth of Nations,* implies, Adam Smith was not concerned with the wealth of individuals. He was concerned with the forces that caused an increase in the aggregate wealth of nations. Briefly stated, Smith believed that the total wealth of a nation increases when each isolated individual in the nation is allowed to act in his or her economic self-interest.[2] *Herein resides one of the most fundamental principles of Capitalist theology, namely, that the freedom of the people engaged in economic transactions should not be impaired by restrictions from government, morality, custom, family, or religion.* Indeed, the only acceptable government regulations are regulations designed to promote such freedom rather than restrict it.

2. Adam Smith, *The Wealth of Nations* (New York: Bantam Books, 2003), p. 572.

Freedom — described as an individual acting in his or her own perceived self-interest — is a fundamental value that all Capitalists share.

Smith's theories make an understandable, but, to our ears, odd assumption. He assumes that, as Jesus even said, "the poor will always be with you." The idea that poverty could somehow be eliminated never crossed his mind. Poverty is a given. Poverty is an inevitable consequence of the "natural order" of human society.

Adam Smith asserted that the "natural order" of human society is *everywhere* divided into three social orders: laborers, businesspersons, and aristocracy. A person's source of income determines the social order into which he or she resides. The owners of capital (businesspersons) receive their revenue through profits, and the aristocracy (landowners) receives its income through rent, and laborers garner their income by labor.[3] A laborer is at an extreme disadvantage in this social order.

Workers, obviously, desire to get the most money possible for their labor, but their employers wish to maximize profits and pay laborers as little as possible. This perpetuates laborers' poverty because "masters" have enormous advantages in most labor disputes. "Masters, being few in number, can combine much more easily; and the law, besides, authorizes or at least does not prohibit their combinations. We have no acts of parliament against combining to *lower* the price of work; many against combining to *raise* it. In all such disputes masters can hold out much longer. . . . Masters are always and everywhere in a sort of tacit, but constant and uniform combination, not to raise the wages of labor above their actual rate. . . . We seldom, indeed, hear of this combination, because it is the usual, and one might say, *natural* state of things which nobody ever hears of."[4]

There is a natural limit to how low wages can fall. They cannot fall below subsistence level.[5] This subsistence wage is the *natural* wage. Since wages could rise above this *natural* subsistence level when revenues and profits rise, there was a possibility that the poverty of labor might be alleviated in countries where revenues and profits were on the rise.[6] The next generation of economists, however, considered such a permanent increase in wages to be remote.

In his book *Essay on Population,* Thomas Malthus (1766-1834) noted

3. Smith, *The Wealth of Nations,* p. 336.
4. Smith, *The Wealth of Nations,* pp. 94, 95, emphasis mine.
5. Smith, *The Wealth of Nations,* p. 96.
6. Smith, *The Wealth of Nations,* pp. 97, 98.

that the number of people who can live in the world is limited by the food supply. Just as the number of deer increases when there is more deer food, human population increases when there is more human food. Since human population rises to meet the food supply, Malthus concluded that there will always be "just enough" food for the vast majority of human beings to live on the edge of starvation. Later he qualified this notion, saying that if laborers exercised "moral restraint" and eliminated "vice" then they could reduce their numbers and live above the poverty level. Without such restraint, however, laborers — who constitute the vast majority of humanity — would be subject to the dire consequences of this *law of nature* that Malthus believed he had discovered.

Adam Smith and Thomas Malthus studied national aggregates. They were concerned about the forces that acted to enrich nations. Just as Sir Isaac Newton had discovered the laws of universal motion, they believed they had discovered universal laws that combined to increase aggregate wealth *and* perpetuate poverty. Smith and Malthus were not interested in the laws that governed the distribution of wealth. This, however, was David Ricardo's (1772-1823) interest. In a letter to Malthus he stated his shift in interest in this way:

> Political Economy you think is an enquiry into the nature and causes of wealth — I think it should rather be called an enquiry into the laws which determine the division of the produce of industry amongst the classes who concur in its formation. No law can be laid down respecting quantity, but a tolerably correct one can be laid down respecting proportions. Every day I am more satisfied that the former enquiry is vain and delusive, and the latter only the true objects of the science.[7]

Ricardo accepted Smith's assumption that the three orders (classes) of society — aristocracy, business owners, and laborers — were determined by how they received their revenues. He denied any intrinsic conflict between business owners and the aristocracy, but since higher wages always lower profits, Ricardo argued that conflicts always exist between labor and owners. In agreement with Malthus, Ricardo thought that higher profits might lead to higher wages in the short run, but higher wages would only increase population, prices, and rents. Eventually this

---

7. Ricardo's letter to Malthus (October 9, 1820), as quoted in Keynes, *The General Theory of Employment, Interest and Money,* p. 4, n. 1.

would lower the relative value of wages and return laborers to a subsistence level. While aggregate wealth increases under these circumstances, ultimately only businesspersons and landowners (aristocracy) benefit. The crushing poverty plaguing labor does not diminish even when the aggregate wealth of the nation increases.

> Adam Smith, David Ricardo, and Thomas Malthus
> thought they had discovered economic laws that were
> of the same status as Newton's laws of motion.

Such logic led Ricardo to the following conclusions:

Labor, like all other things which are purchased and sold, and which may be increased or diminished in quantity, has its natural and its market price. The natural price of labor is that price which is necessary to enable the laborers, one with another, to subsist and perpetuate their race, without either increase or diminution.

These then are the laws by which wages are regulated, and by which the happiness [a word to be duly noted] of far the greatest part of every community is governed. Like all other contracts, wages should be left to the fair and free competition of the market, and should never be controlled by the interference of the legislature.[8]

This constitutes Ricardo's famous Iron Law of Wages. No one is to be blamed for this oppressive state of affairs. The misery of poverty and the few instances of individual wealth are just the way things are. This is the order of things. God or perhaps nature established this irreversible dismal state of affairs.

Several doctrines from Smith, Malthus, and Ricardo abide as fundamental theological teachings of Capitalism. The first says that the essence of humanity is our capacity to engage in exchange. The second states that this free competition of people in pursuit of their self-interest is both the best way for human nature to express itself, the only way to distribute wealth, and the way the aggregate wealth of the nation will increase.

---

8. *The Works and Correspondence of David Ricardo,* vol. 1, pp. 93, 105, as quoted in John Kenneth Galbraith, *The Affluent Society* (Boston: Houghton Mifflin, 1958), pp. 33, 34. The words in brackets are Galbraith's.

Third, the only way to increase labor's standard of living is to increase aggregate wealth, but these theologians think this possibility is remote. Finally, Smith, Malthus, and Ricardo considered their economic "laws" to be on the level of Newton's laws of planetary motion. In other words, these dismal projections are deemed natural or God-given laws. As such, moral objections to these natural laws are as useless as a moral objection to a tornado or snowstorm. These newly discovered economic laws were simply the way things are designed to be. Understanding such laws, however, might help someone avoid their most disastrous consequences, but these laws could never be eliminated. Moreover, their absolute status introduced *struggle* as one of the abiding subplots in Economic theology.

The Economic realm is a realm of struggle where only the fittest survive. Ricardo himself promoted this view, saying that aiding the poor just makes matters worse because aid violates economic laws. Charity just depletes aggregate wealth. It does not change the plight of the poor.[9] For Ricardo this struggle was necessary but not particularly welcome. Social Darwinists welcomed this struggle.

Struggle was the way Charles Darwin's (1809-1882) theory of evolution worked in the Economic Market. Just as Darwin contended that species survive because they are better fit for survival than their competitors, Social Darwinists believed The Market was a place of struggle and competition where the fittest not only survived but prospered. Market competition selected the strong and devoured the weak. In eliminating the weak, Economic competition ensured that the weak would not pollute the gene pool.

Herbert Spencer (1820-1903) first applied (some would say misappropriated) Darwin's ideas to economics. He, not Darwin, coined the phrase "survival of the fittest." He used it to explain why *individuals* (Darwin's theory of evolution concerned the evolution of entire species and not individuals) thrived and others died in the market place. Spencer gloried in the success of the rich and opposed almost all aid to the poor, arguing that such aid helped the inferior human beings that nature had selected for destruction. Accordingly, he opposed state ownership of the post office, the mint, public education, and any aid to the needy including public sanitation because such "luxuries" enabled the most vulnerable to survive.[10]

---

9. Galbraith, *The Affluent Society*, p. 56.
10. Galbraith, *The Affluent Society*, p. 57.

There was no moral condemnation for the wealthy, for, according to Social Darwinism, the rich were rich because nature had selected them for survival and the poor were poor because nature had selected them for death. The rich were in no way responsible for this state of affairs. Indeed, caring for the poor was contrary to natural law. The rich were just required to get richer. As America's first billionaire John D. Rockefeller (1839-1937) would explain to his *Sunday School Class(!)*, "The growth of a large business is merely the survival of the fittest. . . . The American Beauty rose can be produced in the splendor and fragrance which bring cheer to its beholder only by sacrificing the early buds which grow up around it. . . . This is not an evil tendency in business. *It is merely the working-out of a law of nature and a law of God.*"[11] The rich serve nature and, in Rockefeller's words, serve God Himself by continuing to do whatever makes the rich people richer.

Karl Marx: The Prophet of The Economy

Joseph Schumpeter (1883-1950), a patriarch of modern neoconservative Capitalism, begins his book *Capitalism, Socialism and Democracy* by calling Karl Marx a prophet. This is an interesting insight, but Schumpeter does not tell us what a prophet actually is, and you need some idea of what a prophet actually is in order to appreciate the implications of Schumpeter's assertion.

Using the prophets of Israel as an example, one might say that *the prophet challenges conventional religious wisdom. The prophet accomplishes this through the creative reinterpretation of the religious myths, rituals, theology, and laws the prophet shares with the people he or she criticizes.* Just as the prophets of Israel challenged Israel's conventional religious wisdom, Marx did the same with respect to the conventional wisdom of those who worship The Economy.

The prophet Amos (c. 780-742 BCE) prefigures Marx. He spoke during a time of prosperity when Israel thought its unprecedented wealth was a consequence of divine favor. Amos had a different interpretation. He said that the real reason for Israel's prosperity was *the exploitation of the poor!* Divine favor had nothing to do with it!

---

11. William Graham Sumner, *Essays in Political and Social Sciences* (New York: Henry Holt, 1885), p. 85, as quoted in Galbraith, *The Affluent Society*, p. 56.

Thus says the LORD: "For three transgressions . . . , I will not revoke the punishment; because they sell the righteous for silver and the needy for a pair of sandals — they that trample the head of the poor into the dust of the earth and turn aside the way of the afflicted. . . ." (Amos 2:6, 7a)

Hear this, you that trample on the needy and bring to ruin the poor of the land, saying, "When will the new moon be over so that we may sell grain; and the Sabbath so that we may offer wheat for sale? We will make the ephah small and the shekel great, and practice deceit with false balances, buying the poor for silver and the needy for a pair of sandals, and selling the sweepings of wheat." The Lord has sworn by the pride of Jacob: Surely I will never forget any of their deeds. (Amos 8:4-7)

Amos was convinced that the people of Israel did not even know they were acting unjustly. Their own rituals and religious practices blinded them to their injustice and even concealed their injustices from themselves. Their Torah (Law) was clear. Israel's God required justice and compassion for the poor, but Israel had substituted ritualistic sacrifices for justice. The rich could neglect the poor simply by fulfilling cultic rituals. This is why Amos wrote:

Thus says the LORD . . . : "I hate, I despise your feasts, and I take no delight in your solemn assemblies. Even though you offer me your burnt offerings and grain offerings, I will not accept them, and the offerings of well-being of your fatted animals I will not look upon. Take away from me the noise of your songs; I will not listen to the melody of your harps. But let justice roll down like waters, and righteousness like an ever-flowing stream." (Amos 5:21-24)

Amos shared the same religion with the people he criticized. His prophetic critiques are based on alternative interpretations of this common religion. For there to be a prophet, a common religion must be practiced between the prophet and his or her adversaries. For Karl Marx to be a prophet, as Schumpeter claims, he must share a religion with those against whom he prophesies.

Karl Marx was a prophet of the religion called Economics. Like Israel's prophets, Marx introduced a moral element into Economic thought.

> Karl Marx refused to accept poverty as part of the natural order of things. In line with the Hebrew prophetic traditions, Marx said poverty was a consequence of the exploitation of the workers. It was neither natural nor God-given. It was a consequence of the design of Capitalism itself.

He rejected the claims that poverty is a consequence of the natural order of things. Amos had proclaimed that Israel's affluence had nothing to do with divine favor and everything to do with Israel's exploitation of the poor. Marx rejected the contention that poverty was the consequence of natural forces. Instead it was the consequence of the owners of capital robbing workers of the value of their labor. Like Amos, Marx predicted the inevitable day when these unjust situations would be remedied. Like Amos, Marx worked *within* an already-established religion. Like Amos, he used the principles of this common religion to criticize the beliefs and practices that perpetuate poverty.

Marx's theory of value illustrates how he did this. In agreement with Adam Smith, Marx had a labor theory of value. He thought that the labor "socially necessary" to produce a given product was the *only* source of a product's value.[12] This theory inspired Marx to insert a prophetic, moral element that is still present in Economic debate; for, if labor is the source of all value, and owners of capital do not contribute labor, then one must ask, "From where do the owners' profits arise?"

Given Marx's labor theory of value, these profits could only result from the vicious exploitation of labor. Marx argues that the owners of capital increase their profits when they "extend the workday," which is a polite way to say that the owners make the laborers work longer hours for no additional pay. They increase profits when they centralize labor. They increase their profits by getting labor to cooperate in the production of the product. They increase their profits when the division of labor makes labor more efficient and productive. New technology increases profits because it makes the strength of men superfluous and allows owners to fire men and hire women and children at lower rates. Admittedly, new technologies or new organizational structures employed to promote efficiency could be understood as the owners' own labor. This could lead

12. Marx, *Capital,* vol. 1, trans. Ben Fowkes (New York: Penguin, 1976, 1990), p. 129.

to the conclusion that owners do contribute their labor to a product and thereby increase its value, but Marx "refutes" such reasoning throughout *Capital.*

These refutations allow Marx to maintain the moral high ground against the Capitalists who, in Marx's view, continue to exploit the workers and keep them in grinding poverty. Marx agrees with Smith, Malthus, and Ricardo who said the business and landowners have an extreme advantage over labor. In this sense he was an orthodox believer in the theological traditions of the religion called Economics. Marx was a prophet because he rejected the belief that grinding poverty was part of the natural order of things. This led him to "prophesy" that the evil of poverty is the consequence of an unjust system whose days are numbered.

Obviously Marx's theories are not beyond dispute. While labor contributes to the value of a product, it is not the only source of value. Sometimes one's context contributes to the value of a given product. For example, in a normal context I would not pay too much for a bottle of water, but if I had been days in the desert without water, I might gladly pay a considerable sum for that bottle. Value is also subjective. Subjective value lies in the eyes of the beholder. It does not matter how much labor is put into a given product; it does not have value unless someone desires it.[13] Marx's labor theory of value may be incomplete or may even be wrong, but prophets are not prophets because of their accuracy. They are people who envision and create alternatives to conventional religious culture.

After Marx, the rich could no longer justify themselves in the presence of the poor because poverty could not simply be attributed to nature or some divine plan. The rich were no longer above moral critique. Marx was, as Schumpeter said, a prophet, but he was a prophet only because he shared the same religion as those against whom he prophesied.

Economic Reformers

As Marx was writing his prophetic words, a growing optimism was emerging in the industrialized world. Colossal developments in technology — railroads, telegraph, and electricity — created unprecedented economic growth. These magnificent innovations introduced optimism

---

13. Georg Simmel, *The Philosophy of Money* (New York: Routledge, 1978, 2004), pp. 61-131.

into the dismal science without violating the economic laws introduced by Malthus and Ricardo. The dramatic expansion of the food supply created by the railroads' ability to bring more food to market led economists to believe that it would take the population a very long time to catch up to this newly created bounty. More food meant that laborers might escape the mere subsistence that Malthus predicted. Likewise, sustained economic growth gave the most ardent followers of Ricardo a reason to celebrate. Ricardo's one exception to his Iron Law of Wages was that wages would remain at subsistence levels *except* during times of sustained economic growth. New technology and innovations were a harbinger of exactly this sort of sustained growth. The destruction of Capitalist society was not inevitable. The entire system did not need to be overthrown, as Marx prophesied.

Poverty could be eliminated by *following* Capitalist principles. Public policies could be constructed to ease the burden of the poor without undermining the innovations that were the strength of Capitalist society. Reformers emerged in Great Britain and the United States with this new vision.

British Reformers

British Economists developed new policies based on a philosophy called utilitarianism. This philosophy challenged policymakers to develop ways to produce the greatest good for the greatest number of people. In theory, the greatest good was a *calculation* that gave positive numbers to pleasures and negative numbers to pain. Assuming that society was no more than the sum of its parts, utilitarian policymakers tried to develop policies that would increase the total amount of pleasure and decrease the total amount of pain within a nation.[14]

John Stuart Mill (1806-1873) was probably the nineteenth century's premier utilitarian philosopher. He generally followed Ricardo and Malthus, but he challenged their contention that wages, rent, and profits are a consequence of *immutable* laws. Instead, he believed that the "laws" that Ricardo and Malthus "discovered" were not natural laws but the consequence of institutional constraints and organization. This meant that

---

14. Utilitarian policymakers might be in disagreement concerning what exactly constitutes pleasure and pain and how to measure this.

> Economic reformers tried to alleviate the socially detrimental aspects of Capitalism without jettisoning the Capitalist system.

these institutional constraints could be changed, and Mill believed they should be changed according to utilitarian calculations. Calculating the amount of pleasure and pain enabled utilitarian policymakers, at least in theory, to change our institutions in more humane ways.[15]

Even Mill called himself a Socialist, but he will not here be classified as such because he was not interested in centralized control of the economy. He thought human freedom was fundamental and firmly believed that freedom could be maintained, while, at the same time, its adverse consequences could be reduced.[16] Capitalist freedom entails that some people — the lucky ones, the smart ones, the hardest-working ones — will be better off than others. It implies social inequality of the sort Socialists think is unacceptable. Yet Mill thought the more inhumane aspects of unfettered Capitalism could be alleviated by social policies based on utilitarian principles. He was not a Socialist. He was a reformer of the Capitalist system.

Mill was concerned with adjustments to the system and not its overthrow. He also represents an important split within Capitalism itself. Whereas the classical Capitalists understood poverty and other detrimental consequences of Capitalism to be necessary, unavoidable processes of nature, reformers like Mill tried to correct the negative features of Capitalism through government policies and laws. They protected labor unions and civil rights. They established graduated income taxes, social security, public education, and national health care. When reformers were successful, welfare states or mixed economies emerged. Today, we often confuse welfare states with Socialist states. They are not the same. A welfare state tries to maintain an individual's economic freedom (a central theological feature of Capitalism) while also trying to protect the citizens from the worst consequences of this freedom. Keeping the means of production in the hands of business owners is essential to freedom. Socialism, on the other hand, places the means of production under

15. Fred Wilson, "John Stuart Mill," *Stanford Encyclopedia of Philosophy*, 2002, 2007. http://plato.stanford.edu/entries/mill/.

16. John Stuart Mill, *On Liberty* (New York: Bobbs-Merrill, 1956).

state control (at least until the state withers away). The central control of the means of production destroys the economic freedom that Capitalists deem an essential and fundamental human right. This important distinction keeps utilitarian economics within Capitalism and introduces a note of optimism into Capitalist thought.

American Reformers

This new optimism had a profound impact in America as well, but American Economists modeled their reform on the Christian Social Gospel Movement instead of utilitarianism. The leader of the Social Gospel Movement, Walter Rauschenbusch (1861-1917), expressed this optimism well in the concluding paragraphs of his classic *Christianity and the Social Crisis*.

> If the twentieth century could do for us in the control of social forces what the nineteenth did for us in the control of natural forces, our grandchildren would live in a society that would be justified in regarding our present age as semi-barbarous.... Humanity is gaining in elasticity and capacity for change, and every gain in intelligence, in organizing capacity, in physical and moral soundness, and especially in responsiveness to ideal motive, again increases the ability to advance without disastrous reactions. *The swiftness of evolution in our country proves the immense perfectibility in human nature....*
>
> Perhaps these nineteen centuries of Christian influence have been a long preliminary stage of growth, and now the flower and fruit are almost here. If at this juncture we can rally sufficient religious faith and moral strength to snap the bonds of evil and turn the present unparalleled economic and intellectual resources of humanity to the harmonious development of a true social life, *the generations unborn will mark this as the great day of the Lord for which the ages waited, and count us blessed for sharing in the apostolate that proclaimed it.*[17]

Contrary to Smith, Ricardo, and Malthus, Rauschenbusch believed that evil in the form of poverty could be eliminated. In fact, the beginning

17. Walter Rauschenbusch, *Christianity and the Social Crisis* (New York: Macmillan, 1907), as quoted in Sidney E. Ahlstrom, *A Religious History of the American People*, vol. 2 (Garden City, NY: Image Books, 1975), pp. 250, 251. Emphasis mine.

of poverty's demise was already underway. No "otherworldly realm" was anticipated. The Social Gospel Movement proclaimed a "heaven on earth" that the "immense perfectibility in human nature" creates through economic progress. The American Economic Association (AEA) emerged from this Christian Social Gospel Movement.[18]

Richard T. Ely (1854-1943) co-founded the American Economic Association, where the Richard T. Ely lecture remains a prestigious forum. In his day, he was better known as a leader of the Social Gospel Movement than as an economist. In one of his first books, *The Social Aspects of Christianity,* he identified himself with "the ethical school of economics," which aimed "to direct in a certain definite manner . . . the economic social growth of mankind. Economists of this school wish to ascertain the *laws of progress* and to show how to make use of them."[19] Like all his economic predecessors, Ely searched for eternal economic laws, but he provided a Christian slant. His laws were laws of progress. The discovery of these laws removes the few remaining impediments to the Kingdom of Heaven on earth. For Ely, Economics was the best way to promote Christianity, but soon American Economists abandoned their Christian origins.

Although twenty of the fifty charter members of the American Economic Association were Christian ministers, talk of God and explicit references to the Social Gospel Movement were soon deemed inappropriate in economic discussion. Nonetheless, the narrative *behind* American economics remained the same. Instead of the Christian God, Economic progress became the power behind history.[20] American Economists remained optimistic. They continued to understand history in the same linear way all Abrahamic religions understand history, believing it to progress from humble origins into a final glorious consummation. But God was not the force behind this change. Economists substituted Economic growth and human innovation as the power behind the emergence of a new, more perfect society. As is true with utilitarianism, this new progressive optimism countered the Marxist/Socialist critique without undermining Capitalism's most important principles like the freedom to engage in the self-interested pursuit of profit and the belief that this self-interested pursuit would increase social well-being.

18. Robert H. Nelson, *Economics as Religion* (University Park: Penn State Press, 2001, 2006), pp. 41, 42.

19. As quoted in Ahlstrom, *A Religious History of the American People,* p. 263.

20. Nelson, *Economics as Religion,* pp. 41, 42.

Indeed, American Economists believed that the free, self-interested actions of these isolated individuals would create so much national wealth that poverty itself could be eliminated. This robbed the Socialists of their issue. The Capitalist system did not need to be overthrown. Practicing the scientifically established Market principles established by Smith, Malthus, and Ricardo was all that was necessary to progress. The exercise of freedom in the economic realm — the very thing that the Socialists thought led to poverty, inequality, and alienation — was all that was necessary to eliminate poverty and create a better society. We did not have to abandon freedom (the fundamental virtue of the Capitalist) to eliminate poverty. To be sure, this would not eliminate inequality, but neither would inequality result in poverty. It was an inequality we could live with.

Economic Terrorism

The Character of Religious Terrorism

Once theology and doctrine emerges to rationalize the rituals and myths of a religion, there is a tendency for certain people of faith to think that their theological doctrines are synonymous with the mind of God. When this happens, violence or terrorism is justified on religious grounds.[21] Acting in accord with these "true" unchanging beliefs is paramount. The actual consequences of these "faithful" actions are secondary.

For example, Yoel Lerner justified the assassination of Prime Minister of Israel Yitzhak Rabin (1922-1995) because his religious doctrine could not tolerate the fact that Rabin's peace treaty ceded the Temple site in Jerusalem to the Palestinians. His divine narrative recognizes the biblical fact that most of God's laws to Israel concern religious rituals that can only be performed in the Temple. Furthermore, Lerner believed that the Messiah of Israel will come only when these Temple rituals are performed. Unfortunately, the Temple was destroyed around 1900 years ago. It does not exist! Since Rabin's peace proposal involved ceding the Temple site to the Palestinians, this would inevitably delay the Temple's reconstruction, and this delay also would delay the Messiah's coming.

21. Mark Juergensmeyer, *Terror in the Mind of God: The Global Rise of Religious Violence* (Berkeley: University of California Press, 2000).

66

This being so, Rabin's peace efforts had to be stopped.[22] Rabin had to be assassinated.

Extreme violent acts like Rabin's assassination are not limited to Judaism. In the recent past, Christianity (Eric Robert Rudolph bombing abortion clinics, a lesbian bar, and the 1996 Atlanta Olympics); Buddhism (Tokyo subway bombing, March 20, 1995); Sikhism (thousands killed between 1981 and 1994, the most prominent being the assassination of Indira Gandhi on October 31, 1984); and Islam (Mahmud Abouhalima's involvement in the World Trade Center bombing in 1993, and its destruction by Osama bin Laden in 2001) have all had their terrorists. Moreover, these acts are justified by theological doctrines believed to reflect the unchanging mind of God.[23] Economics is not immune from such violence. Economic violence may not be obvious because it often is supported by governments or international agencies, and our understanding of terrorism does not extend to governments. Nonetheless, there is more than ample evidence to suggest that both Capitalists and Socialists have extremists whose actions, when implemented, often have violent, death-dealing consequences.

Capitalist Terrorism

Nobel Prize–winner Gary Becker's thought borders on Capitalist extremism. He extends the utilitarian idea that everyone seeks to maximize his or her utility beyond the purely economic realm and into all areas of human endeavor. For example, in Becker's view, criminals are not different because of moral defects. They differ because a criminal receives more benefits from criminal activity than a law-abiding citizen.[24]

According to this logic, I, a pastor, will refrain from stealing food from a grocery store not out of moral superiority, but because I stand to lose much more than would be gained if caught. The possible costs of stealing food far exceed the benefits I would receive. On the other hand, a man whose family is on the verge of starvation has different costs and

22. Juergensmeyer, *Terror in the Mind of God,* p. 46. Had Juergensmeyer been able to interview those who had killed heretics and "witches" and conducted religious crusades, jihads, or pogroms in previous centuries, he probably would have had similar conversations among "the faithful" who also justified religious violence using theological propositions.

23. Juergensmeyer, *Terror in the Mind of God,* p. 46.

24. Nelson, *Economics as Religion,* p. 172.

benefits to consider. He might choose to steal because the benefits he and his family would receive from stolen food exceed the cost of possibly getting caught and punished. We both conduct a cost/benefit analysis, in Becker's view. Traditional moral considerations are not involved.

On this level, Becker seems intuitively correct; but his reasoning becomes more and more questionable the further it extends into the social world. He does not back down from the challenge. He extends his cost/benefit analysis into other aspects of human life. He discusses marriage, divorce, and procreation as utilitarian acts of consumer choice. Marriage, for example, works because the sum of the individual gains (benefits) exceeds losses (costs).

> It is not only that Becker was describing an evolving trend in society. He was also giving it greater legitimacy. He was presenting the new world of marriage in the language of economic exchange, efficiency and productivity. In the progressive gospels of the twentieth century, maximizing efficiency in the use of the productive resources of society is the path to heaven on earth. If (former) patterns of marriage had been blessed by God (or his representatives in the church), the newer forms of marriage would now be blessed by a more contemporary god who would save the world by eliminating scarcity and bringing on a state of complete material abundance. . . . *[T]he technical content of Becker's economics is secondary to the preaching of a powerful underlying value system. It defends a new set of values that manifest a strong individualistic and libertarian trend not only in marriage but in almost every area of society as it has been spreading in American life from the 1960s onward.*[25]

While those who adopt Becker's assumptions may find it easy to agree with him even in this rather unromantic analysis of marriage, extending his logic to *all* aspects of human life becomes increasingly problematic. Following Becker's cost/benefit logic, Nazi Germany's persecution, concentration, enslavement, and murder of millions of Jews could *only* be condemned if it could be shown that these despicable activities diminished the aggregate utility or overall efficiency of Germany.[26] Now such an argument would appear ridiculous from any traditional religion's

---

25. Nelson, *Economics as Religion*, p. 184. Emphasis mine.
26. Nelson, *Economics as Religion*, p. 174.

perspective. Indeed, *the only way such a cost/benefit analysis of the Holocaust makes any sense whatsoever is if The Economy is in fact God!* Without this religious perspective, a cost/benefit analysis of the Holocaust is itself an immoral act. Now Becker never extends his analysis to the Holocaust. This is a bit extreme even for him, but this sort of cost/benefit logic was used by Lawrence Summers when he was the Chief Economist for the World Bank.

On December 12, 1991, he circulated a memo throughout the World Bank. Under the title "Dirty Industries," Summers wrote:

> Just between you and me, shouldn't we the World Bank be encouraging MORE migration of the dirty industries to the LDCs [Less Developed Countries]? I can think of three reasons:
>
> 1) The measurements of the costs of health impairing pollution depends on the foregone earnings from increased morbidity and mortality. From this point of view a given amount of health impairing pollution should be done in the country with the lowest cost, which will be the country with the lowest wages. *I think the economic logic behind dumping a load of toxic waste in the lowest wage country is impeccable and we should face up to that.*
>
> 2) The costs of pollution are likely to be non-linear as the initial increments of pollution probably have very low cost. I've always thought that under-populated countries in Africa are vastly UNDER-polluted, their air quality is inefficiently low compared to Los Angeles or Mexico City. Only the lamentable facts that so much pollution is generated by non-tradable industries (transport, electrical generation), and that the unit transport costs of solid waste are so high prevent world welfare enhancing trade in air pollution and waste.
>
> 3) The demand for a clean environment for aesthetic and health reasons is likely to have very high income elasticity. The concern over an agent that causes a one in a million change in the odds of prostate cancer is obviously going to be much higher in a country where people survive to get prostate cancer than in a country where under 5 mortality is 200 per thousand. Also, much of the concern over industrial atmosphere discharge is about visibility impairing particulates. These discharges may have very little direct health impact. Clearly trade in goods that

embody aesthetic pollution concerns could be welfare enhancing. While production is mobile the consumption of pretty air is a non-tradable.

[Summers continues] The problem with the arguments against all of these proposals for more pollution in LDCs (intrinsic rights to certain goods, moral reasons, social concerns, lack of adequate markets, etc.) could be turned around and used more or less effectively against every Bank proposal for liberalization.[27]

In case you missed it, Summers proposed a policy based on a cost/benefit analysis. While nineteenth-century utilitarian economists argued about how utility should be calculated, Summers offered a simple solution. Money measures utility. The more money a particular act generates, the greater is the utility. The worth of an individual human being, for example, can be calculated in terms of his or her earning potential. A person projected to earn $100,000 in his life would be worth less than a person projected to make $2,000,000. This is the utilitarian logic behind Summers's memo. He proposed that pollution should be dumped on LDCs for the simple reason that the human lives hurt by such actions are less valuable than are the human lives in the developed states. He was doing a simple cost/benefit analysis. His logic was impeccable!

> Both Capitalist and Socialist often use impeccable logic
> to reach insane conclusions, demonstrating that insanity
> and the ability to reason are not mutually exclusive.

This memo became public in February of 1992. What happened next is interesting. Brazil's Secretary of the Environment Jose Lutzenburger (1927-2002) responded: *"Your reasoning is perfectly logical but totally insane.* ... Your thoughts (provide) a concrete example of the unbelievable alienation, reductionist thinking, social ruthlessness and arrogant ignorance of many conventional 'economists' concerning the nature of the world we live in. ... If the World Bank keeps you as vice president it will lose all credibility. To me it would confirm what I often said ... the best

---

27. Lawrence Summers, "The Bank Memo," The Whirled Bank Group (2001), www .whirledbank.org. Emphasis mine.

thing that could happen would be for the Bank to disappear."[28] Jose Lutzenburger was fired for writing this letter. Lawrence Summers, the author of the memo, went on to become Secretary of Treasury in the Clinton administration, President of Harvard University, and a top economic advisor to President Obama. In 2013 he was a leading candidate for Federal Reserve Chairman.

Lutzenburger's response helps us recognize that perfect logic and insanity are not mutually exclusive. Being insane is neither the same as being stupid nor is it necessarily always psychological. It is often the consequence of a strict "religious" adherence to principles thought to be divinely instituted. Summers *religiously* believes that his principles of utility are sacred. He realizes that other people — maybe the unenlightened unbelievers not associated with the World Bank — could view his proposal as a touch strange; for, he starts his memo saying, "Just between you and me," and he ends noting that moral arguments could be used against his proposal. But, he adds, these same moral arguments could be used against any proposal for "liberalization" (a word one must pause to duly note) that the World Bank has proposed. In other words, Summers says that the World Bank *always* employs the logic he uses, but it is just not as obvious.

Like all religious extremists, Summers makes the merely plausible into an absolute, and he is willing to sacrifice innocent people to his false absolute. If, as Lutzenberger said, Summers's memo is both logical and insane, it is insane because all calculations determining the relative value of human beings are doomed if all human beings have intrinsic worth apart from such calculations. Socialists recognize this. They think that human equality is an absolute value. But history demonstrates that Socialist extremists have performed death-dealing acts of even greater scope. To some of these we now turn.

Socialist Terrorism

Socialists believe that poverty and human inequality are a consequence of private control of the means of production; hence, emancipation requires removing the means of production from private, Capitalist control and placing them in the hands of a central government authority.

---

28. Summers, "The Bank Memo," www.whirledbank.org.

Unfortunately the implementation of this plan has had many terrible consequences.

According to Vladimir Lenin (1870-1924), a central authority is essential to socialism. Without its guidance workers can only develop "a trade union consciousness." Workers will form labor unions. They can compel the government to enact reforms. Workers will fight employers for higher wages, but they will not seek to overthrow the Capitalist system. Absent the philosophical support of a central committee, the workers will work within the Capitalist system and will not eliminate the structures (mainly the private ownership of the means of production) that are the source of poverty and inequality. An educated ruling elite is necessary for Socialists' consciousness to be complete.[29]

> I assert: 1) that no movement can be durable without a stable organization of leaders to maintain continuity; 2) that the more widely the masses are spontaneously drawn into the struggle and form the basis of the movement and participate in it, the more necessary is it to have such an organization, and the more stable must it be . . . ; 3) that the organization must consist chiefly of persons engaged in revolutionary activities as a profession; 4) that in a country with an autocratic government, the more we *restrict* the membership of this organization to persons who are engaged in revolutionary activities as a profession and who have been professionally trained in the art of combating the political police, the more difficult will it be to catch the organization; and 5) the *wider* will be the circle of men and women of the working class or of other classes of society able to join the movement and perform active work in it.[30]

The central group of educated professional revolutionaries is to the working class as intelligence is to brute force. Indeed, nothing better con-

---

29. Vladimir Lenin, *What Is to Be Done?* (1902), in *Essential Works of Lenin*, ed. Henry M. Christman (New York: Bantam Books, 1987), p. 74. This book has the same title as Lenin's older brother's favorite book by Nicholas Chernyshevsky. In Chernyshevsky's book a "new man" of intelligence destroys the old order and rules autocratically to establish a social utopia. Lenin himself states, "I became acquainted with the works of Marx, Engels and Piekhanov, but it was only Chernyshevsky who had an overwhelming influence on me." See James C. Scott, *Seeing Like a State: How Certain Schemes to Improve the Human Condition Have Failed* (New Haven: Yale University Press, 1999), p. 148.

30. Lenin, *What Is to Be Done?* pp. 147, 148.

veys this relationship than the word "masses" — a physical metaphor that implies only weight and numbers, has no mind of its own, and needs to be managed by an intelligentsia.[31]

Just months before taking power in the new Soviet Union, Lenin published *The State and Revolution* (1917) in which he argued for the dictatorship of the proletariat.[32] This dictatorship would last until the state withered away. "The economic basis for the complete withering away of the state is the high stage of development of communism in which the antithesis between the mental and the physical labor disappears, that is to say, when one of the principal sources of modern *social inequality* . . . disappears."[33] The trouble is that the state has yet to wither away, and the dictatorship of the proletariat lasted as long as Lenin's Soviet Union lasted.

Lenin's absolute adherence to a central planning committee that set prices, determined what is produced, who is to produce it, and how production should happen was *meant* to be the source of equality. It was *meant* to free Russian citizens from want and need. Instead it became the source of oppression and death. Some have suggested that in his later years Lenin was disillusioned because he did not advocate authoritarianism simply for the sake of authoritarianism. He had hoped it would be a short period in which the state withered away, creating a society of

31. Scott, *Seeing Like a State*, p. 150.

32. It is not that Lenin represents the only Socialist view with respect to an elite central committee in the Party or government. He represents an extremist view that led to state terrorism. In response to Lenin's *What Is to Be Done?* Rosa Luxemburg wrote *Organizational Questions of Russian Social Democracy* in which she argued that the class struggle operates within a "dialectical contradiction" that requires those engaged in revolution to make adjustments as the revolution progresses. This fact precludes a "ready-made predetermined and detailed tactic of struggle that the Central Committee could drill into the . . . membership." Rosa Luxemburg, *Organizational Questions* (1905) in *The Rosa Luxemburg Reader,* ed. Peter Hudis and Kevin B. Anderson (New York: Monthly Review Press, 2004), p. 252. Lenin was also critiqued from an anarchist's perspective by Emma Goldman who wrote of her involvement in the Russian Revolution in books titled *My Disillusionment in Russia* (1923) and *My Further Disillusionment in Russia* (1924). She came to realize that "the centralized political State was Lenin's deity, to which everything else was sacrificed." With its nationalized, central economy in which the state owned the means of production, with its rigid central planning and wage system, with its class divisions and privileges, Goldman came to believe that Lenin's state was not much different from state capitalism. See Peter Marshall, *Demanding the Impossible: A History of Anarchism* (Oakland, CA: PM Press, 2008), p. 400.

33. Lenin, *The State and Revolution*, in *Essential Works of Lenin*, p. 343.

freedom and equality.[34] If this is true, Lenin's disillusionment is a consequence of power's tendency to become an end in itself.

Whatever goal those in power once had, this initial goal usually becomes subordinate to the goal of power's perpetuation. Only very remarkable people like Gideon (Hebrews), Cincinnatus (Romans), George Washington (America), and Mikhail Gorbachev (Soviet Union) refused absolute power when offered. But in the act of refusal, each person changed the course of history in one liberating way or another. These are the exceptions. More often than not, people aspire to such power and will fight to the death in order to keep it. Joseph Stalin (1879-1953) was such a man.

Stalin assumed absolute control of the central committee and controlled the means of production. He continued Lenin's efforts to collectivize and control agriculture.[35] This goal entailed the "transfer of peasants, whose mothers and fathers had worked the same land as they, from their small farms to big, public farms capable of producing, using the best science of the day, the greatest quantity of grain for the market."[36] Now this is an admirable undertaking and it was an important step toward the Socialist goal of freedom from life's necessities. But the means to this end — collectivization of farming — had many life-threatening consequences.

Centralization transferred the means of production *from* the small peasant farms *to* the large, centralized collective farms. The peasants were forced to relocate and work on collective farms. This relocation obviously meant the confiscation of peasant property and their forced removal from the lands of their heritage. But of more importance to agricultural production itself, it eliminated the peasants' local knowledge of the land, soil, climate, and times to plant and harvest that they had acquired over the centuries in the practice of farming in their traditional locales. Soviet farming suffered as a consequence of this lost knowledge, and peasants

---

34. Henry M. Christman, "Introduction," in *Essential Works of Lenin*, p. 10.

35. Stalin's Soviet Union was not alone in the collectivization of farming. Americans were toying with the idea in 1934 when, under the auspices of the American Planning Board, the United States studied the centralized planning of four countries — Germany, Italy, Russia, and Japan — as instances of modern approaches to agriculture. By 1946 Western nations were calling these nations "totalitarian." The United States had fought a war with three of them and was beginning a cold war with the other. F. A. Hayek, *The Road to Serfdom* (Chicago: University of Chicago Press, 1944, 2007), p. 43.

36. Sheila Fitzpatrick, *Stalin's Peasants: Resistance and Survival in the Russian Village After Collectivization* (New York: Oxford University Press, 1995), p. 39.

changed from knowledgeable, autonomous persons capable of making creative decisions into a people in bondage. The extent of their bondage is revealed in an August 1932 decree from Stalin that branded anyone who withheld grain — declared by the state as being sacred and untouchable state property — an enemy of the people. They were to be arrested and shot![37] It is well known that Stalin in particular arrested and killed millions of people. Some probably were killed for eating the "state's" grain which they themselves had cultivated.

Socialist extremists like Lenin and Stalin are often disowned by contemporary Socialists because of the death-dealing consequences of their actions. But these dire consequences are in fact the result of strict, religious adherence to the centerpiece of Socialist doctrine, namely, the government's ownership of the means of production. Lenin and Stalin adhered to this principle come what may, and their "faithful" adherence had death-dealing consequences. We do not call them terrorists, only because our definition of terrorism precludes government actions from being terrorist acts. Nonetheless, the collectivizing acts of the Soviet Union mimic actions of religious terrorists who adhere to their religious principles despite the carnage. Sadly, the carnage created by central planning was not limited to the Soviet Union.

The infamous policies of Chinese leader Mao Tse-tung (1893-1976) may have been responsible for more deaths that those of Lenin and Stalin, but the lesser-known practices of two African nations are more recent illustrations of the extremes to which our religious devotion to the Socialist doctrine of centralized planning will take us.

Julius Nyerere (1922-1999) of Tanzania believed he had learned from Soviet and Chinese mistakes. He insisted that the creation of Tanzania's collectives would be gradual and voluntary. He declared, "Socialist communities cannot be established by compulsion (and) can only be established with willing members; the task of leadership and of Government is not to try and force this kind of development but to explain, encourage, and participate."[38] But, since the program was voluntary, it was resisted.

Resistance prompted Nyerere to compel people to join the collectives. He simply could not allow his people to "choose death over life." He thought peasant refusal proved their ignorance, and ignorance should not determine government policy. Since they did not know what was good

37. Fitzpatrick, *Stalin's Peasants*, p. 73.
38. Scott, *Seeing Like a State*, p. 231.

for themselves, peasants were evicted from their lands and forced into planned villages where they grew cash crops on communal fields using state-owned and -supplied machinery. Their housing, government, farming practices, and workdays would be overseen by the state. They were forced to farm "scientifically."

This, of course, was the plan, but the outcome was the same as that on the Soviet collectives nearly a half-century before. *Forcing farmers to move from places where they possessed local knowledge to areas were this local knowledge did not apply made the farmers much less effective in their work.* "The forced villagization campaign itself had such a disastrous effect on agricultural production that . . . [h]uge imports of food were necessary from 1973 through 1975. Nyerere declared the 1.2 billion shillings spent for food imports would have bought one cow for every Tanzanian family. Roughly 60 percent of the new villages were located on semiarid land unsuitable for permanent cultivation, requiring peasants to walk long distances to reach viable plots. The chaos of the move itself and the slow process of adapting to a new ecological setting meant further disruptions of production."[39]

Nyerere knew of the brutalities involved in collectivization. He publicly decried the failure to compensate peasants for their property destroyed in their forced relocation. But it never occurred to him to blame centralized authority itself. Central planning alone established where people should live, determined what they should do, the crops they should plant, the fields they should cultivate, and the methods they used in cultivation. Despite Nyerere's stated hopes, this centralized power structure had to be authoritarian if it were to achieve its stated goals. Once again we see that "heads roll" when a plausible premise (central planning) becomes a religious absolute.

If the means of production are in the hands of the state, in all likelihood, the state will eventually become authoritarian. In Nyerere's case, this happened despite his stated intentions, but in Ethiopia, Colonel Mengistu Haile Mariam (1937-) believed that Nyerere failed because the transition to collectivization was too slow and too pacific. In Ethiopia, peasants were given only three months to leave places where they and their families had lived for generations. Settlements were more like a penal colony than a village.[40] It was a crime to flee. Sanitation was nonexis-

39. Scott, *Seeing Like a State*, p. 239.
40. Scott, *Seeing Like a State*, p. 248.

tent. Roads were often impassable. As was the case in Tanzania, this was done for "humane" reasons. Colonel Mengistu Haile Mariam declared: "The scattered and haphazard habitation and livelihood of Ethiopian peasants cannot build socialism. . . . Insofar as efforts are dispersed and livelihood is individual, the results are only hand-to-mouth existence amounting to fruitless struggle and drudgery, which cannot build a prosperous society."[41] Once again disastrous consequences occurred despite the admirable goal to build a prosperous society.

People were removed from settings in which they had the knowledge, skills, a supportive community, and the resources to meet their basic needs, and they were placed into settings where such local knowledge and talents were of no avail. Communal ties, family, networks of cooperation — the principal way these forced exiles once managed to survive periods of want — were gone. Stripped of these social resources and forbidden to leave, the settlers were much more vulnerable to starvation and other afflictions. The pain and suffering were so great that in 1991 the people rebelled. Colonel Mengistu Haile Mariam went into exile in Zimbabwe. In 2006, Ethiopian courts found him guilty of genocide and sentenced him in absentia to life in prison. The next year this case was appealed, and the colonel was sentenced to death.

In *The Road to Serfdom*, F. A. Hayek argues that the oppression of which we are speaking is the direct consequence of the Socialist objective to remove the means of production from private hands and place them in the hands of the government. To be sure, the dire consequences of such centralization never were the outcome the Socialists desired. In fact, Socialism attracts many because of the admirable ends it wishes to achieve: social justice, greater equality, security, and freedom from want. Yet, those who desire these ends do not understand that the means are diametrically opposed to the envisioned ends.[42] "The situation is still more complicated by the fact that . . . 'economic planning' which is the prime instrument of socialist reform, can be used for many other purposes. . . . *But such planning is no less indispensable if the distribution of incomes is to be regulated in a way which to us appears to be the opposite of just.* Whether we should wish that more of the good things of this world should go to some racial elite, the Nordic men, or the members of a party or an aristocracy, the methods which

41. Scott, *Seeing Like a State*, p. 248.
42. Hayek, *The Road to Serfdom*, p. 83.

we shall have to employ are the same as those which could ensure an equalitarian distribution."[43]

Centralized planning also presupposes a universal moral agreement that never exists. People can agree on lesser items of importance, but we will never agree on the all-encompassing worldview that central planning needs if it is to reflect the actual will of the people. In fact, the idea of a universal morality is becoming less and less plausible in our increasingly diverse world. Centralized planners think the lack of universal moral agreement is a consequence of people's ignorance and that they, the planners, know these absolutes. Their belief in such absolutes as centralized planning or social utility combined with the contention that a core group (centralized planning authority or the World Bank) knows these moral absolutes, allows extremist beliefs to be imposed on the people despite the consequences. These policies have proved to be death-dealing, as the recent histories of the Soviet Union, Tanzania, and Ethiopia indicate.[44]

The need for a core group that possesses "true" knowledge that it must impose on an ignorant population is not simply a phenomenon of Socialism. Special people are needed in all Economic schools of thought, though the consequences are seldom as death-dealing. In traditional religions these special people are priests. In Economics these priests are called professionals.

The Economy's Priests and Their Training

Like the other religious leaders, Economic professionals are bound by moral standards to which the general public need not submit. Whereas members of the public (the laity) are always expected to act in their own economic self-interest, Economic professionals are slightly restricted in this regard. Their profession compels them to reject money if they are paid to distort or bias advice to the benefit of one party over the other — even though it is clearly in their self-interest to do so. This is a contradiction for any Economist who believes that self-interest should determine all economic behavior. But the morality of Economic professionalism is not that of the marketplace. It better reflects the morality of priests, monks, and

43. Hayek, *The Road to Serfdom*, p. 84.
44. Hayek, *The Road to Serfdom*, pp. 101-5.

other religious officials who have always been able to accept donations for their services but only in limited and appropriate circumstances.[45]

Economic professionals are like the priests of ancient religions because both function to keep chaos at bay. In ancient Egypt or Babylon, the responsibility for drought or famine fell on the priests. Likewise, the High Priest of the American Economy, the Chairman of the Federal Reserve, is responsible for preventing recession or depression. The rituals these priests perform minister to their respective gods. If they perform their tasks properly, their God and their people thrive. Otherwise, the people suffer. The need for priests for The Economy is acknowledged in both Capitalism and Socialism. Marxist Lenin needed a special class of educated people to create the conditions for the classless society to come. Socialist Auguste Comte (1798-1857) not only understood that there was a need for an educated, scientific elite to govern a socialist state, but he actually argued that a religion should be developed that worshiped humanity with a Socialist elite that would function in much the same way popes and bishops had ruled in the medieval church.[46] Capitalism also has a professional class that establishes and maintains the conditions under which The Market Economy flourishes. In certain instances, all denominations of the religion we call Economics call on their leadership to abandon their self-interest to serve The Economy. This is what priests of all other religions have always been called to do. We expect the high priests of The Economy to resist their "natural" self-interest and serve the interests of The Market instead. They are bound to a higher standard of moral behavior than are other mortals.[47]

This is quite consistent with the way priests are viewed in other religious traditions, where priests are always understood to be different from regular, ordinary people. For example, even though my Lutheran Protestant tradition pays lip-service to Martin Luther's notion of "the priesthood of all believers," this egalitarian idea is not a "lived-in" practice. As a Lutheran pastor, I've noticed that people routinely apologize to me if they curse or swear in my presence. On occasion, they even ask my permission and/or apologize in advance before telling an off-color joke. Let's just say that, in this regard, I am treated quite differently from when

45. Nelson, *Economics as Religion*, p. 11.

46. Frederick Copleston, S.J., *A History of Philosophy, Volume IX: Main de Biran to Sartre* (New York: Newman Press, 1974), pp. 93-98.

47. Nelson, *Economics as Religion*, p. 9.

I worked as a construction worker. As a priest, I am subjected to a higher standard — at least in the minds of many of my parishioners.

Paul Samuelson (1915-2009) expressed a Capitalist version of these expectations for the Economic priesthood. He promoted the reformers' view that if society could be managed according to economic laws, poverty could be eliminated and universal prosperity achieved. Samuelson believed that government could provide society's "proper management." He assumed that most people behave in accord with their self-interested nature. Only these educated managers — these priests of The Economy — would depart from their nature and reject their selfish ways by acting in the public interest. Samuelson speaks as if there are two types of human beings. One type acts according to his or her self-interested nature. The other inexplicably acts in the public interest.[48] Obviously there is no scientific basis for such a bifurcation of humanity, but if we understand Economics as a religion and Economists as priests, a *religious* explanation emerges.

This bifurcation in humanity that distinguishes an educated priesthood from an unenlightened populace has parallels in many world religions and philosophies. Plato's *Republic* distinguishes between an educated guardian class that acts in the interest of the state and ordinary people who seek their own self-interest. This "priestly" understanding of humanity is also reminiscent of the medieval Western Christian notion that ordination makes the priest fundamentally different from regular, ordinary people who simply cannot live by elevated priestly standards. It reflects the relationship between Buddhist monks and Buddhist laity, where a split exists "between the *Sangha* (the fellowship of Buddhist monks) and the laity. Today the main spiritual responsibility of lay Buddhists is not to follow the path themselves, but to support *bhikkhu* monks. . . . In this way lay men and women gain *punna* 'merit,' which can lead to a more favorable rebirth next time."[49] In all cases, education or enlightenment creates these "special" people.

Just as Christianity created universities and seminaries and Buddhism developed monasteries, The Economy has business schools to educate its own enlightened people who will minister to needs of The Economy. This analogy between business schools and Christian seminaries

48. Nelson, *Economics as Religion*, p. 99.
49. David R. Loy, *Money, Sex, War, Karma: Notes for a Buddhist Revolution* (Boston: Wisdom Publications, 2008), pp. 5, 6.

may break down somewhere, but it does provide a religious way to understand the training of economic professionals. As a seminary student's goal is ordination, a business student's goal is an MBA. As ordination allows entry into the priesthood, an MBA allows access to the higher echelons of the business world. As ordination makes a person suitable to minister to the Christian God, an MBA makes a person suitable to minister to The Economy.

The way professional Economists minister to The Economy varies depending on the perceived threat. Some are "called" to make sure that no undue restrictions are placed on The Economy by government regulations. This way of ministering to the Economy happens within a corporate structure or an Economic think tank. Other Economic priests are "called" to protect The Economy from clandestine or illegal practices of corporations and individuals that undermine fairness within the Market itself. These professionals usually work from within government, and they serve The Economy by making sure that the Market's free workings are not destroyed by the excessive self-interest of individuals and corporations. Sometimes Economists find themselves "called" to temporarily abandon raw, free-market practices when these practices become so detrimental to the social fabric that their continuation might lead to social disorder (and the accompanying breakdown of the Markets themselves). These economists freely move from business to government and back throughout their careers. Like former CEO of Goldman Sachs and former Secretary of the Treasury Hank Paulson, those who serve The Economy in this way are sometimes called upon to abandon every free-market principle they hold dear in order to protect civilization itself from the ravages of free-market capitalism run amuck.

> **Like all religions, Economics has its priests whose function has always been to keep chaos at bay.**

Finally, a new sort of ministry to the Economy has emerged in the last couple of decades. These are the cheerleaders for The Economy that we call the business media. While the media has always followed business, these cheerleaders have clearly taken their "ministry" to a new level. In their round-the-clock coverage of the world's businesses, these professionals delight in Economic growth or profits no matter what creates the profits. They assume economic growth and profits are an unequivocal good. They generally disregard any negative consequences of growth caused by the unbridled quest for profit. They spend little time reporting on job loss and even less on environmental pollution or the destruction of communities that may occur when a corporation "in legitimate pursuit of maximum profits" abandons a community in search of cheaper labor. The business news seldom notes that Economic growth is not always good for everyone. Indeed, Economic growth is assumed to be the remedy for our ills and ultimately always good for everyone. This assumption is proposed as a universal truth, but, in fact, such an assumption can only be true if The Economy is in fact God. If, however, the economy is a human creation, then what is good for the economy might not always be good for human beings.

These ministries take a variety of forms because The Economy must be ministered to in many ways. Occasionally these ministries are at odds and conflict arises. For example, those who want to protect The Economy from the illegal or clandestine practices of some corporations often find themselves in conflict with those who promote unregulated markets. In practice these differences are no more than theological debates that occur within any religion, and are not in contradiction with the priestly task of ministering to The Economy.

Business School Curricula: What They Don't Teach Can Hurt Us

All business schools have a core curriculum that includes: accounting, marketing, finance, corporate leadership, and operations management. In addition, our business schools teach a variety of subjects like negotiation, international finance, game theory, knowledge-based strategy, and risk management to enrich these core courses.

Much is excluded from a business school's curriculum simply because all disciplines have their boundaries. Quantum physics is not part of an art school's curriculum and courses in portrait painting will not be found in medical schools for the simple reason that such subjects are not a part of the disciplines in question. Religious institutions, however, often reject certain subjects for ideological reasons.

Christian seminaries that claim the Bible is unerring in all factual details do not include topics that undermine this belief. By the same token, most Roman Catholic seminaries and many mainline Protestant seminaries rarely discuss the *merits* of the so-called heretics of the Church. Usually only their alleged demerits are discussed. Seldom do we give our opposition an honest hearing. Since business schools are like seminaries, we might expect the same practice.

Two subjects that usually are not taught in business schools, yet might be considered pertinent to economics, are economic history and economic anthropology.[50] These omissions are curious from an educational standpoint, but understandable from a religious perspective because these two disciplines undermine important, but untested religious assumptions of the religion called Economics. Specifically, economic anthropology discredits the ideas that human beings *by nature* engage in exchange, that we have forever engaged in such exchange, and that human beings are *isolated* units who only interact through economic exchange.

A student of economic anthropology might discover no society ever used barter without first knowing about money. This could create an intellectual dilemma similar to the one created when geological facts are set beside the Bible's seven-day creation story. Business schools, however, prefer to let the barter myth go unchallenged because this myth supports their fundamental assumptions.

The barter myth imagines a time when markets existed and governments did not. It references a fantasy world where people do what comes naturally (engage in economic exchange) in a free market.[51] This uncritically adopted myth undercuts all debate concerning the role of business and government in the economy. If the free market becomes the *natural* stage on which human beings do what we were created to do, any action that intervenes in this natural, pristine environment is deemed unnatural. In contemporary moral theory, the natural is always counted good while the unnatural is often deemed evil.

In telling us that money originates in barter exchange, the barter myth also prejudices discussions of the origin and nature of money. If we

---

50. It is not 100 percent accurate to say that business schools never offer students the opportunity to take courses in these disciplines. Harvard Business School has a professor of business history, and good business schools like Stanford and Georgetown allow their students to take up to four electives in disciplines outside the business school, and these universities do offer courses in economic history and anthropology that a business student can take. It is, however, unlikely that a large number of business school students will routinely take these electives.

51. See David Graeber, *Debt: The First 5000 Years* (Brooklyn, NY: Melville House Publishing, 2011), p. 25.

think from the start that barter exchange leads to exchange in precious metals which culminates in coins, we are unlikely to see that money first appears as credit ciphers in Babylonian writing almost 3000 years before mass-produced coins.[52] If credit money existed before coin money, money originates in our *promises* to repay debt (as most anthropologists assert) instead of the intrinsic value of precious metals (as Economists mistakenly believe). The fact that money is based on promises is an inconvenient truth for Economists because it undermines their fundamental beliefs.

> **Business school curricula do not routinely include economic history or economic anthropology because the study of these subjects undermines Economic ideology and myths.**

The barter myth also creates the illusion that our social world is composed of isolated individuals who are untouched by others except when engaged in market exchange. This view has dramatic philosophical consequences that are based on myth (the barter myth) rather than reality. As David Graeber points out on numerous occasions, the act of economic exchange does not require any further social relationship between the parties to the exchange. Once the exchange is made, the individuals can go their separate ways. They never have to be in contact again. The centrality of economic exchange in the barter myth logically entails that our social world is composed of isolated individuals who remain untouched by others except when engaged in market activities.

If, however, money originated as credit rather than barter, money is credit based, and we live in a credit/debtor-based society. A credit-based society implies that human beings are fundamentally related rather than isolated. Credit demands that relationships must be maintained, and the debtor's life ordered in certain ways until the debt is paid. Our understanding of economic matters would be quite different if our society were fundamentally credit based instead of exchange based. But these possible differences will not even be entertained if the barter myth persists as money's foundation narrative. As long as Economists live under the barter myth, they cannot know the nature of money, the nature of humanity, or the true character of society.

52. Graeber, *Debt,* p. 38.

Economic history is another discipline that remains largely unknown to MBA recipients. Its study reveals that until recently no society was ordered in accord with market dictates. Instead, they were ordered in one of three ways: reciprocity, distribution, or householding.[53]

Reciprocity is giving a fellow member of one's community help in time of need. In return, there is the expectation that you can call on that person when you are in need. A monarch might run a distribution-based economy where items of value are collected by the authority figure and redistributed among the subjects with the authority figure, of course, often taking the lion's share. The feudal system of medieval Europe is a somewhat benign version of a distribution economy. There each class had their obligation to fulfill. The peasants supplied the food for everyone. The nobles protected everyone, and the priests prayed for everyone. Each group received goods and services from other groups and distributed their own particular goods and services throughout the social system. Aristotle (382-322 BCE) discusses the householder form of social organization. An *oikos* or household was a semi-fortified compound occupied by landowners with their families, craftsmen, slaves, and livestock. Its aim was self-sufficiency, which required the application of budget and thrift. Aristotle contrasts Greek household economies with the emerging market economies of his day, and he attacks the market economy because he thinks it is antisocial.[54] Economic history reveals a myriad of societies organized in ways other than a market-exchange economy. This fact could be known by all priests of the Economy, but, once again, such knowledge would undermine the universal status of The Market Economy. This factual knowledge is marginalized in the training of business professionals (Priests) not because it is irrelevant to their discipline, but because such knowledge undermines the supreme status of the God we call The Economy.

Summary

In his book *Idiot America: How Stupidity Became a Virtue in the Land of the Free,* Charles P. Pierce narrates his visit to Hebron, Kentucky's Cre-

53. Karl Polanyi, *The Great Transformation: The Political and Economic Origins of Our Time* (Boston: Beacon Press, 2001), p. 57.

54. Chris Hahn and Keith Hart, *Economic Anthropology: History, Ethnology, Critique* (Malden, MA: Polity Press, 2001), p. 20.

ation Museum — a museum dedicated to the "biblical" notion that the earth is less than 7000 years old. To those who think that fossil evidence of dinosaurs and other prehistoric animals is conclusive evidence against the earth being so young, think again. These facts only lead the "true believers" to assert that dinosaurs and human beings coexisted. The Creation Museum takes this a step further. Some of its "exhibits" maintain that dinosaurs were domesticated! They show dinosaurs wearing saddles, pulling plows, and engaging in races.[55] The Creation Museum demonstrates the extent of the mental gymnastics necessary if certain religious worldviews are to be accommodated.

Unfortunately, the many debates between Economists are based on assumptions just as shaky as those undergirding the Creation Museum's exhibits. The difference is that the public religiously assumes the scientific validity of Economic assumptions and uncritically accepts Economic ritual as natural and Economic myth as scientific fact. In short, Economics functions as a religion for most people. It has its orthodox theologians like Smith, Malthus, and Ricardo, who without any historical evidence assumed that private property always existed; the barter myth is historically true; it is human nature to engage in economic exchange; self-interested behavior always leads to greater social well-being; the poor are a product of nature; and nothing can be done to eliminate poverty. The religion called Economics also has prophets like Karl Marx who challenged the assumptions of orthodox Economists and proposed alternatives to their understanding of economic reality. He denied the orthodox assertion that Economic laws — laws that explained perpetual poverty — were natural and claimed that poverty was the consequence of the Capitalist *system* instead. Moreover, like many prophets before him, he proposed an apocalyptic vision of the future in which the dire conditions created by Capitalism would be violently overthrown by historical forces.[56]

The religion that worships The Economy has its reformers as well. These theologians recognize the moral cogency of Socialist critiques, but are not willing to jettison Capitalism. They want to preserve economic

55. Charles P. Pierce, *Idiot America: How Stupidity Became a Virtue in the Land of the Free* (New York: Random House, 2009), pp. 2, 3. In commenting on the Creation Museum, comedian Lewis Black once opined that the curators of this museum must think *The Flintstones* was a documentary.

56. On this level Marx himself is in need of a prophet. While he may have correctly denied the Capitalist claim that poverty was "natural," his claim that history has a predictable direction is a religious claim.

freedom, and, at the same time, help alleviate some of the most inhumane aspects of Capitalism. They want to guarantee minimum wages, adequate food, housing, healthcare, sanitation, and education without obliterating an individual's economic freedom to engage in exchange and innovation, to freely move, and to change his or her employment. Today these people are often called Socialists by classical Capitalists and neoconservatives, but, in my view, they are not. The principal feature of Socialism is state control of the means of production, and these reformers seek to address Capitalist abuses *and* keep the means of production in private hands. They want a welfare state or a mixed economy. They do not want a Socialist state. The reformers have no interest in jettisoning the Capitalist idea of individual freedom. They want to eliminate some of the injustices associated with this freedom and create a more humane sort of Capitalism than the original classical Capitalists dreamed possible.

Finally we come to the extremists. Like all religious extremists, Economic extremists equate theology or doctrine with their religion. They fixate on correct belief, correct doctrine, and the implementation of their doctrines in social life. Sometimes, like the case with Kentucky's Creation Museum, the consequences are comical. Often, they are not. Osama bin Laden's destruction of the World Trade Center and Eric Robert Rudolph's bombing of abortion clinics and the 1996 Atlanta Olympics are examples from two religions of the death-dealing consequences of religious extremists' fixation on correct belief and doctrine regardless of the consequences. Economic extremism might have a greater history of carnage. Lenin, Stalin, Julius Nyerere of Tanzania, and Colonel Mengistu Haile Mariam of Ethiopia were illustrative of the actual carnage that might have been the consequence of Socialist extremists, while Lawrence Summers's cost/benefit analysis leading him to argue that pollution should be exported to "underdeveloped" nations is one example of extreme Capitalist policy — the logic of which, in Summers's view, is employed by the World Bank.

Even in Economics, violence and death have been a consequence when people think that correct belief and the correct doctrines are always more important than the human cost! The danger of Economic extremism becomes more acute when we refuse to entertain the notion that Economics is a religion. The consequences of our unspoken denial of this possibility cannot be overstated. As long as the religious status of Economics remains a part of our unspoken, subconscious knowledge, we cannot even begin to deal with the negative consequences that arise when we act as though The Economy is God. The examples from Socialist Lenin and Capitalist Summers give some indication of the human cost of such Economic religious extremism. These death-dealing facts of Economic extremism are largely due to the sacred status of our Economic doctrines and beliefs. The fact of the matter is, however, that our corporate life may have even greater death-dealing consequences. It is to these we now turn.

CHAPTER 4

Corporations: The Religious Communities of the Economic Faithful

Corporations are people too, you know.

Republican Presidential candidate Mitt Romney, 2012

All religions have places where people gather to serve their gods and receive benefits from their gods. Modern Jews gather in synagogues. Christians congregate in churches. Buddhists express their devotion in monasteries, and Muslims worship in mosques. The Economic faithful have their gathering places as well. We call these places companies, businesses, and, more than ever before, corporations.

According to the Internal Revenue Service, businesses manifest themselves in three ways. A business can be a sole proprietorship owned by one person who receives the profits and bears the risk involved in the business. The owner of a sole proprietorship places at risk more than his or her monetary investment. If a sole proprietorship goes bankrupt, its owner's wealth is at stake. If necessary, the owner must sell his own personal property until the debts of his business are paid. A business can also be a partnership. Here two or more people own the company and share the profits and risks of the company. As is the case with a sole proprietorship, the partners' risk can exceed the amount of their monetary investments in the company. The modern Limited Liability Corporation (corporation) is the third way a business can organize.

The corporation is a legal construct in which the government limits the liability of the owners (called shareholders) to their monetary investment. Unlike the owners of a sole proprietorship or partnership, the private property of a shareholder is not subject to risk in case of bankruptcy. This arrangement obviously gives the shareholders a tremendous advantage! A suit against a sole proprietorship could result in the owner losing his or her home and personal property along with the business. Moreover, if the sole proprietorship is convicted of criminal activity, the owner could go to jail for the crime. On the other hand, if someone sues a corporation, only the monetary investment of the shareholders is at risk. No private property of the shareholders is liable for seizure. When a corporation is convicted of a crime, it normally pays a fine (often less than the amount of money it gained by virtue of its criminal activity), and it is highly unlikely that a human being would be incarcerated as a consequence of the corporation's crime. Shareholders not employed by the criminal corporation are always exempt from criminal prosecution.

Some of the characteristics of modern corporations are as follows:

1. Corporations are legal entities constructed and chartered by a state.
2. Once chartered, the government limits the liabilities of corporate shareholders to their monetary investment in the corporation.
3. The limited liability of shareholders reduces a corporation's incentive to pay certain costs of operation — like the costs of pollution.
4. Corporations have evolved to become persons under the law with the same rights and privileges as human persons.
5. Corporate persons are much more long-lived than human persons.
6. Corporations can dissolve in one place and reassemble, under a different name but with the same personnel, in another.
7. Corporations are legally responsible to make money for their shareholders.

One important difference between the classical capitalism of Adam Smith and modern capitalism is that Adam Smith understood business largely in terms of sole proprietorships and partnerships. Modern capitalism, on the other hand, understands business in terms of large corporations. One important contention this chapter makes is that the evolution of the modern corporation dramatically alters the dynamics of business as well as the principles of classical capitalism. Corporate persons now compete with human persons in The Market.[1] *Both pursue their self-interest,*

---

1. In what follows, do not confuse corporate persons with the human persons who work for the corporations — even with the corporate executives. Corporate persons are

but the self-interest of corporate persons is quite different from the self-interest of human persons. This fact alone has already had some very negative consequences for human beings.

This chapter begins with a discussion of the evolution of the modern corporation, but it understands corporations in a religious way. The modern corporations are to The Economy as churches and synagogues are to Christians or Jews. All are places where the faithful congregate to serve their God and to receive benefits from their God. In Christianity, the benefits the faithful receive are objectively expressed in sacraments. In corporations, money has this sacramental function. This chapter is like the branch of Christian theology called ecclesiology that explores the nature of the church. The next chapter discusses money as the sacrament of the corporate and business enterprise. After that the global mission of the religion that worships The Economy will be discussed.

The Origin of the Limited Liability Corporation

The earliest record of a Limited Liability Corporation is in Florence, Italy, in 1532. In 1498 Vasco da Gama sailed around Africa to India and returned with a cargo worth sixty times the cost of the voyage. The Europeans were hooked. The possible profits of such exploration and trade were immense but so were the risks. The chances of a ship sinking or pirates capturing it were considerable, and, according to the laws of the day, if you could not repay your debts from such a loss, debtor prisons awaited you, your family, and perhaps even your descendants.[2] The Limited Liability Corporation was designed to decrease the risk of an unsuccessful voyage.

This required a special government charter that governments like Florence approved because of the riches a sanctioning jurisdiction could expect from a successful voyage.

> The self-aggrandizing state that we know today developed along with the royally chartered corporation, because they were dependent on each other. . . . The enormous wealth extracted from the New World,

---

legal persons, but they are not human persons. All legal persons have certain legal rights as described in the Bill of Rights of the U.S. Constitution. Corporate persons have the same rights as human persons.

2. David R. Loy, *The Great Awakening: A Buddhist Social Theory* (Somerville, MA: Wisdom Publications, 2008), pp. 92, 93.

in particular, enabled states to become more powerful and ambitious, so rulers assisted the colonization and corporatization process by dispatching their armies and navies to "pacify" foreign lands. As this suggests, there was a third partner that grew up along with the other two: the modern military. Together they formed an "unholy trinity" thanks to new technologies (gunpowder for aggression, the compass for navigation) and (thanks) to this clever new type of business organization that minimized the financial risk. In short, the modern nation-state and its military machine matured by feeding on colonial exploitation, in the same way that chartered corporations did.[3]

England began its own experimentation with Limited Liability Corporations in 1580 when Queen Elizabeth I gave Sir Francis Drake's ship *The Golden Hind* "legal freedom from liability," and, at the same time, she became the largest shareholder in the ship. There is no record of the queen's return on her investment, but, since Drake's other shareholders recorded a 5000 percent return, the queen's investment was probably well rewarded.[4] The success of Drake's enterprise eventually led the queen to authorize a group of 218 English merchants and noblemen to form a Limited Liability Corporation called the East India Company. Its corporate charter was issued on December 31, 1600.

In 1607 the East India Company established Jamestown, England's first permanent colony in North America, and by 1681, most of the members of Parliament and most royalty were stockholders in this company. These important stockholders enabled the East India Company to begin an extremely important corporate tradition. The company lobbied the government for legislation that would enrich the company. Under the influence of corporate pressure, Parliament passed "An Act for the Restraining and Punishing Privateers and Pirates." This law required licenses to import any product into America and granted licenses only to the East India Company and a few other British corporations.[5] The British government continued to pass laws that gave the East India Company a competitive advantage, and the power and influence of the East India Company grew.

3. Loy, *The Great Awakening*, p. 93.

4. Thom Hartmann, *Unequal Protection: How Corporations Became "People" — and How You Can Fight Back,* 2nd edition (San Francisco: Berrett-Koehler Publishers, 2010), pp. 64, 65.

5. Hartmann, *Unequal Protection,* p. 70.

In 1773, Parliament passed the Tea Act. Today most Americans think the Tea Act of 1773 increased the taxes the colonists had to pay for their tea. This is not true. The Tea Act of 1773 *exempted* the East India Company from paying taxes on the tea the company sold in the colonies. This gave the East India Company a competitive advantage over other suppliers of tea who had to pay a tax on their tea. Even though the Tea Act reduced Britain's tax revenue, it was passed by the British Parliament because it increased the revenue of members of Parliament who were shareholders in the East India Company.[6] The Boston Tea Party was in fact a protest against the union between big business and the state. It was a protest on behalf of smaller businesses and others who recognized that the global power of a corporation can seriously undermine the economic vitality of a community. The American Revolution, therefore, has its roots in the rejection of legislation that compelled the poor and middle class to support large, wealthy corporations.

If government-sponsored support of a large business enterprise at the expense of regular human beings and small businesses was, in fact, the root cause of the American Revolution, one might ask, "How has it come to pass that the United States government consistently supports corporations in a manner quite similar to the way eighteenth-century British government supported the East India Company?" It is an interesting story that culminates in the now universally accepted belief that corporations are persons under the law.

The Rise of the Modern Corporation

Following the American Revolution and consistent with its spirit, the United States were quite suspicious of their large Limited Liability Corporations; however, corporations did exist. When a group wanted to limit their risk to their cash investment, they still petitioned the government to obtain the legal limits to their liability through a Limited Liability Corporation. *But in the early days of the Republic, the government actually demanded certain responsibilities* from such corporate arrangements and actually placed certain restrictions on the sort of company these legal petitions created. Thom Hartmann summarizes these limits and responsibilities:

6. Hartmann, *Unequal Protection*, p. 71.

- State legislatures could revoke a corporate charter if the corporation either exceeded or failed to fulfill its chartered purpose.
- State legislatures could revoke a corporate charter if the corporation misbehaved.
- Corporate charters did not relieve management from liability for illegal corporate acts.
- Directors were required to come from among the stockholders.
- Charters were granted for a specific period of time.
- Corporations were prohibited from making political contributions.
- Legislatures could set pricing limits on some monopolies.
- All corporate records were open to legislature or state attorney general scrutiny.[7]

Today we believe restrictions such as these are harsh and perhaps immoral. In fact, these conditions were more a *quid pro quo* than a regulation. In return for the stockholders' limited liability (which one must admit is quite a benefit!), state, local, and federal governments placed certain restrictions and obligations on corporate behavior. These restrictions and obligations, however, gradually eroded.

In 1816, the state of New Hampshire decided to revoke the corporate charter of Dartmouth College and make it a state-run institution. Dartmouth sued, claiming that its charter, granted by King George of England before the Revolution, was still valid. Since the original charter had neither time limitations nor a clause indicating that it could be revoked, Dartmouth argued that New Hampshire could not revoke Dartmouth's corporate charter. In *Dartmouth College v. Woodward,* the Supreme Court agreed with Dartmouth's argument. A state like New Hampshire did not have the right to revoke a charter if the original charter had no such revocation clause.

The Court pointed out that this ruling in no way undermined a state's right to place revocation clauses in corporate charters, but this case became the first chink in the armor of a state's ability to regulate corporate activity. The court's ruling prompted many states to pass laws reinforcing their right to revoke a corporate charter, but the federal system allowed a corporation to charter itself in any state it desired. Eventually this led to corporations shopping from state to state in order to get the "best deal" on their charter.[8] Even today, certain states like Delaware, New Jersey,

7. Hartmann, *Unequal Protection,* pp. 95, 96.
8. Hartmann, *Unequal Protection,* p. 101.

and Nevada are preferred states for corporate charters because they impose fewer restrictions on corporate behavior.

Railroads dramatically expanded corporate power. In 1840 there was little more than 2700 miles of track used in the United States. This expanded to 9000 miles by 1850 and 30,000 miles by 1860. In 1890 over 180 million acres of public land had been *given* to the railroads by federal local and state governments. The railroads were the most powerful corporations America had ever experienced.[9] Communities died or thrived depending on whether or not the railroad came to town. In this life-and-death struggle, nearly everyone was willing to give just about anything to railroad corporations. Bribes, land grants, tax exemptions, and much more were given by small towns and villages to the railroads for a depot in one's hometown. The climate of bribery and corruption reached the highest echelons of government. As a matter of fact, the Grant administration (1869-1877) was rendered nearly impotent by scandals related to the railroads. As a consequence, when Chief Justice Samuel Chase died in 1874,[10] President Grant could not get his nomination for Chief Justice of the Supreme Court through Congress.

Grant put forth six candidates. His seventh, Morrison Waite, was approved. Waite had never been a judge. He was an attorney who defended railroads and other large corporations. His Court presided over *Southern Pacific Railroad v. Santa Clara County.*

Southern Pacific Railroad was suing the county because they were being taxed at a rate that was different from the tax rate of human persons and this, Southern Pacific argued, violated the fourteenth amendment right to equal protection under the law. The fourteenth amendment was supposed to guarantee the rights of former slaves. For it to apply to corporations, corporations had to be persons under the law. The case was decided in favor of Southern Pacific, but on different grounds. Nevertheless this case is largely thought to have established the legal personhood of corporations.

The preamble to the court's decision, written by the court reporter

---

9. Hartmann, *Unequal Protection,* p. 104.

10. Before his appointment to the Supreme Court, Samuel Chase had been Secretary of the Treasury. In this capacity, Chase inaugurated paper money called the greenback to help finance the Civil War. In a rather strange twist of fate, Chief Justice Chase presided over a ruling where the Court declared these greenbacks unconstitutional! Not only did Chase deem them illegal, but these unconstitutional greenbacks had Samuel Chase's face printed on them.

J. C. Bancroft, says, "The Court does not wish to hear argument on the question of whether the 14th Amendment to the Constitution, which forbids a State to deny to any person within its jurisdiction the equal protection of the laws applies to corporations. We are all of the opinion that it does." Technically, this was not Chief Justice Waite's opinion. It was that of the court reporter. Nevertheless, the idea that the Supreme Court believed a corporation was a person under the law receives legal precedent here.[11] Later, in *Minneapolis & St. Louis Railroad v. Beckwith* (1889), the Supreme Court explicitly stated that a corporation is a "person" for both due process and equal protection. Few realize how these rulings changed Capitalism and Economics.

> Corporate persons have material resources and potential longevity that greatly exceed that of human persons. Material resources allow corporations to alter the political landscape by pursuing political solutions too expensive for human persons to pursue. Longevity allows corporate persons to wait until opposition to corporate agendas decreases or the political climate becomes more favorable.

Corporate Persons and Capitalist Competition

Corporations are legal entities. Our own laws created them; yet, these human creations have taken on a life all their own. They now function independently of living human beings, and it is possible that they are now beyond human control. Our inability to control that which we create is not an unusual phenomenon. It often happens that creations, sometimes creations of nonhuman origin, develop in ways far beyond the intentions of their creators. Karl Popper describes how even the simplest of creations grow beyond the control of their creator:

> How does an animal path in the jungle arise? Some animal may break through the undergrowth in order to get to a drinking-place. Other animals find it easiest to use the same track. Thus it may be widened

11. Hartmann, *Unequal Protection*, pp. 30-32.

and improved by use. It is not planned — *it is an unintended consequence* of the need for easy or swift movement. This is how a path is originally made — perhaps even by men — and how language and any other institutions which are useful may arise, and how they may owe their existence and development to their usefulness. *They are not planned or intended,* and there was perhaps no need for them before they came into existence. *But they may create a new need, or a new set of aims: the aim-structure of animals or men is not "given," but it develops,* with the help of some kind of feedback mechanism, out of earlier aims, and out of results which were or were not aimed at.[12]

The autonomous power of the corporation is much like this path. *Homo sapiens* had lived for perhaps 150,000 years without needing a corporation; yet, the creation of a corporation created a path of least resistance for human beings trying to both reduce their risk and increase their monetary rewards. As a consequence, corporations evolved in an unplanned way that exhibited what might be called corporate autonomy. Just as the path attracts animals because of its easing of travel and further use alters it in an unintended way, corporate limitations of risk attract human beings and evolve in ways unforeseen by their innovators. The gradual evolution of corporations from being held in suspicion to becoming persons under the law is evidence that this process benefited corporations perhaps even at the expense of their human creators.

The emergence of the corporation as a person under the law shattered classical Economic theory and Economic practice in many unintended ways. Adam Smith thought that economic reality was composed of isolated individuals who by their very nature engaged in economic exchange. In Smith's world each individual would pursue his or her own self-interest, and, if this pursuit was unencumbered by external restraint, the nation as a whole would benefit. It is safe to say that Adam Smith thought that all the isolated individuals engaged in the self-centered pursuit of profit were *human* persons. The Supreme Court made this assumption obsolete.

Corporations have become the richest, most powerful, and long-lived legal persons engaged in the self-interested pursuit of profits. Some of these nonliving, legal constructs currently possess more wealth than

---

12. Karl Popper, *Objective Knowledge: An Evolutionary Approach,* revised edition (Oxford: Oxford University Press, 1979), p. 117, emphasis mine.

entire nations. The consequences are enormous and unnoticed. The most ominous is that *the self-interest of these extremely powerful corporate persons is different from the self-interest of the weaker human persons with whom they compete.*

The difference between corporate self-interest and human self-interest can be summarized as follows: It is in the interest of the corporate persons to *survive.* It is in the interest of a human person to *live.* This is not simply a silly play on words. Corporations exist, but they are not living, biological beings. They are legal constructs. In order to *survive,* a corporate person needs labor, property, raw materials, equipment, human creativity, and money. The corporate person will attempt to obtain what it needs to survive in the most efficient way possible. In order to *live,* human persons need food, shelter, water, air, clothing, healthcare, companionship, arenas in which to exercise creativity, and perhaps a means of exchange like money to ease the acquisitions of many of these necessities. What a corporation needs to survive is not *completely* different from what humans need to live, but these respective needs are different enough to create problems. Given the advantages corporate persons have over human persons in The Market, over time, corporate needs will be met, and sometimes they will be met at the expense of human needs because corporations are far more powerful than mere human persons. They have more wealth, longevity, and power, which enable them to eventually meet most of their needs.

For example, corporate persons have been extended first amendment rights of freedom of expression. This allows them to lobby Congress (as of 2005 there were roughly sixty-four registered lobbyists for every member of Congress) or use their nearly unlimited funds to oppose any political candidate. These rights allow corporations to influence Congress and even elections to a far greater extent than human persons can. By the same token, as persons under the law, corporations do not have to submit to random government inspections like inspections for violations of labor laws, environmental pollution, unsafe work practices, etcetera because such searches violate their fourth amendment rights against random searches and seizure by the government.[13] These constitutional amendments were written to protect the less powerful human persons from the more powerful government. Now they protect the extremely powerful

---

13. Hartmann, *Unequal Protection,* pp. 188-92.

corporate persons from a government when it tries to protect the less powerful human persons.

Corporate longevity dramatically increases the advantage of corporate persons over human persons.[14] Longevity allows a corporation to bide its time in ways that human persons cannot. If a court gives a corporation an unfavorable ruling, it merely waits until a more favorable climate exists to receive more favorable treatment. To be sure, corporations are not idle while they wait. They use their resources to change perceptions, and perhaps to make sure that more favorable government officials are in office. Moreover, their unlimited resources — something human persons do not generally have — allow corporations to keep on suing, petitioning, and lobbying the government so that the government will act more positively toward corporations. Corporate persons have unlimited resources, power, and life expectancy. This gives them a decided advantage in their effort to promote corporate values over human values in the marketplace.

Corporate Values versus Human Values

Corporate persons value efficiency, and efficiency has become synonymous with reason. While human persons are often bewitched by this corporate value, efficiency is often opposed to an even more important human value called life. Conflict between these two value systems lurks behind nearly all political/economic discussions.

James C. Scott reveals the nature of this conflict in his analysis of the "achievements" of nineteenth-century German forestry science. German forestry science imposed the corporate value of efficiency on nature in an attempt to "improve on nature" in the forests of Germany. "The fact is

---

14. Compound interest is a simple way to understand this advantage. The way to figure out how long it will take your principal to double given a particular interest rate is by dividing the interest rate into the number 72. The result gives you the time it will take for your principal to double. For example, if the interest rate is 6 percent, it will take twelve years for your principal to double because $72/6=12$. After twelve years a $1000 principal would become $2000 at a 6-percent rate. In twelve more years the $2000 would become $4000. This means that your $1000 would be $256,000 after ninety-six years, $512,000 after 108 years, and $1,024,000 after 120 years. Human persons do not have the time to wait for such returns. Corporations do, and should they do so, their financial power will be far greater than it is now.

> The self-interest of a corporate person is quite different
> from the self-interest of a human person.

that forest science . . . had the capacity to transform the real, diverse and chaotic old-growth forest into a new, more uniform forest that closely resembled the administrative grid of its techniques. To this end, the underbrush was cleared, the number of species was reduced (often to monoculture) and plantings were done simultaneously in straight rows on large tracts. . . . The German forest became the archetype of imposing on disorderly nature the neatly arranged constructions of science."[15] At first, these techniques were amazingly productive. Things soon changed. A new German word, *Waldensterben* (forest death), was coined to describe the consequences of this efficient, rational activity that had destroyed the biological relationships involved in soil-building, nutrient uptake, and the symbiotic relationships between fungi, insects, animals, and flora. In short, efficiency created *Waldensterben!*[16]

Efficiency abstracts what it needs and discards the rest. It eliminates redundancies because redundancies are, by definition, inefficient. As the German forestation effort suggests, life is not efficient. Life often depends on the very things that are discarded in the name of efficiency, and life's abundance *depends on these redundancies* (in an ecosystem we often call such redundancies diversity). Two value systems are in conflict here. One is the corporate person's value of efficiency, and the other is the human person's value of life. Both have their own logic, and these logics are often in conflict.

The logic of efficiency demands calculability, predictability, and control, which are the central values of the corporate value system.[17] Efficiency is the search for the optimum means for a given end. Calculation determines what is optimal. Whatever produces the greater number of desired results is deemed most efficient. Hence, calculability demands that every-

---

15. James C. Scott, *Seeing Like a State: How Certain Schemes to Improve the Human Condition Have Failed* (New Haven: Yale University Press, 1999), p. 15.

16. Scott, *Seeing Like a State,* p. 20.

17. Jacques Ellul, *The Technological Society,* trans. John Wilkinson (New York: Vintage Books, 1964), was probably the earliest, most systematic study of the corporate value of efficiency. His is a voice of prophecy in the sense that one wonders, upon reading the book, how it could possibly have been written in the early 1950s.

thing be reduced to number and counted. This demand entails the division of tasks into given (calculated) units and the production of predetermined (calculated) weights and sizes. Both human labor and production become more predictable when quantified in this way. Such predictability leads to control over production, workforce, and to an increasingly larger extent, customers. George Ritzer calls the end result of this corporate mindset "McDonaldization."[18]

Ritzer also contends that corporate rationality has irrational consequences that, using the words of Max Weber (1864-1920), he calls "the irrationality of rationality." But, I would suggest that two sorts of rationality are operative here. On the one hand is corporate rationality with its emphasis on efficiency, and on the other hand is human rationality with its emphasis on life. What is rational from the perspective of corporate values is often irrational from the perspective of human values.

> Take the famous case of the Ford Pinto. Because of competition from small foreign cars, Ford rushed the Pinto into and through production, even though preproduction tests had indicated its fuel system would rupture easily in a rear-end collision. Because the expensive assembly line machinery for the Pinto was already in place, Ford decided to go ahead with the production of the car without any changes. Ford based its decision on a quantitative comparison. The company estimated that the defect would lead to 180 deaths and about the same number of injuries. Placing a value, or rather a cost, on them of $200,000 per person, Ford decided that the total cost from these deaths and injuries would be less than the $11 per car it would cost to repair the defect. Although this may have made sense from the point of view of profits, it was an unreasonable decision in that human lives were sacrificed and people maimed in the name of lower costs and higher profits.[19]

Ford's decision was rational from the perspective of corporate values. The corporate values of efficiency, calculability, predictability, and

18. George Ritzer, *The McDonaldization of Society: An Investigation into the Changing Character of Contemporary Social Life,* revised edition (Thousand Oaks, CA: Pine Forge Press, 1996), pp. 35-120.

19. Ritzer, *McDonaldization,* p. 141. More recently (2014) it was disclosed that General Motors used the same logic in their refusal to fix the starting mechanism on the Cobalt. This refusal resulted in twelve deaths that GM viewed as cost-effective.

control gave Ford its "Better Idea."[20] This "Better Idea" reasoned that it would be more efficient (cost-effective) to deal with the deaths of 180 people than to deal with the known defect. From the perspective of human persons whose core value is life rather than efficiency, Ford's idea was insane. This clearly illustrates that the interests of corporate persons are not the same as the interests of human persons, and these differences are not benign. This antagonism between corporate persons and human persons exists throughout The Economy because what is good for corporate persons is not necessarily good for human persons. In recent years this antagonism has been greatly augmented by an interesting corporate ideology that has its roots in the corporate values of efficiency, calculability, predictability, and control.

Corporations were not always the way they are today. Today they exist to "increase shareholder value." All other constituencies of a corporation — management, employees, pensioners, and the communities in which the corporations are located — are immaterial when it comes to the shareholder value or the bottom-line. But the purpose of a corporation has not always just been to increase shareholder value.

The postwar period provides a more humane example of corporate life. From roughly 1945 until 1980 we thought of our corporations as social institutions with constituencies and responsibilities far beyond corporate shareholders.[21] Workers, managers, pensioners, and the corporation's immediate community also had a stake in corporate affairs. Corporations were, to a greater degree than they are now, loyal to their workers, and, to a far greater degree than now, workers were loyal to their corporation. Many worked for the same company for life, and they were rewarded with a relatively comfortable retirement for their loyalty. Moreover, the communities in which corporations were located could rely on a corporate presence as an important economic foundation for social and economic cohesion. American communities from Bethlehem, Pennsylvania, to Detroit, Michigan, once thrived on their relationship with the corporations that inhabited these cities.

Since the emergence of shareholder value as the only metric of corporate viability, however, other corporate constituencies — employees, managers, pensioners, and community — are routinely jettisoned in the

20. One of Ford's slogans was "Ford has a Better Idea."

21. Karen Ho, *Liquidated: An Ethnography of Wall Street* (Durham, NC: Duke University Press, 2009), p. 124.

name of efficiency, and efficiency is determined by the "bottom-line." Money and money alone measures corporate efficiency. And, as was the case with "efficient" German forest management, the result might be the corporate equivalent of *Waldensterben* (forest death).[22] In Germany, the first twenty or thirty years of efficient forest management created a great deal of growth. Such growth was measured by increases in the forest products *that could be measured.* But this tunnel vision led to neglect of anything in the forest that did not contribute to the bottom-line. As a consequence, the German forest technicians neglected the very things — diversity present in soil and the forest ecosystem — that allowed the forest to live. As a consequence, the forest died. Could this be the future of modern corporations? Could the emphasis on the bottom-line and shareholder value destroy all that is living in the modern corporation?[23]

The belief that shareholder value is the only metric for corporate success has created a new environment within modern corporations. Corporate management has a dilemma. Are they going to be driven by the product or service they are creating, or are they driven by an exit strategy whereby they cash out when they have made an adequate profit?[24] In other words, a publicly held company must be focused on short-term profits or risk being bought out and split up in the name of shareholder value. This new corporate environment also has a great impact on employees. Because the corporation must focus more and more on short-term profits, labor becomes expendable. Laborers can no longer count on a regular paycheck if they just do their jobs. This means that they can no longer plan their future — as they once did when corporations had constituencies in addition to shareholders. Their loyalty to the company is diminished if not extinguished, and, as a consequence, they simply seek the most money possible because money is the only thing they can now

22. Richard Sennett, *The Culture of the New Capitalism* (New Haven: Yale University Press) and *The Corrosion of Character: The Personal Consequences of Work in the New Capitalism* (New York: W. W. Norton, 1998), are two excellent analyses of the destructive potential involved in the corporate worldview that has emerged since 1980.

23. Scott, *Seeing Like a State,* pp. 15-20 uses the image of forest death to describe the way that our nation-states "think." This image also helps us understand how corporations think.

24. In a CNBC interview (March 4, 2014) Dennis Crowley, the founder and CEO of *Foursquare,* expressed this corporate dilemma. If he reinvests too much money into his company in an attempt to keep the company robust, this action might be conceived as inefficient because such investments in the future are deemed destructive of the bottom-line.

rely upon.[25] Workers can no longer rely upon friends at work, pride in the company, and many other nonmonetary considerations with respect to work. All that is left is money to measure their worth and status.

Money and money alone has now become the measure of both corporate worth and human worth. Not only has the emphasis on shareholder value made money the only measure of the value of a company, it is rapidly becoming the only measure of the value of a human being. It is in money that corporate values and human values coincide. Money is the reason human beings cooperate with the nonhuman corporate agendas. The problem is that money may only be a life-giving value if it serves values other than efficiency, and these alternative values have been eroded by the triumph of corporate persons over human persons.

Money as an Expression of Corporate Values

Corporate persons are not alive. They make decisions, but they are not alive. Their decision-making process differs from the human decision process. Human beings are not always logical, and our decisions are often emotional. Sometimes we favor one person or place or thing over another because our emotions dictate that we do so. Greed is often an emotion related to our quest for money. A greedy person desires more money long after he or she has enough money to last several lifetimes. Corporate persons are not subject to emotions. They are not greedy; yet, they pursue money even more than the greediest of human persons. The reason for this resides in corporate values of efficiency and calculability. These values, not greed, lead to the universal corporate quest for money.

Efficiency must be measured in order to be known. This means that corporate activities must be reduced to number, and money allows corporations to make such numerical measurements. Money provides an easy comparison between product A and product B, action Y and action Z, or even action Y with product A. In order to make a decision regarding efficiency, all that needs to be known is the relative value of numbers. If action Y results in 400 units and competing action Z results in 300 units, action Y is more efficient and will be pursued. All decisions become obvious once such calculations are made. Indeed, human beings are not necessary to make such decisions. Machines can easily make them. Nothing

25. Sennett, *The Corrosion of Character*.

but number is relevant to this process. Human needs, human interests, and the needs of other life-forms are simply irrelevant.

Monetization not only makes corporate efficiency possible, it also removes human beings from the decision-making process. Corporations do not need human persons to recognize that 400 is greater than 300. Machines routinely make such calculations. Indeed, machines can make far more complex calculations at a speed human beings cannot match, and unlike human calculations, the goal of corporate calculations is quite simple. It is only to find the one number that is always greater than all other numbers. The outcome of such measurements reveals the most efficient decision. Human beings are becoming both unnecessary to these calculations and less and less capable of even performing them.[26] Human beings are slowly being made redundant, and, according to corporate values, redundancy is inefficient and should be eliminated.

William Dugger envisions a bleak outcome to this state of affairs. The contemporary habit of corporations buying back their own stock leads Dugger to wonder if a corporation will own itself if it purchases 100 percent of its stock. This could allow a corporation to dispense with shareholders from the species *Homo sapiens* or even dispense with human workers and managers. "It would exist physically as a network of machines that buy, process, and sell commodities, monitored by a network of computers. Its purpose would be to grow ever larger through acquiring more machines and to become ever more powerful through acquiring more computers to monitor the new machines. It would be responsible to no one but itself in its mechanical drive for power and profit. It would represent capitalism at its very purest, completely unconcerned with anything save profit and power."[27]

Instead of eliminating people altogether, the corporation, in pursuit of its self-interest, might have better luck turning people into machines! This scenario is not too farfetched, as Ray Kurzweil enthusiastically argues in *The Age of Spiritual Machines: When Computers Exceed Human Intelligence.* He begins with a discussion of Moore's Law, which observes that transistor-based computing has doubled its power every eighteen months for the last thirty years. He extrapolates this growth into the future

---

26. Ellul, *The Technological Society,* pp. 158-83.

27. William Dugger, *Corporate Hegemony* (New York: Greenwood Press, 1989), p. 13. As quoted in David C. Korten, *When Corporations Rule the World,* 2nd edition (San Francisco: Berrett-Koehler Publishers, 2001), p. 223.

(assuming doubling every two years instead of every eighteen months, probably for ease of calculation). He states that if this trend continues, computers will have powers equal to the human brain's powers by 2018. And they will have double those powers by 2020, and quadruple those powers by 2022. In other words, by 2030, computers will have sixty-four times the capacity of the human brain, and by 2040 they will have 2048 times the capacity of the human brain.

Other things will also become possible in the name of corporate efficiency. For instance, it should soon be possible to implant a computer chip in the human brain giving the recipient the "brain power" of a computer. If someone with whom you are competing for a promotion gets such an implant, you will too. Once developed, corporate efficiency and competition will demand that all workers be equipped with such devices. This will be done in the name of efficiency and by our own "volition" because corporate efficiency has become synonymous with reason itself.[28]

Although Kurzweil happily anticipates his very reasonable prediction that human beings will become more machinelike, and Dugger fears the time when corporate persons will no longer need human persons, their hopes and fears express two radical outcomes in a struggle between the human person and the corporate person. Both corporate persons and human persons are capable of acting in the world to achieve their own self-interested goals. Their needs and goals differ because, unlike human persons, corporate persons are not alive. Their actions have little to do with life. They have everything to do with efficiency. Humans cannot be completely efficient because we are alive, and life is not efficient. Life is full of inefficient redundancies and is, in the final analysis, nonlinear and messy.

Human persons cooperate with the corporate agenda and adopt corporate values because we are paid to do so. Since money is a value held by both human persons and corporate persons, and since money is rapidly replacing all other human values, corporate persons use money to get human persons to willingly serve them. Corporations now distribute money to their people like the medieval Church distributed sacraments to believers. As the Church and its constituency believed that sacraments transformed people from sinners to saved, so does money transform its holder into anything its owner desires. In other words, money now pos-

---

28. Ray Kurzweil, *The Age of Spiritual Machines: When Computers Exceed Human Intelligence* (New York: Penguin Putnam, 1999), pp. 9-40.

sesses a sacramental quality. It can transform its recipients into whatever they may want to be. Indeed money is the central sacrament of the religion called Economics, and it is to a discussion of money as a sacrament that we now turn.

CHAPTER 5

Money: The Sacrament of The Market Economy

*The Word comes to the element, and so there is a sacrament . . . a
sort of visible word.*

St. Augustine of Hippo[1]

The benefits bestowed by a given deity depend on the attributes of the
deity in question. To make complex matters far simpler than they are,
it might be said that the Christian God's primary attributes are love and
grace; therefore, love and grace are what the Christian God bestows.
Likewise, since each *Sura* of the *Qur'an* begins "In the Name of God,
the Compassionate and Merciful," God's compassion and mercy are bestowed on the Muslim faithful.

The *way* a believer attains the benefits his or her deity bestows also
differs from religion to religion. Muslims receive these benefits through
the observance of the Five Pillars of Islam: (1) Profession of Faith, (2) Ritual Prayer, (3) Zakat, (4) Ramadan fast, and (5) Hajj (a pilgrimage to
Mecca). Likewise, many Christians believe that they receive benefits
their God bestows through sacraments, which they often call the means
of grace.

*Sacraments are corporately recognized rituals that express in one uni-
fied act both the benefits a specific deity bestows **and** the religious one's subjective trust or faith in these benefits and promises.* While religions other
than Christianity do not use the word *sacrament* to describe such acts,

1. Augustine, *In Johannem*, 80, 3.

they all have recognized public actions, rituals, or ceremonies that are acknowledged by all the faithful to be public or objective expressions of a person's inner, subjective faith. Christian sacraments like baptism, confession, and Holy Communion are such expressions. Circumcision is one such expression for Jews. The Five Pillars of Islam are also such objective expressions of Muslim faith. Similar corporately recognized expressions of subjective faith are observable in the relationship between Buddhist monks and laity.

> Both in the case of begging for food and in the case of the donation of shelter, one observes a strong reliance of monks on the laity. But the laity receive something in return, namely the merit accrued from giving gifts to a virtuous person. Indeed, monks do not thank laypeople for the food they receive; laypeople thank monks for providing them with the opportunity for giving. . . . Buddhist laypeople have generally considered themselves incapable of doing the things that monks and nuns do and thus have devoted themselves instead to their support, in the hope of accruing the merit that will allow them to become monks and nuns . . . in a future lifetime.[2]

Most religions have corporately recognized rituals that express, in one unified act, both the promises of the deity and the religious person's trust or faith in these promises. The word *sacrament* will be used as a cipher for these corporately recognized phenomena in the discussion below.

> A sacrament is a corporately recognized expression of a subjective trust in the promises of a god. Money is the sacrament of The Economy because it is an external expression that embodies our subjective trust in The Economy's promises. Without such subjective belief, money would not "work."

In one respect, a person's trust in God is purely subjective. By subjective I mean that a believer might have faith or trust that they never need to express in the external world. But when God's promises and our

2. Donald S. Lopez, Jr., *The Story of Buddhism: A Concise Guide to Its History and Teachings* (San Francisco: Harper, 2001), p. 17.

belief in those promises are ritualized in the external world, what was once only an internal subjective belief becomes external and objective. *When a religious body agrees that a particular observable act actually expresses a faithful, subjective belief, we have a sacramental event.* These sacramental acts are all objective in the sense that a person need not be a believer in order to recognize the act. An unbeliever might think that the Christian sacrament of baptism, for example, is a meaningless waste of time, but this person would have to admit the event called "baptism" happens in the external world. Such objectivity is characteristic of all sacraments.

The way The Economy bestows benefits on its faithful is similar in structure to this understanding of a sacrament. As a sacrament of baptism is the objective means by which the Christian God bestows grace on believers, money is the objective means by which The Economy bestows Its blessings on Its faithful. Since money makes objective both the promises of The Economy and our trust in these promises, money functions as a sacrament of the religion called Economics. It is The Economy's "means of grace." The more money a person has, the more blessings The Economy has bestowed. Just as some Christians think that salvation is impossible without baptism, many think that The Economy's benefits are impossible to obtain without money, and they are probably quite correct in believing so.

Money's actual function compares quite favorably with the Roman Catholic doctrine of transubstantiation, except money's power is more extensive. Transubstantiation declares that when the priest pronounces the Words of Institution over the bread and wine in the Eucharist (Holy Communion), the substance of the bread and wine *literally becomes* the substance of the body and blood of Jesus Christ. Karl Marx first made the comparison between money and transubstantiation, arguing that when a woman sells food and uses that money to buy fuel, the substance we call food *literally becomes* the substance we call fuel by *means* of money.[3] In agreement with Marx, Georg Simmel wrote that all commodities can only be exchanged for money, but money can be exchanged for any commodity whatsoever. "By contrast with labor, which can rarely change its applications, and the less easily the more specialized it is, capital in the form of money can almost always be transferred from one use to another,

3. Marx, *Capital: A Critique of Political Economy,* vol. 1 (New York: Penguin Group, 1976, 1990), pp. 197, 203.

at worst with a loss, but often with a gain. The worker can hardly ever extricate his art and skill from his trade and invest it somewhere else. By comparison with the owner of money (the worker) is at a disadvantage so far as free choice is concerned, just as the merchant is. Thus, the value of a given amount of money is equal to the value of free choice between innumerable other objects, and this is an asset that has no analogy in the area of commodities and labor."[4]

Money has the power to transform anything into anything else. Shakespeare's ode to gold expresses the extent of money's transformative powers.

> Gold? Yellow, glittering, precious gold? . . .
> Thus much of this will make black white; foul fair;
> Wrong right; base noble; old young; coward valiant.
> . . . What this, you gods? Why this
> Will lug your priests and servants from your sides;
> Pluck stout men's pillows from below their heads.
> This yellow slave
> Will knit and break religions; bless the accursed;
> Make the hoar leprosy adored; place thieves
> And give them title, knee and approbation
> With senators on the bench; this is it,
> That makes the wappen'd widow wed again.
>
> William Shakespeare, *Timon of Athens,* Act 4, Scene 3

The irony is that modern Christians are far more likely to deny the Roman Catholic doctrine of transubstantiation than reject money as a means to transform one substance into another. One wonders if this is an honest expression of what we clearly see every day, or whether what we *think* we see every day reflects our belief in the sacramental status of money. Belief and trust are not innocuous. As we are about to see, our beliefs about the character of money have transformed society, human thought, and even nature itself on a number of crucial points in human history.

Money is a human invention. Indeed, it is one of our greatest creations, but, as we have seen with reference to corporations, our creations

---

4. Georg Simmel, *The Philosophy of Money,* trans. David Frisby and Tom Bottomore (London: Routledge, 1978, 2004), p. 228.

have a habit of taking on a life of their own and changing us. Money has achieved a great deal of power over human beings. On the positive side it has enabled us to achieve goals far beyond the wildest dreams of our predecessors. On the negative side, money has made many of us its slaves. Above all, money is The Economy's sacrament. It is the means through which The Economy bestows its benefits on its faithful. It did not start out as a sacrament, but it has become one. It is, therefore, important to try to understand its origin to gain further clarity concerning its sacramental nature.

The Origin of Money

Money has one or more of the following functions: It is a means of exchange. It is a store of value, and it is an accounting mechanism that records who owes what to whom.[5] In the following discussion money will be said to originate when one or more of these functions operates.

Money has not always existed. Our hunter-gatherer ancestors did not use money for many millennia. Money evolved from the social, political, and intellectual dynamics created by the agricultural revolution. Eventually, these dynamics created two sorts of people that we currently call creditors and debtors, and the way we conceive of this creditor/debtor relationship is reflected in how we understand the relationship between money's functions.[6]

As the following discussion will demonstrate, ancient archaic empires conceived of money only as an accounting mechanism that recorded who owed what to whom. This was reflected in the tributary system of ancient empires. The emergence of coins in Greece meant a different understanding of money. Coins allowed people to think of money as a means of exchange as well as an accounting mechanism. This reconfiguration of money was accompanied by a reconfiguration of Greek society and the entire ancient world. Likewise, when coins went out of use after the fall of Rome, Europe developed a new social configuration called feudalism. But, we are getting ahead of ourselves. There was a time when money was

5. Bill Mauer, "The Anthropology of Money," *Annual Review of Anthropology* 35 (2006): 20, and Geoffrey Ingham, *The Nature of Money* (Cambridge: Polity Press, 2004), p. 3.

6. Ingham, *The Nature of Money*, and David Graeber, *Debt: The First 5000 Years* (Brooklyn, NY: Melville House Publishing, 2011).

not. While its origin is obscure, an analysis of the dynamics of the agricultural revolution does give us clues.

The agricultural revolution was a technological revolution, and technologies are never ideologically neutral. Even a small technological innovation contains social and intellectual biases that the people who created these innovations did not foresee.[7] Air conditioning is an example.

The people who invented air conditioning were just trying to cool a home or workplace, but they inadvertently undermined neighborhood life in the process. Before air conditioning, people spent hot summer evenings in the coolest place they could find, namely, outside on their porches. They got to know their neighbors. They knew the neighborhood children and their parents. They even made some friends. Neighborhoods had an identity as a consequence. After air conditioning, people continued to spend hot summer evenings in the coolest place they could find. But now the coolest place they could find was inside their homes. Eventually neighbors became unfamiliar and neighborhoods lost their identities. In short, the technology we call air conditioning has an institutional bias toward the isolation of neighbors from neighbors. This bias can be overcome, but doing so requires work because knowing one's neighbor must now be a priority rather than merely a consequence of living close to each other.

The agricultural revolution was one of humanity's greatest technological innovations. Accordingly, it created certain social, institutional, and intellectual biases. Eventually money emerged as a consequence of these biases. As noted in the introduction, the agricultural revolution was not simply about farming. Certainly farming was important, but farming alone does not exhaust the social ramifications of the agricultural revolution. The agricultural revolution was also a revolution in the way we *thought* about food. For the first time we thought of food as a commodity — as something that can be owned, hoarded, and traded for other goods and services. Before the agricultural revolution food was not owned, and

7. Neil Postman, *Technopoly: The Surrender of Culture to Technology* (New York: Alfred A. Knopf, 1992), discusses biases within technological innovations like the printing press, television, medicine, etc. In an earlier book, *The Disappearance of Childhood* (New York: Vintage Books, 1994), he argues that childhood is not biological. Childhood, at least as we know it, was created by the technological innovation created by the printing press, and childhood is now under assault because television has replaced the printing press as our primary technology.

generally it was not bought and sold. After the agricultural revolution the buying and selling of food was the norm.[8]

It is important to emphasize that the commodification of food happened before the emergence of money. This had one extremely important implication. Without money as a guide to determine the exchange value of food, nonmonetary criteria had to be established to determine who merits food and who does not. These criteria are arbitrary in the sense that they differ from one agricultural center to another. These criteria are also the source of what we now call morality. In other words, morality emerges when the commodification of food demands that a distinction be made between those who merit food and those who do not, and morality begins when this distinction is made. But morality achieves full power over society when religious leaders — through rituals and myths — convince the people that the divide between those who merit food and those who do not is of divine rather than human origin. When this happens, morality becomes universal at least within civilization.[9]

When religion justifies a given morality, those who merit food are deemed, by God and society, to be good. Those who do not merit food are deemed, again by God and society, to be evil. Morality exists wherever this distinction between good and evil exists. Morality does not exist where the distinction between good and evil is not universally drawn.

This is not to say that hunter-gatherer societies did not distinguish between some things we might call "good" and other things we might now call "bad or evil." It is to say that hunter-gatherers did not universally

<hr />

8. Daniel Quinn, *Beyond Civilization: Humanity's Next Great Adventure* (New York: Three Rivers Press, 1999), *Ishmael* (New York: Bantam/Turner, 1992), *The Story of B* (New York: Bantam, 1996), and *My Ishmael* (New York: Bantam, 1997). What is important about Quinn is the idea that in order to understand our current status, we must recognize that human beings lived for 2 million years before civilization as we know it began in the agricultural revolution. For one anthropological confirmation (among others) of Quinn's contention that the commodification of food was hardly the social norm for hunter-gatherer cultures, see John Gowdy, "Hunter-gatherers and the mythology of the market," in *The Cambridge Encyclopedia of Hunters and Gatherers,* ed. Richard B. Ley and Richard Daly (Cambridge: Cambridge University Press, 1999), pp. 391-98.

9. It is important to note once again that civilization is the sort of human culture that emerged out of the agricultural revolution. It is one sort of human culture among many, but it is now the dominant form of human culture. No positive or negative connotations are meant from the term. If, for example, I were to call a group uncivilized, it would simply mean that the social configuration in question predated the agricultural revolution and has not been overcome by it.

> Once food becomes a commodity, criteria are simultaneously
> developed that determine who merits food and who
> does not. This is the origin of morality. Later, money
> emerges from morality and becomes the criterion that
> determines who merits food and who does not.

draw the moral divide. For us, it is as if we are in a drug-induced state whereby we cannot evaluate our friends or select a cut of meat without distinguishing between good and evil and thereby drawing the moral divide.[10] Not only must we distinguish between the good and the bad, we also must distinguish between the good, the better, and the best as well as the bad, the worse, and the worst. No such compulsion existed in hunter-gatherer bands because they did not make food a commodity. Any moral criteria they may have developed to distinguish between good and evil did not pertain to food. When food became a commodity, it was incumbent upon the entire society to draw the moral divide. It could not be otherwise because the distinction between good and evil determined who merited food and who did not.[11] Since food is a universal need, it follows that criteria that determined who merited food and who did not, namely morality, would also be a universal concern.

Morality's universal act is to draw the line between good and evil. But where this line is to be drawn differs from place to place, culture to culture, and even person to person. This is a consequence of different agricultural centers using different criteria to distinguish between those who merit food and those who do not. This is also why there has never been an agreed-upon universal morality, and why there probably never will be one. But our focus on our apparent inability to construct a universal moral scheme leads us to overlook one very important feature of morality, and this feature is, in fact, universal to all moral schemes no matter how much they disagree about what is good and what is evil.

In every instance morality's function is always the same. When any given moral system draws the line between the good guys and the bad

10. Jay Williams, "Genesis 3," *Interpretation: A Journal of Biblical Theology* 35, no. 3 (1981): 278.

11. Scott W. Gustafson, *Behind Good and Evil: How to Overcome the Death-dealing Character of Morality* (West Conshohocken, PA: Infinity Publishing, 2009).

guys, it tells us who can be justifiably killed or simply left for dead.[12] This is why, even today, many of our conversations about helping the poor or homeless are expressed in terms of morality. We are quite willing to help a homeless person whom we have placed on the good side of the moral divide. If such a person's plight is a consequence of events over which he or she had no control, we are likely to help. If, however, the homeless one is a drug addict and a thief, our morality places them on the evil side of the moral divide, and we are very unlikely to assist them. The former homeless person, we deem good. The latter, we deem evil. We never ask ourselves the question, "What becomes of the people we turn away?" This is because we do not want to face the fact that we have left them for dead. Moreover, it is our moral reasoning that enables us to justify ourselves when we leave someone for dead.

Morality emerged with the agricultural revolution's commodification of food. Religious leaders contributed to this new social arrangement. Through myths and rituals they made it appear that the moral criteria used to determine who merited food and who did not were established by the Gods instead of human beings. Moreover, morality justified those who owned the food when they refused to distribute food to the unworthy ones. In short, morality sanctioned the agricultural revolution's new social order. Any social order derived from the agricultural revolution has therefore been composed of two sorts of persons who might now be called creditors and debtors, but they may have been called patricians and plebeians, nobility and common, master and slave in the past. In all cases morality required that the inferior group always justify itself to the superior group by fulfilling the moral requirements of the superior group. We now call this social arrangement civilization. It is based on this creditor/debtor relationship that began with the commodification of food.

In one form or another, this creditor/debtor relationship provides social coherence to civilization, but the creditor/debtor relationship has not always been the basis of social cohesion. The hunter-gatherer bands in which human beings lived prior to the agricultural revolution cohered around trust and autonomy, and trust and autonomy were objectified (sacramentalized) in the act of sharing. Anthropologist Tim Ingold describes sharing as acting "with that person in mind, *in the hope* that

---

12. Enrique Dussell, *Ethics and Community* (Maryknoll, NY: Orbis Books, 1986), pp. 49, 50.

they will do likewise by responding in favorable ways to you."[13] Recently R. I. M. Dunbar has argued that sharing, so defined, is limited by the human brain's capacity to "keep in mind" about 150 people. This means that trust (and sharing) can be a socially cohesive force only in small groups.[14] When agricultural societies became more populous, they needed a new way to cohere. The creditor/debtor relationship became this new force.

This new power of social cohesion was far more coercive than trust and autonomy. Hunter-gatherer bands were generally nomadic and operated on a subsistence level. Accordingly, a person's property was limited to what that person could carry. As a consequence, a person could not ask for what another person did not have. Agricultural societies were different. They were sedentary. A person's property could be stored, and it was not limited to what that person could carry. The one who stored food could ask for almost anything in exchange for food. They could even ask for things that a person did not have. To be sure, creditors or food owners relied on the promises of their debtors to repay, but these promises of repayment did not honor the autonomy of the debtors. Instead, the promise of the debtor created a new sort of person — a person capable of honoring his debt. This is not as innocuous as it first appears. In order to create the confidence (within the creditor) that the debtor will repay, the debtor must guarantee repayment with something that is already owned. Today we call this collateral. We offer our creditors our property or proof of employment to guarantee repayment. In the past, all a debtor had to offer was his own body, his wife, or his children.[15]

Force is the most obvious way that debtors are "encouraged" to repay. But morality, internalized by the rituals, myths, and other religious practices, remains a preferred alternative. Morality's function is to make the repayment of debt synonymous with moral goodness in the minds of the debtors themselves. But eventually even morality and force were not enough to guarantee repayment. As more and more people owed their creditor more and more, the creditor had to remember who owed him what. Money may have emerged to address this issue.

We first encounter money *circa* 3500 BCE, and we encounter it as

13. Tim Ingold, "On the social relations of the hunter-gatherer band," in *The Cambridge Encyclopedia of Hunters and Gatherers*, p. 407.

14. R. I. M. Dunbar, "Coevolution of Neocortical Size, Group Size, and Language in Humans," *Behavioral and Brain Sciences* 16, no. 4f (1993): 691.

15. Maurizio Lazzarato, *The Making of the Indebted Man*, trans. Joshua David Jordan (Los Angeles: Semiotext[e], 2012), p. 41.

an accounting mechanism. About 70 percent of ancient extant writings record who owes what to whom. *It is quite likely that money as an accounting mechanism evolved because the creditors found it difficult to remember their debtors, and they used writing (they may have invented writing for this purpose!) to remind themselves who owed them what.*

When we first find money it is configured in a surprising way. We find money as credit. The barter myth tells us that money evolved differently. It says that money evolved from barter through the use of precious metals made into coins. But historical facts do not support the barter myth. Nearly 3000 years before the emergence of coins, we find accounting ciphers that record who owes what to whom. Since sacraments are an external, objective expression of a person's internal, subjective promise, these ciphers, which are also objective expressions of a person's subjective promise to repay, are sacramental in form. Moreover, these ciphers justify a social configuration that has always dominated agricultural civilizations, namely, the creditor/debtor relationship. Our modern global Economy still coheres around this social relationship, and money depicts how the creditor/debtor relationship functions in culture.[16]

Money and Social Transformation

When a socially dominant religion alters the way a sacrament is understood, society as a whole changes quite dramatically. For example, the Protestant Reformation of the sixteenth century proposed a different way to understand the sacrament of confession and absolution, and this new understanding coincided with the emergence of revolutionary new social structures. Medieval theology said that an ordained priest was necessary to mediate between God and the penitent person. A person confessed to a priest, and the priest could then absolve the penitent one. Only an ordained priest possessed the power to forgive a person's sins. As a Church official, he had access to a store of merits from Jesus and the saints that could be used to "pay for" a person's sins. Such forgiveness was impossible without access to the Church and its merits, and priests provided this access. As strange as it might seem to modern ears, life revolved around

16. That money depicts how the creditor/debtor relationship functions in any given culture is Geoffrey Ingham's argument in *The Nature of Money*.

forgiveness and absolution in medieval Europe because everyone "knew" that an unrepentant sinner suffers in hell for eternity. The fact that the Church's sacrament of confession and absolution was the only way to avoid such a terrible fate was the source of the Church's political and social power.

The Protestant Reformation changed this notion of confession and absolution, and, in the process, initiated a tremendous social transformation in Europe. In arguing that a person could receive forgiveness directly from God, the Protestants claimed that a priestly intermediary was nice but unnecessary. This new understanding of the sacrament undermined the Church's authority. The Church's monopoly on forgiveness was broken. Since it was now possible to receive forgiveness from sources other than Catholic priests, political leaders could reject Church authority. Before the Reformation, the pope could keep a king in line by threatening excommunication. Once accomplished, excommunication cut off the king and his kingdom from forgiveness and destined everyone in the kingdom to hell. Threatened by eternal damnation, the people might revolt. After the Reformation, the Church lost its monopoly on forgiveness and absolution. Since forgiveness could be obtained and eternal damnation avoided apart from the Church, kings could oppose the Church without the threat of losing their thrones.

New social and political configurations arose as a consequence of this shift in the understanding of the sacrament of forgiveness and absolution. Specifically European nations independent of Church control emerged. The nations that we now take for granted became realities. It is quite unlikely that this would have happened if the Church had maintained its monopoly on confession and absolution.

There are a variety of ways any one sacrament can be interpreted, and when these interpretations change, society is often transformed. This is true with the sacrament we call money. Geoffrey Ingham and David Graeber have demonstrated that a shift in the way we understand money is always accompanied by a massive social transformation.[17] As noted, money has three functions. It is an accounting mechanism that records who owes what to whom. It is a store of value, and it is a means of ex-

---

17. Ingham, *The Nature of Money*, pp. 89-150, and Graeber, *Debt: The First 5000 Years*, pp. 223-391, who relies on Ingham's thinking. Both give historical evidence supporting the contention that a shift in our understanding of money is always accompanied by new social configurations.

change. Sometimes one of these three functions dominates a culture's understanding of money. Sometimes all three function together. *History clearly demonstrates that whenever we make a significant shift in the way we understand the relationship between money's three functions, society is transformed.* Such transformation reveals money's sacramental status. Just as the shift in medieval Europe's understanding of the sacrament of confession and absolution led to the transformation of Europe's social, political, religious, intellectual, and institutional life, so has a shift in our understanding of money led to comparable social changes in nearly all aspect of our social life. This transformation often takes a century or more, but the process of transformation begins when our understanding of the sacrament of money changes.

Credit and Ancient Empires

As noted, the first evidence of money is found in the archaic civilization in Mesopotamia around 3500 BCE. Here money was chiefly an accounting mechanism that recorded who owed what to whom. This understanding of money supported hierarchical, far-flung archaic empires. These were tributary systems where goods and services flowed from the periphery to the center. Money as an accounting mechanism recorded what was owed to the empire. As a written account, money enabled the emperor's military forces to "remember" which portions of the empire they had to "visit" to assure that tribute would be paid.

Coins and Social Transformation

Invention of coins around 600 BCE was a transformation in the way money was understood. Coins presumed that money was also a means of exchange and a store of value. Money understood as an accounting mechanism lost its exclusivity.

Coins had at least two and possibly three independent origins — all of which occurred around 600 BCE. In Greece, coins were made of precious metal. In China they were made of common metals, and coins may also have been independently invented in India as well. The reconfiguration of society, religion, and philosophy in all these civilizations was immense, and these reconfigurations occur at the same time as the invention of coinage.[18] In fact, the invention of coins corresponds to the greatest transformations of society since the agricultural revolution. Karl Jaspers (1883-1969) calls this transformation the Axial Age.[19] Modern religions like Buddhism and Judaism emerge to challenge the archaic religions of ancient empires. Philosophy begins in Greece and in China, and new social configurations emerge that allow new ways to deal with the adverse consequences of debt. The following discussion focuses on Greece and Europe, but similar social and intellectual transformations were happening in China and India where coins were also being used.

Coins provided a new answer to the policy dilemmas that were a consequence of understanding money primarily as an accounting mechanism. Money so understood allowed only two policy options with respect to the creditor/debtor relationship. The creditor could demand payment. In this case the debtor's options were debt peonage, slavery, escape, or revolt. Forgiveness of debts was the second option.

> Since money is the sacrament of a dominant religion, massive intellectual and social changes occur when a given society changes the way it thinks about money.

This amnesty option was not without precedent in ancient civilizations. Massive debt amnesty was practiced in Samaria and Babylonia when a new king or a conqueror assumed power. Amnesty usually meant returning land to its original owners and allowing all debt-peons to return to their families. In Samaria, debt amnesty was called a "declaration of freedom." Such declarations provide us with the first recorded word for freedom *(amargi)*. It literally means "return to mother" which is exactly what a freed debt-peon would do when the decree was issued.[20] The Jubilee codes in the Bible (Leviticus 25) are an effort on the part of the entire Hebrew culture to institutionalize the practice of debt amnesty. Among other important codes benefiting the poor debtor class, the Jubilee codes

18. Walter Scheidel, "The divergent evolution of coinage in eastern and western Eurasia," Version 1.0, *Princeton/Stanford Working Papers in Classics,* www.Princeton.edu/~pswpc/scheidel/040603.pdf, 2006, p. 2.

19. Karl Jaspers, *The Origin and Goal of History* (London: Routledge & Kegan Paul, 1953), p. 1.

20. Graeber, *Debt: The First 5000 Years,* p. 65.

decreed that every forty-nine years all debts should be abolished and land returned to its original owners.

Coins gave creditors and debtors other options. When Athens distributed coins to its citizens in 483 BCE, the Athenian debtors used them to pay off debt and avoid peonage. Creditors accepted coins as payment because the Athenian government guaranteed that these coins would be accepted for all payments due the city.[21] The Athenians also began to pay their soldiers in coin. This had tremendous implications for Greek warfare.

Before the advent of coins, armies had been composed of aristocrats who led the men who were in their (debt?) service into battle. Aristocrats were rewarded for their participation by dividing the spoils of war. Aristocrats had the resources to wait until the war's end to be paid. Nonaristocrats (we might call them soldiers) had no such resources and could not wait. Moreover, these soldiers were not in the position to train for war. They needed to work in order to pay off their debts. Coins permitted the state to train professional soldiers who, because of coined money, no longer had to worry about the origin of their next meal. Professional training allowed the Greek military to develop and practice new techniques. In the period in which the Greeks developed coins, they also developed and practiced new phalanx tactics that gave them a tremendous advantage on the battlefield — an advantage that had much to do with their ability to defeat and later conquer the archaic Persian Empire.

Roman policy also reflected the profound social changes coins enabled. According to Livy (59 BCE-17 CE), there was always conflict between the patricians (creditors) and the plebeians (debtors). Periodically, the plebeians would cease work and camp outside the city, threatening a mass defection that would shut down society.[22] Here too, the patricians

---

21. Graeber, *Debt: The First 5000 Years*, pp. 226, 227. In fact, it is not gold or silver that gives coins their value, it is the promise of governments to honor these coins (or checks or bank notes) in the payment of taxes. Ultimately, money is accepted as payment for goods and services because the government guarantees it as payment for taxes and other government services and fines.

22. This is an interesting phenomenon because it represents another way debtors responded to the weight of their debt. The Hebrews abandoned their oppressive Egyptian captors. The Mayans of Central America may have walked away from their civilization as well. The Roman plebeians probably had nowhere to go, so they went on strike. In China, people were known to revolt. The Han (206 BCE-220 CE), Tang (618-906), Sung (960-1179), and Ming (1368-1644) dynasties were all a product of peasant (debtor) insurrections.

only had two choices if money were to remain strictly a way to account for debt. They could deal with the crisis by force which, if successful, would turn the plebeians into a class of bonded laborers. Alternatively, they could meet their demands with some kind of debt amnesty that would diminish the status of the creditors. Coins provided another option.

The Roman creditors could, as the Athenians did, preserve a free peasantry and employ the male peasants as soldiers. Grudgingly and over time they did this. As a matter of fact, the traditional date of the first Roman coinage (338 BCE) is nearly the same date as a law outlawing debt bondage (336 BCE). Ultimately, the emergence of an imperial structure of Rome (*circa* 45 BCE) accelerated this process of social transformation. To make a complex story very simple, it was through the popular support of the plebeian, debtor class that emperors came to power and ruled. In turn, nearly all the emperors of Rome pacified the plebeians with a Roman version of a welfare state.[23]

Coins and the Beginning of Philosophy

Coins had a profound influence on the human intellect. Both coins and philosophy emerged in the same city, Miletus (a Greek colony located on the coast of what is now Turkey), at the same time (c. 600 BCE). Thales (615-545 BCE), a resident of Miletus, is credited with being the first philosopher. Aristotle narrates that when mocked about his strange philosophical interests, Thales drew upon his knowledge of the heavens to predict a bumper crop in olives. As a consequence of his investigations, he gathered investors and purchased all the olive presses in the region. When the bumper crop came in, there was a sudden demand for olive presses for which he charged rent, becoming a rich man in the process, and, I suppose, the first person to corner a specific market through scientific investigations.[24]

Little is known about Thales' philosophy *per se*, but he was in search of an ultimate principle from which everything emerges and into which everything dissolves. He suggested water, one of the four basic elements, to be the principle from which everything emerges and into which everything dissolves. It is very important to note that coined money has the same characteristics as Thales' ultimate principle. When we purchase

23. Graeber, *Debt: The First 5000 Years,* p. 230.
24. Aristotle, *Politics,* 1259 a.

something, money is that from which the purchased item springs, and when we sell something, money is that into which our sold item dissolves. Thales' younger countryman Anaximander (610-540) reveals even more similarities between the principles of philosophy and the function of coined money.

Anaximander proposed the "Unlimited" *(apeiron)* as the first-principle of things that are. "The Unlimited is that from which the coming-to-be (of things and qualities) takes place, and it is that into which they return when they perish, by moral necessity, giving satisfaction to one another and making reparations for their injustice, according to the order of time."[25] The unlimited *(apeiron)* is neither water nor any of the other so-called elements. It is altogether different. The unlimited is something out of which everything springs and into which everything "of moral necessity" perishes. Again, coin money has the same characteristics as Anaximander's "Unlimited."

Recently Richard Seaford has argued exactly this, namely, that Anaximander's "Unlimited" functions exactly as coin money functions.

1. Both the Unlimited and coin money are *unlike other things* and separate from them.
2. Both *contain all things* in the sense that everything else emerges from the Unlimited or coin and is transformed back into the Unlimited or coin.
3. Like Anaximander's Unlimited, coin money "precedes and persists" beyond all other things, and in this sense is, like the Unlimited, immortal and indestructible.
4. The Unlimited is in eternal motion yet maintains its identity. Money too is in constant circulation (eternal motion) and keeps its identity.
5. As the Unlimited "surrounds and steers" all things, coin money regulates market activity.
6. Both are *impersonal.* Both philosophy and money begin the quest to develop impersonal, objective knowledge. Philosophy begins the modern quest to explain the unexplainable in terms of impersonal natural forces, and coins function in a purely impersonal matter. It does not depend on who a person is. A coin transaction is impersonal. It can be made with anyone.

25. Anaximander, *Fragment 1,* as quoted in Philip Wheelwright, ed., *The Presocratics* (New York: Odyssey Press, 1966), p. 54. The "moral necessity" by which an entity might return to the Unlimited mimics "the moral necessity" to repay debts.

7. The Unlimited is homogeneous and internally undifferentiated. The same is true with money.
8. Money, like the Unlimited, is concrete and abstract, visible and invisible.
9. The Unlimited has the power to unite opposites in the sense that opposites are absorbed into the Unlimited. Coined money also has this power. In monetary transactions enemies can become friends and one commodity can become another when the sold commodity is absorbed into money and the purchased commodity proceeds out of money.[26]

The existence of coined money in his hometown gave Anaximander a "lived-in" experience of diverse things being swallowed up by money and different things emerging from money. His first principle, the Unlimited, expressed this same dynamic. Like money, the Unlimited was also the principle into which things were destroyed and from which everything emerged. Money as coin set Anaximander's mind on a path that led to a new, impersonal way of thinking called philosophy.[27]

The Demise of Coins and the Rise of European Feudalism

Many modern historians and philosophers do not like to admit it, but Western philosophy and Western civilization nearly came to an end with the fall of the Roman Empire. We once called this period the Dark Ages. There are many mysteries surrounding this period in European history, but only recently have Ingham and Graeber recognized that transformation into the Dark Ages was accompanied by a shift in our understanding of money. Around 600 CE coins ceased to exist. Money was once again conceived primarily as an accounting mechanism, much less so as a store

---

26. Richard Seaford, *Money and the Early Greek Mind: Homer, Philosophy, Tragedy* (Cambridge: Cambridge University Press, 2004), pp. 204-7.

27. Marc Shell, *The Economy of Literature* (Baltimore: Johns Hopkins University Press, 1978), takes this issue even further, noting how "the money form" dominates the philosophy of Heraclitus (535-475 BCE). According to his ninetieth fragment, "All things are an equal exchange for fire and fire for all things, as goods are for gold and gold for good" (p. 52). The money form is either criticized or an unspoken background of much ancient philosophy, leading one to suspect that philosophy would not have developed without the shift in our understanding of money provided by coins.

of value, and hardly ever as a means of exchange. This shift in our understanding of money was also accompanied by a transformation of European society.

Feudalism emerged. The new social structure was still built on obligation and debt, but, since money was no longer used as a means of exchange, debts were paid in ways other than a monetary transaction.[28] In medieval Europe, every social class had its own particular obligations and duties. Each class owed something to the others. The nobility was obligated by God to *protect* everyone. The peasants were obligated to *feed* everyone, and the religious ones were obligated to *pray* for everyone. Goods and services were distributed based on the fulfillment of these obligations. This new feudal system was unlike anything humans had yet devised. It was composed of self-sufficient, relatively isolated political units in which monetary exchange was unnecessary. A peasant could probably live his or her entire life without touching a coin. In return for a peasant's produce, the nobility would protect him from the threat of thieves and marauders, and the priests would protect him from the threat of hell. This self-sufficient system was upset once again when, in the late fifteenth century, coins reemerged. Money once again became a means of exchange, a store of value as well as an accounting mechanism.

The Reemergence of Coins and the Reformation

The role of coins in the social transformation called the Reformation is not appreciated. But it might be crucial. The Reformation may not have happened without coins being widely circulated. The Reformation is said to have begun in 1517 when Martin Luther (1487-1546) nailed ninety-five theses he wished to debate to the door of the Wittenberg church. *Luther's action was prompted by the literal monetization of God's grace in the form of indulgences.* In the discussion of the sacrament of confession and absolution that began this section, it was noted that the Church had a deposit

---

28. During this same period Islamic society also understood money principally as an accounting mechanism. It developed a different social configuration from medieval Europe's feudalism; yet, Islamic society was also a society built on justice and trust. It outlawed usury, for example, and commerce relied on promises and trust between merchants. The Indian Ocean was instrumental in the trade between Muslims in much the same way as the Mediterranean Sea had been in the Roman Empire, but credit and trust rather than coins dominated this region of commerce.

of merits it could use to literally pay God for the debts average Christians had acquired due to their sins. Indulgences literally sold these merits for coins. As a matter of fact, the popular advertising slogan for indulgences, "As soon as *the coin* in the coffer rings, the soul from purgatory springs," demonstrates the relationship between coins and indulgences.[29]

The use of a coin in the purchase of an indulgence undermined some basic tenets in medieval theology. Prior to the Reformation, theologians had devised ways one could buy or purchase one's salvation or forgiveness that were not as immediate as an exchange using a coin. Prior to the re-emergence of coins, an indulgence could be a prayer, a small act of service, a pilgrimage, or even a crusade, but the key to all these transactions is that they took time. The duration of the transaction allowed theologians to place God's act of grace *before* the act of penance and say an act of penance was a person's *response* to the grace God. This maintained the primacy of God's grace and, on paper at least, made it appear that grace was still a free gift. An indulgence, bought and paid for by coin, however, could not be rationalized in this way. The first act was obviously the payment of a coin. God was obviously being bribed! Reformers like Martin Luther recognized that the coin that purchased the indulgence totally undermined God's initiative, and, therefore, an indulgence bought and paid for by coin could not be a response to God's grace. It was a bribe to get God to perform God's forgiving work. It is in this way that the reemergence of the coin in the Renaissance was instrumental in the theological debates that initiated the Reformation and transformed European society.

Paper Money, Public Debt, and the Emergence of the Modern World

How people thought about the sacrament of money continued to change social configurations and societies. The emergence of modern banking and paper money, for example, coincided with the demise of England's absolute monarchy and the rise of a limited, constitutional monarchy. The demise of absolute monarchy in England began when Charles II defaulted on his debt. His creditors did not sit idly by. They rejected Charles and invited William of Orange to assume the British throne. King William's power was no longer absolute. In 1689, he accepted a constitutional set-

---

29. Eric Gritsch, *A History of Lutheranism,* 2nd edition (Minneapolis: Fortress Press, 2010), p. 16.

tlement that intentionally provided him with insufficient funds for normal expenditures. William was forced to go to Parliament for additional funds whenever they were needed. At that time Parliament also adopted a policy of long-term borrowing that set aside a portion of the government's yearly proceeds to pay interest on debts.[30] This began a new way to think about money that is based on public debt.

This "Glorious Revolution" was, in fact, a revolution in money. It was the culmination of a process whereby governments gradually had lost their monopoly on the creation of money. The governments' monopoly began to erode during the Renaissance when bankers began to exchange bills of exchange (written IOUs) among each other. If person A owed banker B money, person A would record this obligation to repay banker B on a bill of exchange (written IOU) that would be held by banker B. On occasion, however, banker B might exchange person A's note to banker C in order to meet an obligation banker B had to banker C. This is one possible origin of paper money — at least in Europe. Until the Glorious Revolution, however, the exchange of such paper debt notes only occurred between bankers. The Glorious Revolution dismissed this limitation.

The Bank of England provided a 1.2-million-pound loan to the government at 8 percent interest and received an annual management fee of 4000 pounds from the government. Of most importance for the evolution of our understanding of money, however, was a royal charter that gave the bank the right to take deposits, and, of most importance for this discussion, issue bank notes and discount bills of exchange.[31] In other words, banks could print money that the government would recognize as legal tender! These bank notes and bills of exchange began to serve as the paper money we now know. "In effect, the *privately* owned Bank of England transformed the sovereign's *personal* debt into a *public* debt, and, eventually in turn, into a *public* currency. Underpinning this transformation in the social production of money was the change in balance of power that was expressed in the equally hybridized concept of sovereignty of the King-in-Parliament. The institutions for the production of capitalist credit-money, and the balance of economic and political interests that underpinned it, were beginning to take shape."[32]

30. Daron Acemuğlu and James A. Robinson, *Why Nations Fail: The Origins of Power, Prosperity and Poverty* (New York: Crown Business, 2012), pp. 191-97.

31. Ingham, *The Nature of Money*, pp. 119-28.

32. Ingham, *The Nature of Money*, p. 128.

Once again, we have a change in the political structure accompanying a change in the way money is understood. Following the Glorious Revolution, bankers had the power to create, on their own and without consultation, sovereign money that would be publicly circulated and acknowledged by the sovereign as legal tender for taxes and all other government services. Here is how the system works today.

When you borrow money from a bank, the accountant records the transaction in two ways. The most obvious way is that the money loaned you is placed in your account and subtracted from the bank's assets. You would think that this is all there is to it, but there is more. The money-*creating* part happens when the accountant also records your (the borrower's) promise to repay the loan as an asset that the bank actually has! If your loan was for $1 million, this means that $2 million now exist where there was once only $1 million. You, the borrower, have $1 million in your account, and your bank, the lender, also has recorded your promise to repay the loan as an asset or $1 million on its books. The bank can, if it desires, loan this $1 million again, and thereby create even more money from the original $1 million. In other words, every time a bank makes a loan, it creates money "out of thin air."[33] This, by the way, is a process quite similar to the Christian doctrine called *creatio ex nihilo* (creation out of nothing), which Christians use to describe how God created the heavens and the earth from nothing but a word or perhaps a promise.

A bank's ability to create money is based on the *promise* of the borrower to repay his or her debt. This obligation is recorded as a cipher on the asset side of the bank's accounting ledger, but it would be impossible to call this money if the government did not acknowledge this cipher to be legal tender. Such acknowledgment first came as a consequence of the Glorious Revolution when the government of England agreed to acknowledge these ciphers as money. In accepting these units of account as payment for taxes, the government assured both the circulation and growth of the money supply, and this growth of the money supply now happens primarily through banks rather than the government. As counterintuitive as it may seem, debt creates modern money. Should the gov-

---

33. David Korten, *Agenda for a New Economy* (San Francisco: Berrett-Koehler Publishers, 2009), p. 23. The system works quite well as long as a sufficient number of debts are paid. Financial crises, the most recent being the Great Recession of 2008-2009 (history may have to extend these dates), happen when the number of defaults achieves critical mass, and money, as an accounting measure, evaporates because lenders can no longer list a debtor's promise to repay a debt as an asset.

ernment ever pay its debts in full, money, as we now know it, would cease to exist.

Money as Capital

Money as capital emerged from credit money. Since it too is a different way to think about the sacrament of money, money as capital led to dramatic social changes.

Capital is not a thing. It is a process in which money is perpetually sent in search of more money.[34] Karl Marx gives classic expression to how this process works. Exchange can be described as a movement of C→M→C where C = commodity and M = money. C→M→C means a commodity is sold for money that in turn is used to purchase another commodity. But an interesting thing happens when a commodity is used or consumed. The commodity ceases to exist, but the money persists as a consequence of the exchange, or as Marx says, "Circulation sweats money from every pore."[35]

Marx further recognizes an interesting fact of this C→M→C process. The C→M phase for the seller of the commodity is always the M→C phase for the buyer. This means that alongside the C→M→C process there springs another form of circulation that can be described as M→C→M. Now from an economic perspective the process M→C→M is a waste of time and effort if M = M. Why bother to make such a transaction if you receive only the amount of money you possessed in the first place? In order to make "economic" sense, the process M→C→M must actually be M→C→M′, where hopefully M′ is greater than M. Money as capital is any money that is the consequence of the process M→C→M′, and a Capitalist is a person who carries this process.[36]

Like Adam Smith, Marx had a labor theory of value. In his view, all commodities have a use value that is intrinsic to the product. Use value can merely be a consequence of a given entity's intrinsic use, or labor can contribute further value to a given product. Labor's ability to create greater use value can be seen, for example, in labor's ability to convert wool into a

---

34. David Harvey, *The Enigma of Capital and the Crisis of Capitalism* (New York: Oxford University Press, 2010), p. 40.

35. Marx, *Capital*, pp. 205-8.

36. Marx, *Capital*, pp. 248-54.

coat. When labor converts wool into a coat it increases use value because a coat is more valuable than mere wool. Since Marx believed that only labor could increase such value, he thought that only the amount of labor "socially necessary" to produce a given product determines its value.[37]

> **Money that emerges as a consequence of the M→C→M' process is capital money.**

Marx's belief that labor alone determines value provoked his contention that *all* profit is due to the exploitation of labor. In order for a Capitalist to make a profit the exchange value must exceed the cost of production. Since labor is the *only* way to add value to a commodity, the Capitalists, in Marx's view, must exploit the difference between the true cost of labor and the lesser amount the Capitalist actually pays labor. Marx's *Capital* discusses many ways Capitalists exploit this difference. As will be discussed below, these methods of exploitation grow in their complexity as the need to increase profit increases. Nonetheless, in Marx's view, they all boil down to denying laborers the true value of their work. For Marx, therefore, money as capital, which it must be remembered is the process summarized in the formula M→C→M', is based on the exploitation of labor.

You do not have to share Marx's theory of value to appreciate the dynamic he exposes in *Capital*.[38] This dynamic indicates that the generation

37. Marx, *Capital*, p. 129.

38. A person can easily maintain that, given certain socio/economic circumstances, a large percentage of profit is due to the exploitation of labor without adopting Marx's theory of value. Personally, I am more inclined toward Georg Simmel's theory, which argues that value is subjective (located in personal desire) as well as objective (intrinsic to the commodity itself as Marx suggests). Sometimes subjective value is contextual. For example, right now, I would not be willing to pay very much for a pint of water. Water, however, would have more subjective value to me if my context changed and I was dying of thirst. In this new context water itself has not changed, but my subjective situation has. To be sure, my subjective situation can be "exploited" but it also cannot be denied that, regardless of the price, the one from whom I purchased the water under such dire conditions did me a service. See Simmel, *Philosophy of Money*, p. 84. This subjective understanding of value does not deny that labor is never exploited or treated inhumanely in the name of profit. It is also not to say that labor does not contribute to the intrinsic value of a product. But a commodity's value usually depends on its subjective as well as its objective value. Moreover, a commodity cannot even be a commodity if is not exchanged, and an exchange

of more and more money each year is essential to the Capitalist process (remember the process itself is capital money according to Marx). This is the case because the process, summarized as M→C→M′, cannot withstand M′ being less than or equal to M for very long. If the process M→C→M′ generates less money for even a short period of time, the carrier of the process, the Capitalist, will go out of business and the system will grind to a halt.

Much of the first volume of *Capital* concerns the means necessary to increase such profits, but to understand how Marx viewed the process, some of his terms and their meaning must be known. Marx calls *constant capital* the money that is invested in the means of production (i.e., expanded work space, new machinery, etc.). This is called constant capital because its cost does not vary. Once the machine is purchased, for example, its cost does not increase. Labor, however, is *variable capital* because the cost of labor varies. Variable capital can be exploited in some of the ways described below. Finally, the price or exchange value of a commodity is constant capital + variable capital + *surplus value* (surplus value would be called profit from the perspective of a Capitalist).[39]

Marx gives us a nineteenth-century answer to how profits annually expand which, because of his labor theory of value, always involves "exploiting" the only source of value that can be exploited, namely, labor. In its most primitive state, a Capitalist captured profits (or surplus value according to Marx) by extending the workday. The laborer was paid a subsistence wage for a day's work. If, in six hours, a laborer could increase the value of the product by the amount he or she was paid for a full twelve-hour day's work, then any work over six hours would create profit or surplus value. The Capitalist uses this surplus value for his own personal benefit or to reinvest in the enterprise. Most of the other techniques Marx discusses involve ways to increase the productivity of the worker while paying the workers less.

Cooperation increases productivity in a variety of ways. For example, it is impossible for one person to move a one-ton object, but one hundred people can do so with relative ease.[40] A Capitalist will use money to create

---

cannot happen unless someone *desires or subjectively values* the potential commodity. This is true no matter how much labor has gone into producing the product. If no one wants the product, it has no value no matter how much work goes into it. (This very book could be an example of this.)

39. Marx, *Capital,* pp. 317-20.

40. Marx, *Capital,* p. 443.

spaces in which workers can work together and increase their productivity through cooperation. When workers are simply brought together in the same place, productivity increases even if an individual worker works on the same product from start to finish. Productivity increases even more when the tasks involved in production are divided among several workers. Thus, *Division of Labor* is another way to increase the productivity of the worker that the Capitalist can "exploit" in the name of profit. Marx also notes that the purchase of machinery also increases the productivity of labor. Marx recognized that machines are not designed to lighten a laborer's toil. They are intended to increase productivity. They actually decrease the number of people necessary to produce a product, but they are also effective at increasing worker productivity and profit. Machines are an obvious substitute for muscle. As a result, the Capitalist is able to hire women and children instead of men. Profit or surplus value increases when this happens because women and children are paid less than men.[41]

With such Capitalist innovations in mind, we can understand some of the ways money, now understood as capital, led to social transformation — for, each new configuration of the workplace brought a new social configuration in its wake. Cooperation, for example, led to larger and larger workplaces, and larger and larger population centers grew up as a consequence. Division of labor reduced the number of skilled laborers or craftsmen — these might be called independent businesspeople — necessary to produce a product. Large-scale machinery may have undermined the family in the sense that it forced families to make their children work. This resulted in early deaths of child workers, and it might also have led to the breakdown of multigenerational family identity. Why, after all, should an adult child express loyalty to a parent who, in an effort to survive, was forced to make the child risk life and limb in a terrible work environment?

Such new configurations of the workplace not only transform Capitalist societies on a regular basis, but they also expand the use of money as capital. According to Marx,

> [t]he advantages of further division can be obtained only by adding to the number of workers, and this means adding not a single individual but multiples. However, an increase in the variable component of the capital employed necessitates an increase in the constant component too, i.e., both in the available extent of the conditions of production,

41. Marx, *Capital*, p. 517.

such as workshops, implements, etc., and, in particular, in raw material, the demand for which grows much more quickly than the number of workers. The quantity of it consumed in a given time, by a given amount of labor, increases in the same ratio as does the productive power of that labor through its division. *Hence, it is a law, springing from the technical character of manufacture, that the minimum amount of capital which the capitalist must possess has to go on increasing.* In other words, the transformation of the social means of production and subsistence into capital must keep extending.[42]

A difference between money and commodities that often gets overlooked is that there is a limit to the number of commodities one can own, but there is no limit to the amount of money that can be acquired. Even Imelda Marcos was limited to the number of shoes she could acquire. Money has no such limits; yet, there are clearly limits in the real world that disrupt the flow of money. These include: insufficient capital, scarce labor, inadequate means of production, inappropriate administration, outdated technologies, and the lack of money (we now call this lack of liquidity) to purchase items necessary for the production of commodities. Any disruption in the circulation or flow of money as a consequence of these barriers can have serious consequences.[43]

In recent years many things have been done to minimize these barriers, and they all have consequences to the way society is configured. The relatively new suburban social structure, for example, compels us to increase our purchases of cars, gasoline, highways, houses appliances, and a host of systems that make suburban living possible.[44] Scarcity of labor, another stumbling block to needed expansion, is minimized by increased unemployment and underemployment, moving worksites to more populated areas, and creating divisions among workers by exploiting differences between gender, race, language, tribe, and sexual orientation.[45] Geographical barriers are minimized through technological advances in travel, communication, computers, and the Internet. Barriers to the flow of capital stemming from governments are also overcome by allowing governments to receive some of the new money generated by capital's

---

42. Marx, *Capital,* p. 480. Emphasis mine.
43. Harvey, *The Enigma of Capital,* p. 47.
44. Harvey, *The Enigma of Capital,* pp. 106, 107.
45. Harvey, *The Enigma of Capital,* pp. 59-68.

quest for more and more money. Even the barrier imposed by the need to create a commodity (for the creation of a commodity to be sold takes time) is being overcome by a new understanding of money that we know as finance.

The Emergence of Finance Money

In 1971 President Nixon initiated another reconfiguration in the way we think about money when he removed the dollar from the gold standard. This gold standard had established a fixed relation between gold (a commodity) and the world's major currencies. In other words, money's value directly related to the value of a commodity, namely, gold. After Nixon's action no external commodity like gold determined monetary value. Money maintained its function as an accounting mechanism and as a means of exchange. But money's status as a store of value was diminished (not eliminated) because money could no longer be valued in terms of a value intrinsic to a commodity like gold. The era of finance money was born.

> Money created through the M→M′ process is finance money. Finance money increases the circulation and accumulation of money because it eliminates the need to produce a commodity in the Capitalist process of "making" money (M→C→M′).

As we have seen, money as capital is the process M→C→M′, where over an intermediate time frame M′ must be greater than M for the system to remain in operation. Money as finance eliminates the need for C in the capitalist process M→C→M′. Thus finance is best described as the process M→M′. The most obvious instance of finance is the interest one receives from a bank. In this case, a person deposits money (M) in a bank and, in the course of time, receives interest (M′) from the bank. Money as finance also operates when a bank loans money (M) to an individual and receives interest (M′) on the loan.

Finance is now essential to our Economy. It is difficult to see how the Global Economy could function without money loaned for interest. What, after all, would the purpose of such loans be if the one lending the money could not make more money from the loan? Those of us who worship the modern Economy cannot understand such behavior. It doesn't make sense. But other religions — at least before they accommodated themselves to the dominant religion called Economics — condemned the financial process where money begets money without the mediation of a commodity (C). These religions simply thought that loans should be made for reasons other than the return of interest plus principal (to simply help someone in need, for example). These religions have always opposed what they call usury, and we call finance.[46]

When money begets money without the sale or purchase of a commodity, money loses its referent, and, in a certain sense, money becomes disconnected from the physical, human world. In other words, the financial process M→M' no longer needs to touch the human world, and as Franco Berardi warns, "The destruction of the real world starts from the emancipation of valorization from the production of useful things. . . ."[47]

We have only just begun the social transformation finance promotes, but we can glimpse it through the dominance of shareholder value briefly discussed in the last chapter. To the extent that stock in a company is not a commodity but the company's currency, buying stock in a company is a classic M→M' financial process. No physical assets are exchanged, and

46. Mir Ahmed Ali, *Prohibition of Usury: Islamic and Jewish Practices* (Denver: Outskirts Press, 2009), pp. 1-24. It is largely thought that Judaism prohibits usury at least among Jews. "If you lend money to any of my people, to the poor with you, you shall not be to him as a creditor; neither shall you lay upon him interest" (Exod. 22:25). Christians, in their inclusion of Gentiles into their ranks, may have extended the prohibitions against usury to all people. Emperor Charlemagne (732-814) used this interpretation when he declared usury a criminal offense. Pope Clement V also banned usury in 1311. Islam continues to condemn usury to the present moment following Qur'an citations like "Allah condemns usury, and blesses charities. O you who believe, you shall observe Allah and refrain from all kinds of usury, if you are believers" (Qur'an 2:276). At the same time, there is no condemnation for commerce because commerce is not the same as usury. "They claim that usury is the same as commerce. However, Allah permits commerce, and prohibits usury" (Qur'an 2:275). If one places this distinction between usury and commerce in the context of this discussion, one might say that the Qur'an permits commerce because in commerce money passes through a commodity M→C→M' whereas usury or finance dispenses with the need for a commodity. Since commodities arise from either nature or human creativity, finance, in bypassing commodities, is opposed because it abandons both God's creation and human creations. This could actually be what these religious prohibitions against usury (which is finance money) intuitively oppose.

47. Franco "Bifo" Berardi, *The Uprising: On Poetry and Finance* (Los Angeles: Semiotext[e], 2012), p. 105.

the hope of a shareholder is that the initial stock price (M) will increase to stock price (M′) without the bother of owning a physical commodity. As we have seen, it is now almost universally accepted that the sole purpose of the corporation is to increase shareholder value, which simply means increase the value of its stock. Anything that does not increase shareholder value is jettisoned from the corporation. The stock price alone determines and evaluates the value of the corporation. Any other corporate constituency — employees, retirees, or the community in which the corporation functions — is subjected to the "bottom-line." If a corporate constituency does not contribute to the bottom-line, it is jettisoned in the name of the corporate values of efficiency, calculability, predictability, and control — corporate values that are often deemed synonymous with reason itself.

Efficiency is simply a matter of numbers, and today money is the number that determines efficiency. If one activity, person, acquisition, or community leads to greater numbers (profit), then that practice will be adopted over other competing practices. If a company's stock price is on the rise, that company is deemed efficient and "good." If a company's stock price declines, the company is very often required to make certain *adjustments* so its profits and its stock price will increase. Under the guise of shareholder value, employees, pensioners, and communities are discarded if they do not enhance profits. Make no mistake, these are institutional and social transformations that are forced by this new configuration of money called finance money — money that seeks money without the intermediary of a commodity.

Once the entire corporation becomes a site for transferring, exchanging, and selling in order to quickly increase the value of its stock, excess cash (formally used to reinvest or save for a rainy day), "overfunded" pension funds, and employees' jobs become assets ripe for liquidation. Any attempt to interpret a corporation as a long-term social institution with responsibilities to stakeholders other than shareholders is anathema.[48] The corporate climate has changed with the advent of shareholder value. Where once loyalty was honored, flexibility is now valued. When people must plan on being liquidated in the name of shareholder value, an entirely different culture with entirely different values emerges.

We must pause to stress what is being eliminated by finance money. It is the employees who are "downsized" in the name of shareholder value. It

---

48. Karen Ho, *Liquidated: An Ethnography of Wall Street* (Durham, NC: Duke University Press, 2009), pp. 150, 151.

is the communities that are abandoned by corporations who hire cheaper labor in another locale. It is the pensioners who thought they were going to have a secure retirement for a lifetime of service to their company. These, along with the goods and services the company actually produces, are the tangible items — what we can see, experience, and touch — that were once the purpose of the corporate enterprise. Today these tangible items are jettisoned in the name of the bottom-line or shareholder value, and in the world of finance, shareholder value is not material or tangible. Instead, such values are numbers on a computer screen. They can vanish into thin air when a financial crisis ensues.

Finance money may bring another, more subtle change. In his best-selling book *Flash Boys,* Michael Lewis exposes a fascinating Wall Street practice called high-frequency trading (HFT). When a brokerage or bank wants to sell a large number of stocks, say 1 million shares of company XYZ, such an amount might be too great to be sold in one market. The seller will have to shop around to find multiple markets (there are about 17) before all 1 million shares can be sold at the best price possible. So the seller will enter the order in one market among the many. In each of these markets HFTs have entered computer programs to buy a small number (100 shares) of almost every conceivable stock at the low ask price. Buying a few shares at such low prices gives the HFT important information, namely, the name of the buyer.

When the HFT program determines that a large brokerage firm such as Goldman Sachs or J. P. Morgan is a buyer, it concludes that the firm is selling far greater quantities of stock than the mere 100 shares that HFTs have programmed their computers to buy. So, the HFT computer programs quickly send orders to other markets to buy the available shares of XYZ company before the large bank or brokerage can. In other words, the HFT computer programs can "outrun" the large firms to the next market, buy the stock they wish to purchase, and turn around and sell these same stocks at a slightly higher price to the brokerage or bank. The amount of money made in each transaction is not high, perhaps less than a penny a share, but these transactions add up. One $9 billion hedge fund, for example, thought that this practice of being outrun by the HFTs cost the fund around $300 million each year.[49] It is as a consequence of this scenario that Lewis asserts that The Market is rigged.

49. Michael Lewis, *Flash Boys: A Wall Street Revolt* (New York: W. W. Norton, 2014), p. 77.

But rigging The Market, if indeed this practice can be described as such, may well be the least sinister aspect of Lewis's "discovery." Of even more importance for the social transformation implicit in finance money is that all of the actions and decisions described above happen in milliseconds (a millisecond is one thousandth of a second). In Lewis's book, the firm that was getting outrun by the high-frequency traders was able to get its order to the closest market in 2 milliseconds. There its order would be filled at the stated ask price.

But here is where the fun begins. This first market usually could not fulfill the entire order at the ask price, so the rest of the order went to other markets. The time to get the orders to market was from 4 to 7 milliseconds depending on the location of these markets. It was in that period of time, 4 to 7 milliseconds, that the HFT program outran the brokerage. The HFT millisecond advantage over the brokerages and banks enabled them to buy XYZ stock and always sell it to the bank or brokerage at a slightly higher price than it had bought it for only 1 or 2 milliseconds before.[50] It is crucial to realize that all this happens in under 10 milliseconds. It takes 100 milliseconds to blink your eyes. Human beings are biologically incapable of perceiving something so quickly, and we are even less capable of making a decision in this time. *Thus, any decision made in 10 milliseconds cannot possibly be made by a human being.* Human beings are, therefore, excluded from this financial process!

While it is true that human beings have in fact created the program that makes these decisions, this is only a comfort if the one who creates something always has control over the creation. This is not always the case. A person who creates a fire, for example, may lose control over the fire and have no say whatsoever in how the fire spreads. This does not always happen, but it happens often enough to demonstrate that sometimes the creator of the fire not only loses control over the fire, but the fire actually consumes its creator. Insofar as the aforementioned trading programs are concerned, human beings simply cannot be in control because we are biologically incapable of making a decision in 10 milliseconds. Such speed is incompatible with human presence.

It cannot be stressed enough that the decisions made in this M→M′ process of modern finance cannot possibly be made by human persons. The time in which humans live requires much longer duration if we are even to be conscious of it, and human decisions require more time even

50. Lewis, *Flash Boys*, p. 49.

after we are conscious of what must be decided. The financial decisions made by HFTs happen outside human time. Any such decisions can only be made by machines programmed to carry out the corporate values of efficiency, predictability, and control.

> In fact, the shared time of financial information no longer exists; it has been replaced by the speed of computerized tools in a time that cannot be shared by everyone and does not allow real competition between operators. We are witnessing the end of the shared human time that would allow competition between operators having to reveal their perspective and anticipation (competition that is vital for capitalism to function) in favor of a nano-chronological time that *ipso facto* eliminates those stock exchanges that do not possess the same computer technology: automatic speculation in the futurism of the instant. . . . Regulation becomes impossible because of this escape into the acceleration of reality.[51]

The flash crash of May 6, 2010, illustrates our inability to regulate such programmed trading. In order to regulate something, we must first know what happened, and we can never know what happened during the flash crash when the market fell 600 points in a few minutes. Explanations for the event are impossible largely because we lack the information needed to understand the event. We lack this information because the unit of trading time is now by the microsecond (unlike the millisecond which is one thousandth of a second, a microsecond is one millionth of a second) and our records are kept by the second. Millions of trades can happen in a second, but we will only receive a summary of what happened. What goes on in the pursuit of finance money is not and cannot be known, and what is not known cannot be regulated or controlled.[52]

Every change in the way we understand the sacrament we call money is accompanied by a change in our social configurations. Today we are in the midst of another change. Removing the dollar from the gold standard released money from its moorings in commodities. When we were on the gold standard, money was thought of as a means of exchange, an accounting mechanism, and a store of value because it could be re-

---

51. Paul Virilio, *The Administration of Fear,* with Bertrand Richard, trans. Ames Hodges (Los Angeles: Semiotext[e], 2012), p. 34.

52. Lewis, *Flash Boys,* pp. 80, 81.

deemed for gold. Nixon's move means our money supply is no longer limited by our supply of gold. Removing this limitation makes more money available and the quest for money more acute. We have seen some of the adjustments to this new situation, but it is difficult to see where this will eventually lead. While it is difficult to see our final goal, we can see where the mission of the Global Economy has taken us so far, and it is to this — the Economy's global mission — that we now turn.

CHAPTER 6

The Economy's Global Mission

Globalization is not about what we all, or at least the most resourceful and enterprising among us, wish or hope to do. It is about what is happening to us all.

Zygmunt Bauman, *Globalization: The Human Consequences*[1]

The Economy's global mission is not a consequence of a conspiracy between business and government leadership. The Economy's mission is not a product of human reason. The Economy's mission is merely the consequence of The Economy's need to grow measured in terms of The Economy's sacrament, money. The need for more and more money is the engine of The Economy's growth. Sometimes we understand this need as a product of the natural order. Sometimes we understand it as divine providence. Sometimes we think it synonymous with reason itself.

To avoid disaster, The Economy must grow each year. Within a nation, growth is measured by the nation's GDP, and the world's economic growth is measured by the combined GDP of all its nations. It is commonly asserted that the world's Economy must average at least a 3 percent growth rate each year. This need for growth fuels The Economy's religious mission that we now call globalization. A few reasonably accurate numbers demonstrate the magnitude of growth necessary for a well-functioning Economy.

1. Zygmunt Bauman, *Globalization: The Human Consequences* (New York: Columbia University Press, 1998), p. 60.

Suppose the world's Economy produced $1 trillion in goods and services in the year 1866. If the world's Economy were to grow at a rate of 3 percent in 1867, the world's Economy would need to produce an additional $30 billion. Such an increase can be achieved if efficiency is increased or new trade routes extended or more railroad track laid or more telegraph lines created. But this is just one year. A 3 percent growth rate must be maintained *every* year for the world's Economy to be robust. Over time, therefore, this rate of growth becomes much more difficult to achieve without major innovation, and, depending on your individual perspective, these innovations might be creative or destructive.

> **The Economy's mission is a consequence of the need to create more and more money whenever and wherever possible.**

"The rule of 72" illustrates the magnitude of an annual 3 percent growth rate over time. This rule states that dividing the interest rate (or in this case the growth rate) into 72 reveals how long it takes money to double. For example, if your interest rate is 6 percent, it takes twelve years for your money to double because *72/6=12*. By the same token the world economy will double every twenty-four years if it averages a 3 percent growth rate because *72/3=24*. This means that an annual 3 percent growth rate makes our hypothetical 1866 $1-trillion economy a $2-trillion Economy by the year 1890, a $4-trillion economy by 1914, an $8-trillion economy by 1938, a $16-trillion economy by 1962. To make a long story short, by 2010 the world's Economy would have to produce $64 trillion and by 2036 we need a $128-trillion economy if a 3 percent growth rate is maintained.[2] This tremendous need for profit fuels the Economy's global mission. To create the huge amount of money needed, more and more places on the planet (and off the planet) must be monetized.

Strange as it may seem, Capitalists generally believe that such staggering growth rates are in fact possible. When the allied powers met at Bretton Woods in 1944 to establish the institutions and rules for the postwar economy, Henry Morgenthau, the Secretary of the Treasury and

---

2. These figures are only slightly off. Public records indicate that the world's economy was $63.26 trillion in 2010 (www.google.com/publicdata).

President of the conference, asked the participants to embrace "the *elementary* economic axiom . . . that prosperity has no fixed limits. It is not a finite substance to be diminished by division."[3] The gathering assumed that economic growth and more world trade would benefit everyone and that economic growth would not be constrained by the limits the planet imposed.

Others believe that there are limits to Economic growth and that we are nearing these limits. I tend to agree with this assessment. Nonetheless, I also must admit that this feeling may not be scientific. I have to admit that in 1860 it was impossible to predict the sort of Economic growth that would occur in the next century and a half. No one predicted electricity becoming as ubiquitous as it is. Air travel and space travel were imagined by very few. Automobiles, roads, television, radio, the discovery of microbes, recombinant DNA technologies, air conditioning, central heating, and a host of other inventions we now consider essential to life were not even imagined. The next 150 years could easily contain innovations of even greater magnitude. For example, what would happen if we could mimic photosynthesis or harness the energy of the sun in efficient ways? The implications to food production, energy, and even the colonization of the solar system are quite staggering and could lead to Economic expansion of exponential proportions!

As I said, I have misgivings about the unfettered Economic expansion that must take place for what we call a robust Economy, but this is not an attempt to discuss whether or not Economic expansion has its limits or if it is good or evil. This is an effort to discuss the mission of The Economy. Just as the Christian Church has a global mission, so does The Economy. The Economy's mission is to expand and grow. The issue is, "What will provide the growth necessary for a robust Economy?" Frankly, it is very difficult to answer this question because future growth requires innovation, and innovation cannot be predicted. What can be done, however, is to note some of the ways The Economy has already grown. The purpose in doing so is to highlight The Economy's mission, and to discuss some of the principles and consequences of that mission.

3. David Korten, "Failures of Bretton Woods," in *The Case Against the Global Economy and For a Turn to the Local* (hereafter abbreviated *CAGE*), ed. Jerry Mander and Edward Goldsmith (San Francisco: Sierra Club, 1996), p. 21. My emphasis.

Globalization and the Decline of National Sovereignty

Globalization is the word proponents of Economic growth use to describe The Economy's mission. "Globalization is not about what we hope to do. It is about what is being done to us."[4] It is a consequence of the increasing need for more capital to fuel The Economy's growth. In the past, national borders limited such growth, but globalization does not abide by national borders. Globalization dismantles national boundaries in its quest for more and more money.

A nation is sovereign insofar as it claims the authority and possesses the resources to enforce its power within specific geographical boundaries. To a large extent, The Economy's need to grow at any price undermines the national sovereignty of even the strongest nations. This is because nations are often understood to be an impediment to Economic growth, and Economic growth is the supreme value of all adherents of the religion we call Economics. "Due to the unqualified and unstoppable spread of free trade rules, and above all the free movement of capital finances, [The Economy] is progressively exempt from political control; indeed, the prime meaning conveyed by the term 'Economy' is the area of the non-political. Whatever has been left of politics is expected to be dealt with, as in the good old days, by the state — but whatever is concerned with the economic life the state is not allowed to touch: any attempt in this direction would be met with prompt and furious punitive action from the world markets."[5] The Economy, not the state, is sovereign.

We are still far from this ultimate destination, but the process goes on. It often appears unstoppable. The Economy's quest for dominance is inherent in words and phrases like "deregulation," "facilitating transactions," "flexibility," "increasing fluidity," and "easing the tax burden." The more consistently a nation employs tactics such as these, the more it cedes its sovereignty to The Economy and The Economy's corporations which, as we have suggested, are the communities in which The Economy's faithful gather. In this new era, corporations are to nations as the Church was to the governments of medieval Europe. Like the medieval papacy, the corporations now have veto power over certain state policies.

Two international trade agreements are indicative of this trend: the

---

4. Bauman, *Globalization*, p. 60.

5. Bauman, *Globalization*, p. 66. Separation of Church and State has remarkable similarities to the quest to separate The Economy from the State.

General Agreement on Tariffs and Trade (GATT) and the North American Free Trade Agreement (NAFTA). In 1994, just before Congress was to vote on policies established by the Uruguay Round of GATT — which established among other things the World Trade Organization's (WTO) power to enforce GATT — Ralph Nader and Lori Wallach offered a $10,000 donation to a charity of choice to any Senator or Congressperson who would sign an affidavit stating they had *actually read* the agreement and successfully answer ten simple questions about the agreement's contents.

Only Republican Hank Brown of Colorado did this! Before the Senate Foreign Relations Committee he signed the affidavit and correctly answered all the questions. He then held a news conference where he said that he had planned to vote in favor of GATT, but after reading it, he was "aghast!" He could not support GATT because it eliminated even the most basic due process guarantees of the U.S. Constitution and U.S. laws.[6] In the language of religion, what Senator Brown saw for the first time was the all-encompassing global mission of the God we call The Economy. Its power exceeds that of nations.

Trade agreements like GATT and NAFTA undermine national sovereignty and democratic processes because they make it possible for a foreign government (often acting on behalf of a corporation) to overturn state, local, and even national laws and policies in the name of competition and free trade. GATT requires each member nation to "ensure that conformity of its laws and regulations and administrative procedures with its obligations as provided in the annexed [GATT] agreement." In other words, a nation is in violation of GATT if a particular jurisdiction adopts laws that are in conflict with GATT. If, for example, California places limits on the amount of pollution from automobiles, it may be in violation of GATT, and a foreign company has the right to sue under GATT. Even if they are not actually in violation, an international agency like the World Trade Organization (WTO), not the Federal government, will ultimately settle a dispute between the local jurisdiction and the foreign accuser. Regardless of what one thinks about any particular law GATT might challenge, GATT requires governments to cede their sovereignty to an international organization in economic matters.[7]

---

6. Ralph Nader and Lori Wallach, "GATT, NAFTA, and the Subversion of the Democratic Process," in *CAGE*, pp. 92, 93.

7. Nader and Wallach, "GATT, NAFTA, and the Subversion of the Democratic Process," p. 104.

Moreover, the values used to determine violations are not neutral. These values assume that competition is always better than cooperation; that progress is synonymous with change, and that the transportation of goods, people, money, and materials is more important than national sovereignty or local customs. These values receive unquestioned support largely because they are the religious values of The Economy. They reflect a global configuration created by The Economy, which is a God that is in the process of placing all nations under Its feet. It is, by the way, a very powerful and unprecedented God that can get *all* the nations of the world to succumb to its values.

Treaties like NAFTA and GATT guarantee that foreign investors, who have no interest in the quality of life within the localities where they invest, will have the same rights as domestic investors. This undermines regional self-sufficiency. This state of affairs is reinforced by a variety of global institutions. The International Monetary Fund (IMF) is one of the most important and powerful. The IMF was created by the United Nations' Monetary and Financial Conference at Bretton Woods in 1944. Its mandate was to finance the rebuilding of postwar Europe and to save the world from future economic depressions. It would accomplish this task by putting pressure on countries that were not doing their fair share to provide loans that stimulate global demand. Originally conceived, therefore, the IMF was based on the recognition that markets often do not work efficiently, and, as a consequence, they need money or "stimulus" to help them recover optimum levels. Over the years the IMF's governing philosophy has changed markedly.

"Founded on the belief that there is a need for international pressure on countries to have more expansionary economic policies — such as increasing expenditures, reducing taxes, or lowering interest rates to stimulate [national economies] — today the IMF typically provides funds only if countries engage in policies like cutting deficits, raising taxes, or raising interest rates that lead to a contraction of the economy."[8] Current IMF policies are now much more concerned with a given nation "repaying its debt" to the banks that have financed them than it is with "development." The stability of the world's banks is now the IMF's agenda. Job creation is not. Taxation and its adverse effects are on its agenda. Land reform is not. Money is available to bail out banks. It is not available for

8. Joseph Stiglitz, *Globalization and Its Discontents* (New York: W. W. Norton, 2003), pp. 12, 13.

education, healthcare, or workers who lose their jobs as a result of IMF demands for repayment of debts.[9]

In short, the IMF now supports the agenda of large corporations and financial institutions whose quest is to increase profits by 3 percent each year. This demands that they search the entire globe for new areas to monetize. We have noted that over time this need for capital increases geometrically, and the communities that serve The Economy, particularly the large corporations, must find more and more persons, places, ideas, and things to monetize. Globalization is the word we use to describe this worldwide mission. This word, however, hides the ever-present need for more and more profit to drive this mission.

The Mission into the Unseen World of Microorganisms

Nothing is too small to be excluded from The Economy's global mission. Even the smallest biological units are subject to monetization. In 1980, there was a little-noted Supreme Court case called *Diamond v. Chakrabarty*. This case began in 1972 when Ananda Chakrabarty, an employee of General Electric (GE), developed bacteria that could digest oil. GE applied for a patent, and their patent was rejected by the U.S. Patent Office under a policy that said life-forms are not patentable. GE appealed this decision to the Supreme Court, which ruled that *this particular life-form* could be patented. This opened the floodgates. In five years the U.S. Patent Office reversed its policy, making it possible to patent genetically engineered plants, seeds, and plant tissue. The entire plant kingdom could now be subject to patents.

Then, on April 7, 1987, the U.S. Patent Office ruled that all multicellular living organisms should be included in this policy. This ruling transformed the Supreme Court decision in *Diamond v. Chakrabarty* — a ruling on the patenting of *one* microbe — into the ability on the part of the biotech industry to patent — *and monetize* — all life-forms on the planet!! On October 29, 1991, the U.S. Patent Office extended corporate reach (and markets) even further. Our legal ability to patent now extends to naturally occurring parts of the human body — specifically stem cells.[10]

9. Stiglitz, *Globalization and Its Discontents*, pp. 80, 81.

10. Andrew Kimbrell, "BIOCOLONIZATION: The Patenting of Life and the Global Market in Body Parts," *CAGE*, pp. 134, 135. Recently (2013) the Supreme Court has ruled that human DNA cannot be patented.

Patenting microbes and stem cells is an example of The Economy's global mission. Just as globalization describes the Economic mission to open more places on the globe to the possibility of corporate expansion and growth, these patents allow profits to be derived from microscopic entities. The Economy's need to grow fuels this process. We must open more and more markets. This quest is both global and microscopic in scope.

The story of the Neem tree further demonstrates the global reach of our microscopic concerns as well as the possibility of resistance. For thousands of years the people of India have used the Neem tree and its seeds for medicine, as an antiseptic toothbrush, for contraception, construction material, for fuel, and to cure ailing soils. After the shift in U.S. patent regulation began to include patents on plants, a dozen U.S. patents were taken out on components of this tree. This global effort to monetize anything capable of monetization made Neem trees and their seeds increasingly expensive. In fact, Neem seeds became unaffordable to the people who, for generations, had had free access to these seeds. All they could do was "steal" what had once been freely given by nature, and, in some instances, they were prosecuted for theft. Fortunately for the local population, and unfortunately for corporations who held patents on the Neem tree, India was able to stop the monopolistic acquisition of the Neem seed. India did this when it rejected a bill that would have put India in compliance with WTO rules regarding patent rights.[11]

Corporate efforts to patent what was readily available to the world were not limited to foreign lands. The Monsanto Company might be considered an American example of efforts to extend The Economy's mission. In the 1960s Monsanto was primarily a chemical company. During the Vietnam War, it made "the defoliant" called Agent Orange, and after the war, Monsanto developed a popular weed killer called Roundup. The trouble with Roundup was that it was too effective. It killed almost everything it touched, including the crops it was supposed to protect. While this did not prevent or inhibit its use on lawns where weeds could be accurately targeted, farming demanded more indiscriminate spraying that would kill the crop along with the weeds. The people at Monsanto began to think outside the box. Instead of redesigning their weed killer so it would be less lethal to desired plants, Monsanto redesigned the plants! They genetically altered the soybean so that it could resist Roundup. Because of

---

11. V. Andina Shiva and Radha Holla-Bhar, "Piracy by Patent: The Case of the Neem Tree," *CAGE*, pp. 146-59.

the genius of Monsanto scientists, all plants in a Roundup-defended field would die except the genetically altered soybeans. They thrived. Later, Monsanto was able to genetically alter corn against Roundup as well.

As we have seen, the Supreme Court ruling in *Diamond v. Chakrabarty* and subsequent policy decisions by the U.S. Patent Office made it possible to patent genetic alterations of plants. Monsanto took advantage of these new regulations and patented its genetically altered soybeans and corn. Monsanto now "owns" and controls the DNA to its genetically altered products. This changed farming. For centuries farmers held on to some seeds from the previous year's crop and used them to plant the next season's crop. Monsanto's control of the patent, however, made this age-old practice illegal. Because of its legal patent, Monsanto owned all seeds that contained its genetically altered DNA. Anyone who planted these genetically altered seeds without authorization was in violation of U.S. patent law. In other words, they were stealing Monsanto's intellectual property.

According to the documentary motion picture *Food Inc.* (a Robert Kenner film), Monsanto has aggressively fought to protect its patent rights. They have hired investigators who investigate anyone rumored to be using Monsanto's seeds without authorization (i.e., without paying for them). If they even suspect that this activity is taking place, Monsanto will sue the person or business they deem responsible for unauthorized use of their product. This is another illustration of the advantages corporate persons have over human persons in court. Corporate persons generally have unlimited time and resources. Most human persons do not. A human person can pay hundreds of thousands of dollars defending him- or herself even before the case comes to trial. Confronted with such an expense, most human persons pay the penalty rather than take on the expense of a prolonged and expensive trial. Farmers that fight a corporation like Monsanto risk everything they have. Monsanto risks little, if anything. Indeed, it ultimately profits from such cases.

Monsanto uses all the advantages corporate persons have over human persons to sue farmers who have never even used Monsanto's seeds. These legal proceedings arise from the fact that seeds from a farm that uses Monsanto seeds cross-pollinate with seeds from farms that do not. When this happens, the next generation of seeds produced by the non-Monsanto farm will have DNA designed, in part, by Monsanto, and those in possession of such seeds are in violation of patent law (at least as Monsanto understands it). Monsanto sues if it can document that this has happened, and, once again, a farmer has the choice of complying or risking financial ruin. The smart ones comply.[12]

Once again we must note how asymmetrical the power relationships are between corporate persons and life-forms like plants, animals, and even human persons. When the U.S. Patent Office did not allow GE to patent its oil-digesting microbe, GE had the time, resources, and legal counsel to overturn the Patent Office decision. *But no one will go to court on behalf of a plant!* This is because no one will profit monetarily from such a challenge. This demonstrates the imbalance of power between corporate persons and all life-forms. While it is arguable that patenting living entities is an affront to the logic of life, this challenge will never be argued in court because it is too expensive (from a monetary point of view) to do so. Corporate persons can challenge policies that are adverse to their profits. But policies that enhance corporate profit yet could hurt life usually go unchallenged because human persons do not have the time or the resources to mount such a challenge. Moreover, they will not benefit monetarily from such a challenge.

Human persons still have one advantage over corporations. Corporations are human creations. As the story of the Neem tree indicates, human persons are still capable of undermining corporate power through direct political action, but, more often than not, we do not do this. We usually comply because direct opposition is too time-consuming and too expensive. Corporations bestow riches on those who serve them, and vengeance and wrath on the few who oppose them. We adapt to the corporation even though such adaptation may not be in the interest of human life. We do so because we believe there is no alternative to corporations and the God they serve, and we believe this largely because we are uncritical believers in the power of this God, The Economy.

---

12. In October 2012, the Supreme Court agreed to hear a case between a farmer named Vernon H. Bowman and Monsanto. Bowman used the patented seeds but also bought cheaper soybeans from a grain elevator and used those to plant a second crop. These cheaper soybeans also proved resistant to Roundup, and Bowman continued to plant the non-Monsanto seeds for eight years. This is why Monsanto is suing Bowman. This is mentioned because "[t]he Obama administration urged the court not to take the case and warned that the outcome could affect patents involving DNA molecules, nanotechnologies and other self-replicating technologies," thus demonstrating once again the government's protection of corporate rights over the human person. Associated Press, "Monsanto seed case going to court," *Washington Post,* October 6, 2012. In May 2013, the Supreme Court ruled in favor of Monsanto in this case.

The Industrial Food Chain

In the first part of his book *The Omnivore's Dilemma*, Michael Pollan traces what is involved in the creation of three typical meals served at McDonald's. In the process, he discloses how fast food extends the mission and scope of The Economy.

In the first three centuries of American farming, the individual farmer was responsible for the quality of his product because it could easily be traced back to him. This system changed with the emergence of railroads and grain elevators. With respect to corn in particular, grain elevators mixed the corn from one farmer with the corn from another, making it impossible to determine its source. At first this disturbed The Market. But, in 1865, the Chicago Board of Trade (CBT) provided a remedy. It introduced a grading system. Corn #2, for example, was an all-purpose corn. The corn so designated from Farm A was considered just as good as the corn so designated from Farm B. Beyond having his corn receive the corn #2 designation, the farmer was no longer responsible for the corn's quality and focused on producing the most #2 corn possible.[13] Quantity not quality became the farmer's concern. This emphasis on quantity set farming on the path to industrialization. The farmer could now count his produce. Once a farmer can make such calculations, he or she can determine the efficiency of the farm and, in the process, employ the corporate values of efficiency, calculability, and prediction.

Nature was still a major limitation to these corporate values, at least on a farm. For example, nitrogen is essential to plant growth, and the soil supplies these nitrates. Crops like corn deplete the soil of its nitrates. This meant that the nitrates in a given field had to be restored by plants capable of replenishing the soil's nitrates. Farmers had to rotate crops or leave some fields fallow from time to time. This natural fact undermined the efficient production of corn.[14] After World War II, however, this natural limit was breached.

---

13. Michael Pollan, *The Omnivore's Dilemma: A Natural History of Four Meals* (New York: Penguin Books, 2006, 2007), p. 60.

14. Along with imposing natural restrictions on the amount of corn that can be grown on a given farm, this restriction made a farmer diversify. American farms once included a whole range of crops, pastures, various domestic animals, and even trees because nature demanded this. Modern farming's emphasis on efficiency and calculability is different from nature's logic of life. See Wendell Berry, "Renewing Husbandry" and "Agriculture from the Roots Up," in *The Way of Ignorance* (Emeryville, CA: Shoemaker & Hoard, 2005), pp. 91-112.

At the war's end, the United States government had a problem. It did not know what to do with the munitions industry that had developed during the war. The war had left the nation with a tremendous surplus of ammonium nitrate — essential to the production of munitions. The future of the industry and its workers depended on finding a peacetime use for their expertise.

To assist in the transition from war to peace, the Department of Agriculture suggested that these nitrates be sprayed on farmland as fertilizer, and the chemical fertilizer industry was born. This launched a new agricultural paradigm. Since the chemical fertilizer industry was petroleum based, agriculture itself moved from a natural, sun-based system to a fossil fuel–based system. The farmer no longer needed to allow nature to replenish the soil's nitrates. Synthetic nitrogen fertilizers could be used instead. Farmers could "improve" nature's efficiency by devoting every inch of land to corn and soybeans without the age-old concern for replenishing the soil's nitrates.[15]

There were still two natural limitations to the efficient production of food. On the supply side, unfavorable growing conditions like drought thwart our attempts to supply food to meet demands. On the demand side is our limited ability to eat all the food produced. Traditionally human beings have adjusted the first limitation by establishing food reserves in abundant years to preserve us through the lean years.[16]

During the Great Depression of the 1930s, the New Deal promoted the creation of such food reserves, and, at the same time, protected the livelihood of small farmers. It set a target price based on cost of a particular crop's production. When the market dropped below this target price, the government granted loans to farmers who used their unsold crop, valued at the target price, as collateral. Farmers had two options. They could store their crop until prices rose to profitable levels, or if prices remained low, they could repay the loan by giving the government the crop, which the government would hold in reserve.[17] This program had at least two

15. Pollan, *The Omnivore's Dilemma*, pp. 43-45.

16. Stories of government intervention of this sort go back to the biblical story of Joseph creating seven years of food reserves in Egypt.

17. This New Deal program is an instance of government intervention to mitigate inefficiencies in the food market. This is based on the Keynesian belief that markets are not always efficient. Indeed, the market for food is one example of systemic inefficiencies that have been addressed by governments in some way ever since the agricultural revolution.

important purposes. It created a food reserve, and it kept the *individual farmer* in business by minimizing losses and debt. This clever policy was abandoned in the early 1970s.

This was a time of inflation, and rising food prices contributed mightily.[18] President Nixon appointed Earl Butz Secretary of Agriculture with the express mandate to bring food prices down. Butz recognized the inflationary tendencies of the New Deal policy. Encouraging farmers to keep their produce off of the market when prices were low, as the New Deal policy did, decreased food supply and increased prices. Butz dismantled this inflationary New Deal program, and, in its place, he instituted the policy of immediate and direct payments to compensate farmers for their shortfalls. This policy removed farmers' incentive to keep their crops from market, and encouraged them to sell as soon as possible. This increased the supply of food and decreased its price. The new policy lowered the cost of food, but had less beneficial ramifications for farmers.

Assured of a minimum price, and denied the incentive to keep their produce off of the market until prices rose, the farmer not only immediately sold his subsidized crop of corn, but planted as much corn as possible.[19] Eventually this proved detrimental to the small farmer. These detriments might not have been so severe if the government had continued to guarantee prices at a high rate, but unfortunately for the farmer, over time, the government lowered and lowered these guarantees to a point where farmers' costs were too often greater than the income they received, even with government subsidies. A business cannot survive very long if its costs exceed its revenues. Small businesses like farms are particularly vulnerable.

There is one more ironic twist. Government policy still makes it in the interest of the farmer to plant as much corn as possible even as the farmer gradually loses the farm. Under the current system, the farmer has a limited number of nonprofitable choices. The farmer can refuse to plant, which guarantees that there will be no income. The farmer can grow a crop and not sell it in hope that prices will rise, but this may never happen and the crop might not be sold at all. Finally, the farmer can sell at market price and receive two checks, one from the buyer and one from the government — checks that often do not meet the farmer's expenses.[20]

---

18. The inflation of this era was probably triggered by the Vietnam War and by Nixon removing the dollar from the gold standard.

19. Pollan, *The Omnivore's Dilemma*, pp. 52, 53.

20. The farmer can also hedge against future price reductions by purchasing an op-

Unlike the New Deal policy, this policy does not benefit small farmers. The "small farmers" — probably the only farmers in the nineteenth and early twentieth centuries — are being driven out of business because the current setup often forces the farmer to sell his product at a loss and go into debt. Eventually this debt becomes so great that farmers are forced to sell the only thing of value that they own, namely, their land. Their land is usually sold at depressed prices to large corporate farms, making large corporate farms and financial institutions the ultimate beneficiaries of government policies.

The land, however, remains "in business." Corporate owners buy large tracts of land and use fewer and fewer farmers to farm the land. They now produce so much subsidized corn that 3800 calories of corn per day are produced for every man, woman, and child in America.[21] A good daily diet for an American male probably consists of 2500 calories. We usually eat more, but even overeating does not take care of the surplus calories provided by subsidized corn.

> (A) way to look at this 10 billion bushel pile of commodity corn — a naturalist way of looking at it — is that industrial agriculture has introduced a vast new stock of biomass into the environment, creating what amounts to an imbalance — a kind of vacuum in reverse. Ecology teaches that whenever an excess of organic matter arises anywhere in nature, creatures large and small inevitably step forward to consume it, sometimes creating whole new food chains in the process. In this case the creatures feasting on the surplus biomass are both metaphorical and real: There are the agribusiness corporations, foreign markets, and whole new industries (such as ethanol), and then there are the food scientists, livestock and human eaters, as well as the usual array of microorganisms (such as *E. Coli 0152: H7*).[22]

This is the second natural limitation placed on the production of food. Someone or something must consume this mountain of surplus corn, and a brief look into who or what consumes it further reveals the extent of The Economy's mission. This mission extends from microorganisms to an-

---

tion from a buyer to sell a future crop at a predetermined price. These are called "futures" and are only a modification of a farmer's choice to sell his crop.

21. Pollan, *The Omnivore's Dilemma*, p. 103.
22. Pollan, *The Omnivore's Dilemma*, p. 62.

imals to human beings to corporations themselves. It is powered by corporate values of efficiency, calculability, predictability, and control, and it is accomplished with government sanction, protection, and subsidies. It also may be one of the best illustrations of the difference between the self-interest of corporate persons and the self-interest of human persons.

The feedlots where our cattle are fattened for slaughter are the largest consumer of this vast mountain of corn. Ruminants, like cows, sheep, and bison, evolved the ability to convert grass into high-quality protein. To do so, they employ a "second stomach" where bacteria eat the grass and convert it into energy for the ruminant. On a grass diet, a cow or steer might take four to five years before it is large enough for slaughter; however, this natural process is too slow, inefficient, and unpredictable for a modern corporation. To increase efficiency, corn and other feeds provided in the feedlot can grow an animal to the desired weight for slaughter in fourteen months. Moreover, this cost to the feedlots is only $1.60 a day for each animal.

While it does enable cattle to grow faster and more efficiently, this process disregards the evolutionary needs of the animal. Cows did not evolve to eat corn, and a corn diet can be lethal. The starch created by eating corn can stop the rumination process and trap gases, inflating the rumen. This can encroach on the lungs and suffocate the animal. Antibiotics treat this condition as well as conditions created by the filth of the feedlot where animals actually stand, sleep, and inhale their excrement. In other words, the $1.60 a day the feedlots pay to feed each animal has hidden costs: the public health costs of antibiotic resistance; food contamination by *E. coli*, salmonella, and other microbes; the taxpayer cost of corn subsidies; and the environmental cost of waste produced by the feedlots.[23]

Feedlots may consume the most corn, but processing plants called wet mills are a close second. These mills convert a large percentage of our corn into the building blocks from which we assemble our processed foods. They begin by dividing the corn kernel into three components. The yellow skin is processed into various vitamins and nutritional products. The germ at the center is crushed for oil, and the largest part, the endosperm, is plundered for its complex carbohydrates.[24] The strange names

23. Pollan, *The Omnivore's Dilemma*, pp. 69-83. In chapter 1 we discussed Disney's need to re-create nature in a way that suits its purposes. Our feedlots do the same, only it's grosser and yuckier.

24. Pollan, *The Omnivore's Dilemma*, p. 85.

we find on food labels are derived from the endosperm: citric acid, lactic acid, glucose, fructose, maltodextrin, ethanol, sorbitol, etc. Pollan calls this process "the industrial version of digestion," and it is highly dependent on fossil fuels. It is so fossil fuel–dependent that every calorie produced by this process requires the use of ten calories of fossil fuel.[25]

The greatest innovation from this "industrial version of digestion" came in the late 1960s when Japanese chemists discovered glucose isomerase, an enzyme that transformed glucose into the sweeter fructose. From fructose the food industry created high fructose — a product that tastes as sweet as sugar. In 1984, Coca-Cola substituted high-fructose corn syrup for sugar in its soft drink products. They did so for the only reason corporations do anything. High fructose was much less expensive than sugar, hence, a more efficient way to produce their product. In good Capitalist fashion Coca-Cola passed these savings along to the consumer, but they did so in an ingenious way.

Instead of decreasing the cost of their product, they increased the serving size from 8 to 12 to 16 and then to 20 fluid ounces.[26] In other words, we now drink more fluid ounces of Coke and other soft drinks. Our wallets do not suffer, but our waistlines expand. This is not the only place in the industrial food processing system that leads to the expansion of our waistlines.

On a per-calorie basis, all food produced by these industrial processes is cheaper (to the consumer) than farm-grown produce. One dollar spent on potato chips, cookies, fries, and other fast foods will buy four times the calories as one dollar spent on fresh fruits and vegetables. People with low incomes, therefore, find it in their economic interest to purchase fast food and other processed items instead of fresh produce. This means that poorer people are more likely to be obese than are wealthy people, and they are more likely to acquire diseases related to obesity like diabetes and heart disease. Here again we find hidden health costs in the diets we subsidize in support of our corporate persons. Our corporate persons are subsidized. Our human persons pay the price in obesity-related diseases.

In his effort to trace the ingredients of a typical fast-food meal, Pollan further exposes the extent of The Economy's mission. In the interest of efficiency, calculability, predictability, and control, corporate self-interest attacks the basic building blocks of life. The mission is to place every-

---

25. Pollan, *The Omnivore's Dilemma*, p. 88.
26. Pollan, *The Omnivore's Dilemma*, p. 103.

thing — even the food we eat and drink — under the rubric of corporate efficiency and calculability, and this mission is not always consistent with human needs. The near-lethal by-products of this corporate mission are many: global warming (due to excess synthetic nitrate evaporation), pollution of our groundwater supply and dead zones in the Gulf of Mexico (both due to nitrate runoff), food poisoning (due to the quest for efficiency in both animal growth and slaughtering procedures), obesity, diabetes, and heart conditions (enabled by government subsidies that make processed and fast foods cheaper than nonsubsidized produce and meats).[27] It is in the interest of corporate persons to extend this mission even though it is often in conflict with the life-needs of human persons.

The Economy's "Spiritual" Formation of Its Young

Like all religions, Economics is concerned with the spiritual formation of their youth. From the cradle these young believers are introduced to two very famous spiritual guides: Santa Claus and Ronald McDonald. Just as Virgil and Beatrice guided Dante through hell and paradise, Santa Claus and Ronald McDonald guide the feet of our children as they walk through a new world of The Economy's design.

> The Economy is concerned with the "spiritual growth" of its young people. From cradle to grave it teaches people to be good consumers and devoted employees.

Santa has happy laborers called elves who never go on strike and who make and distribute free toys to all good little boys and girls. They

27. The relationship between corporate persons' self-interest and human persons' self-interest may not be as stark as is depicted here. The food generated by the industrial food process could prevent starvation — particularly starvation of America's poor. True, the diet that is promoted by corporations and the government has many unhealthy consequences, but it may also mean that people who eat these diets live longer than they would without them. Even if this is true — and to a certain extent it is true — this does not detract from this description of the extent of the corporate *mission*. It also does not mean that one cannot use the hidden costs of this mission as evidence that there is some difference between corporate self-interest and human self-interest. The difference exists, but the extent of these differences is debatable.

work in a factory at the North Pole that produces free toys for all the world's children without exploiting labor or creating environmental damage. Santa subliminally introduces children to the fun side of Capitalism without exposing its negative features.[28] To be sure, children normally cannot articulate the beliefs implicit in the Santa story, but Santa rituals, festivals, and stories influence children even after they know that Santa does not exist.[29]

In a survey of American school children, 96 percent identified Ronald McDonald. Only Santa was recognized more.[30] In the early 1960s McDonald's was looking for a new mascot because its first one was a little chef called Speedy, and Speedy was already the name of the Alka-Seltzer mascot. This connection between a restaurant and an upset stomach was not one that McDonald's wished to promote, so they searched for another mascot.

In 1960 a Washington, D.C., franchise owner, Ben Goldstein, decided to sponsor a local children's TV show called *Bozo's Circus*. After the show was canceled, Goldstein hired its star, Willard Scott, to invent a new clown to appear at Goldstein's restaurants. An ad agency designed the clown's look. Willard Scott created the name. Ronald McDonald was born. Two years later McDonald's introduced Ronald McDonald as its mascot without Willard Scott, whose large physical stature may have prevented his being chosen to sell burgers, shakes, and fries.[31] McDonald's added other characters to attract children, and it soon "loomed large in the imagination of toddlers, the intended audience for the ads. The restaurant chain evoked a series of pleasing images in a youngster's mind: bright colors, a playground, a toy, a clown, a drink with a straw, and little pieces of food wrapped up like a present. (McDonald's) had succeeded . . . at selling something intangible to children, along with their fries."[32] McDonald's, along with Disney, was the first to target children in its advertising.

---

28. Richard H. Robbins, *Global Problems and the Culture of Capitalism* (New York: Pearson Education, 2008), p. 33.

29. In fact, one of the greatest conspiracies of modern life is the effort to keep the Santa fantasy alive among our children. On the day when one child figures out that it is impossible for Santa to personally deliver toys to all the world's children, adults enlist the child into the conspiracy. We seldom pause to acknowledge how odd this is.

30. Eric Schlosser, *Fast Food Nation: The Dark Side of the All-American Meal* (New York: HarperCollins, 2001, 2002), p. 4.

31. Schlosser, *Fast Food Nation*, p. 41.

32. Schlosser, *Fast Food Nation*, p. 42.

Soon toy makers, candy companies, and breakfast cereal manufacturers followed McDonald's lead. Today nearly all companies target children in some way. Major ad agencies have children divisions, and a variety of marketing firms focus only on kids. Industry publications like *Youth Market Alert, Selling to Kids,* and *Marketing to Kids Report* study ways to increase current and future consumption of children.[33] If one understands The Economy as a religious undertaking, these efforts concern the spiritual growth necessary to grow and maintain The Economy's faithful.

This corporate focus on children is similar to that of traditional religions. Lawrence Kohlberg and James Fowler are the leaders in the study of the moral and faith development of children (and adults). Both contend that children and adults pass through certain stages of moral and faith development. *Wikipedia* accurately summarizes Kohlberg's levels of moral development:[34]

> Level 1: Pre-conventional
> > Stage 1: Obedience and punishment orientation (avoiding punishment)
> > Stage 2: Self-interest orientation (What's in it for me?)
> Level 2: Conventional
> > Stage 3: Interpersonal accord and conformity
> > Stage 4: Authority — law and order morality
> Level 3: Post-conventional
> > Stage 5: Social contract orientation
> > Stage 6: Universal ethical principles

Similarly, Fowler offers seven levels of faith development: primal, intuitive, mythic-literal, synthetic-conventional, individual-reflective, conjunctive, and universal faith.[35] Both Kohlberg and Fowler instruct us to consider the stage of moral and faith development in which a person is and to allow that stage to determine how to teach morality or the content of faith. The purpose of such teaching is to move the person to increasingly mature levels of development. The corporate education of young people recognizes similar developmental passages.

33. Schlosser, *Fast Food Nation*, p. 45.

34. See Lawrence Kohlberg, *Essays on Moral Development,* vol. 1 (New York: Harper & Row, 1981).

35. James Fowler, "An Agenda toward a Developmental Perspective on Faith," *Religious Education* 69 (March-April 1974): 209-19.

Ronald McDonald, Happy Meals, and finger food make McDonald's a friendly, fun place for young children. When children and their parents arrive at McDonald's, McDonald's goes to great lengths to make sure the kids have a good time. By the year 2000, McDonald's operated more than 8000 playgrounds in the United States. (Burger King has 2000.)[36] They are built for two reasons. The first is immediate. Playgrounds attract the children and the children bring their parents. The second reason is future oriented. Playgrounds and gifts of popular toys make a favorable and lasting impression on children — particularly if they remain uncritical believers in The Economy.

One day, these children will become parents themselves. They will remember the good times they had at McDonald's. They might even remember a hymn or two from McDonald's advertising, and they will take their own children to McDonald's because, as the "ancient" song said, "You deserve a break today. . . . So get up and get-a-way. . . . To McDonald's. . . ." In the same way a Christian always remembers the Christmas carols learned in youth, so are we, from our earliest and faintest memories, initiated into the spirituality of McDonald's and The Economy.

Corporate America's efforts do not stop with small children. They reach adolescents as well. In the past, these efforts were hampered by school attendance where, for seven or eight hours each day, corporate advertising could not reach our children. This has changed. Today, fast-food chains, soft drink companies, large consumer companies, oil companies, and defense contractors provide schools with teaching materials, lunchroom franchises, and advertising. This began in 1997 when Dr. Pepper gave $3.7 million to the Grapevine-Colleyville School District in Colorado for the rights to market its products in the school system. Since then there have been far more lucrative deals made between corporations and American public schools, all of which subject children to advertising while they are in school.[37]

Corporate persons do not just give money to our nation's schools out of the kindness of their hearts. (Corporations are actually legal constructs and have no hearts.) Just as religious gatherings like mosques, synagogues, and churches are very concerned with instilling religious values in their young followers, so are corporations. Access to schools has allowed the pursuit of these spiritual objectives. "A 1998 study of these teaching materials by the Consumers Union found that 80 percent were biased, providing

36. Schlosser, *Fast Food Nation*, p. 47.
37. Schlosser, *Fast Food Nation*, p. 53.

students with incomplete or slanted information that favored the sponsor's products and views. Procter and Gamble's *Decision Earth* program taught that clear-cut logging was actually good for the environment; teaching aids distributed by Exxon Education Foundation said that fossil fuels created few environmental problems and that alternative sources of energy were too expensive; a study guide sponsored by the American Coal Foundation dismissed fears of a greenhouse effect, claiming that "the earth could benefit rather than be harmed from increased carbon dioxide."[38]

Lifetime Learning Systems was once the nation's largest marketer of corporate-sponsored teaching aids. It claimed its products are used by 60 million students. Its sales pitch to potential *corporate* clients reveals that the central focus of corporate sponsorship of these teaching aids was to aid in what might be called the long-term spiritual development of the students. In other words, they wanted to make the values and goals of the corporation the same as the values and goals of the students. To this end, Lifetime Learning promotional materials said their teaching aids were ". . . the centerpiece in a dynamic process that generates *long-term awareness and lasting attitudinal change*" toward the sponsoring organization.[39]

Many religious communities say that their future depends on their children. To help their children grow up to be faithful people, these communities provide for their spiritual development. The religion that worships The Economy is no exception. It too is concerned with the spiritual development of its young people. Its teachings try to instill a "consumer spirit" and also begin a mentality that is conducive to future service in corporations themselves. The corporate mission is not just about global domination. It not only extends to microbes and food, but it seeks to mold the hearts, minds, and spirits of our children. In the name of The Economy, huge sums of money are spent to educate young people into the values and goals of the corporate worldview.

Evangelism: How The Economy Gets Converts

Christianity and Islam actively seek converts, and all religions receive converts. Christians call activities designed to convert the unbeliever "evangelism," and while other religions do not use this term, "evange-

38. Schlosser, *Fast Food Nation*, p. 55.
39. Schlosser, *Fast Food Nation*, p. 56.

lism" is being used here to describe how The Economy carries out its mission to unbelievers.

When Christianity was being persecuted by the Roman Empire, its "evangelism program" was mostly verbal, but reinforced by behavior that demonstrated a particular Christian's commitment to the truth of his or her words. Sometimes such a commitment involved martyrdom! (The Greek word *martus,* often translated as "martyr," means witness.) When Christianity became the official religion of Rome, however, its "evangelism program" became more than verbal. It could now use its new state support to gain converts. Sometimes these actions were overtly violent, but, more often, they involved social pressure. For example, when the population was largely Christian, a non-Christian might find it in the interest of his business or professional success to "convert" to Christianity.

Islam was founded in a political rebellion, but that should not prevent us from seeing that Islam nearly always used relatively nonviolent methods to convert people to Islam. Mohammad specifically refused to act violently toward his enemies when he conquered Mecca, and even when Islam's political power stretched from Spain to the Philippines, Islam was far more tolerant of other religions than was Christianity of this time. While Islam, like Christianity, did make some conversions "by the sword," most were of a far less violent nature.

The religion that worships The Economy also seeks converts. Like Christianity and Islam, it has done so violently, and, like Christianity and Islam, it also has accomplished its goals by less violent means. Historically, violence has often been used when a Capitalist power tries to "open markets" in foreign lands.[40] Examples of this are numerous. The French in Southeast Asia, the British in India and Africa, the Dutch in South Africa and Indonesia, and the United States in Central and South America are but a few efforts on the part of Capitalist powers to "open" foreign markets that took violent turns.

The Opium Wars of 1839-42 and 1856-60 are typical of such violence perpetrated in the name of The Economy. In the early nineteenth century, Britain began to smuggle opium into China. They did so because of a "trade imbalance" with China. Now most Capitalist nations like Britain or the United States have a tendency to think that there is something immoral about a "trade imbalance," particularly when they are the victims of the imbalance. But the trade imbalance with China was anything but

---

40. Socialist violence happens when there is resistance to centralized planning.

immoral. It was a consequence of the fact that China was exporting tea to Britain, and Britain had nothing the Chinese wanted in return. Since the money Britain paid for Chinese tea stayed in China, Britain needed something for which the Chinese would pay to get their money back.

Britain decided opium would be a great product to sell to the Chinese in order to "balance" its trade. The problem was, however, that China had laws against the importation of opium. The Opium Wars began when China destroyed a large quantity of illegally imported opium possessed by British merchants in Guangzhou (Canton).

Britain had always been trying to end Chinese "restrictions" on trade, and this "attack" on British merchants offered them the opportunity to use force to end these restrictions. Britain attacked several Chinese coastal cities, and China, unable to withstand British weapons, signed the Treaty of Nanjing in 1842. This treaty ceded Hong Kong to the British and opened several Chinese ports to "free trade" with the British as well. In 1856 another war broke out, which compelled the Chinese to accept the Treaties of Tianjin in 1858. France, Russia, and the United States were also parties to these agreements, in which China agreed to open eleven more ports, permit foreign legations in Beijing, sanction Christian missionaries, and legalize the importation of opium. Later, Chinese attempts to block the entrance of foreign diplomats into Beijing reignited hostilities. The French and British occupied Beijing and burned the imperial summer palace. The fighting ended with the reaffirmation of the Treaties of Tianjin and with additional concessions on the part of China.

The Opium Wars were a consequence of China's resistance to the "free market." They resisted because, unlike the twenty-first-century Chinese, the nineteenth-century Chinese were unbelievers. They did not hold the orthodox belief that unrestricted free trade always benefited society. Not only do the Opium Wars demonstrate that the Chinese may well have been quite correct in this belief, but they also show that violence and the threat of violence often stand behind the more benign-looking efforts to extend the range of The Free Market Economy.

In this day and age we assume "the free market" is value free, but, as the Opium Wars illustrate, "free trade" is actually a moral or spiritual system. Progress is one of its supreme values, and progress means change. Free trade asserts other unquestioned values as well. It contends that the transport of goods, people, money, and materials is more important than national sovereignty and local culture. It holds that competition is always better than cooperation, and it believes that profits are more important than people. While some think these values are undesirable, many more believe they are essential to life itself. Whether they are good or bad, however, is not the issue. The issue is that these are values perpetuated by an Economic system in much the same way as Islam and Christianity sought to expand their value systems.

Like most religions, The Economy does not always use force to convert the unfaithful. As a matter of fact, The Economy prefers non-violent ways to gain converts. Helena Norberg-Hodge (b. 1946) was the first foreigner allowed to live in the Himalayan province of Ladakh (a part of Kashmir). Over the decades she learned the language and saw the subtle ways that our Economic culture makes inroads into another culture. She recalls that prior to the introduction of money, the Ladakhis were not conscious of the fact that they lacked it. After its introduction, however, they thought that their lack of money meant that they were poor. When television was introduced, the Ladakhis saw images of wealth and power heretofore unseen. They began to think of themselves as inferior to the rich people who lived in the West. Their perception of their own history changed dramatically. Norberg-Hodge notes, "In my early days in Ladakh, people would tell me there had never been hunger. I kept hearing the expression *tungbos zabos:* 'enough to drink, enough to eat.' Now, particularly in the modern sector, people can be heard saying, 'Development is essential; in the past we couldn't manage, we didn't have enough.'"

The shift in self-image led the Ladakhi people to seek Western education for their children. This divided the children into grades, and diminished the sense of responsibility the older children traditionally had for the younger ones. Work became more technological, and men, the normal beneficiaries of this technological training, became the only valuable members of society. In short, the Ladakhi people adopted different attitudes toward their lives and social relationships as a consequence of the subtle inroads The Economy made into their culture. They now hold a different set of values. They evaluate themselves differently and have changed their understanding of what it means to be Ladakhi. It is testimony to the effectiveness of The Economy's "evangelism" practices that Norberg-Hodge — a non-Ladakhi — is one of the few who bemoan this change![41] Again, this is not an attempt to argue that such change is pos-

41. Helena Norberg-Hodge, "The Pressure to Modernize and Globalize," *CAGE,* pp. 34-42.

itive or negative. It is an effort to demonstrate how The Economy motivates people to adopt its ways and values.

Similar stories exist elsewhere. The indigenous populations of the northern parts of North America once spent their evenings listening to the stories of their elders. These stories were not just important for entertainment value. Their telling also passed the traditions and values from one generation to the next. With the advent of television, however, programs like *Dallas* and *Happy Days* were watched and traditional stories heard less frequently. This quickly undermined both the authority of the elders and the cohesion of the social group. Once again we see The Economy's quest to make converts of unbelievers. It is often nonviolent unless, of course, such conversions themselves are actually a subtle form of violence.

Summary

Large, multinational corporations are to The Economy as megachurches are to Jesus. They are the place where the vast majority of the faithful gather to serve their God and receive benefits from their God. In the United States there has been an alliance between corporations and the government. The government has decreed that corporations are persons under the law, and, as a consequence, corporations receive the benefits and protections afforded human persons. This act gives corporate persons — the communities of the Economic faithful — a considerable advantage over human persons. Corporations possess unlimited resources that most human persons do not have. This enables them to engage in expensive projects like lawsuits and lobbying, which are normally denied human persons because of human limitations in resources. Corporations also are much more long-lived than human persons. This gives them time that human persons do not have to wait for favorable legislation and judgments. Corporations continue to use these advantages to change the sociopolitical landscape.

Since the values of corporate persons are different from those of human persons, further complications exist. The values of human beings are biological. Corporate values concern efficiency and numbers. Since at the very least efficiency tries to eliminate redundancies, and since biological life needs redundancies in order to thrive, it follows that corporate values are not the same as human values. In fact, corporate values are often opposed to human needs and values.

Nonetheless, corporations attract human persons through the sacrament of money. As a sacrament, money is the way the subjective trust that human persons place in The Economy's promises is embodied in the material world. As the supreme corporate metric, money allows a corporation to calculate its efficiency and its fitness. Monetization allows the corporation to determine if it is better off this year than last year by simply checking the "bottom-line." Human persons can use money to achieve almost any want or desire.

The need to monetize leads to The Economy's global mission. If The Economy and its corporations are to grow and develop, more and more money must be made. Thus more and more areas must be monetized. What once was not monetized — childcare, care of the elderly, medicinal plants, care of the sick, microbes, water, air, death, etc. — now is monetized, and this extends The Economy into more and more areas of life.

CHAPTER 7

Is Economics Civilization's Primal Religion?

What, precisely, does it mean to say that our sense of morality and justice is reduced to the language of a business deal? What does it mean when we reduce moral obligations to debts? What changes when the one turns into the other? And how do we speak about them when our language has been so shaped by the market?

David Graeber, *Debt: The First 5000 Years*[1]

This study's goal was to show how Economics functions as a religion in our culture. This has been accomplished. Like all religions, Economics has rituals, myths, priests, prophets, theologians, reformers, and terrorists. It also has places where people gather to serve its God and receive benefits its God, The Economy, bestows. Economics has sacraments. It even has a global mission. While all religions do not have all of these functions, it is a near certainty that anything providing these functions is in fact a religion whether or not it is consciously recognized as such. It is important to at least entertain the possibility that Economics is a religion because merely entertaining this notion creates enough cognitive dissonance to make a person more critical of the economic issues when encountered in politics, on the job, and in daily life.

Economics is, however, a little different from other religions. As strange as it may seem, Economics could be the seminal or primal reli-

1. David Graeber, *Debt: The First 5000 Years* (Brooklyn, NY: Melville House Publishing, 2011), p. 13.

gion of all post-agricultural religious expressions. This is so because Economics created the creditor/debtor relationship. The creditor/debtor relationship was not present in the hunter-gatherer bands that pre-date the agricultural revolution. As will be discussed immediately below, trust and autonomy were the principal form of social cohesion in those cultures. This form of social cohesion was replaced by the creditor/debtor relationship, and at the present moment the creditor/debtor relationship is fundamental to all modern religions and philosophies. This means that Economics is the primal religion because it provides the conceptual metaphor — debt — on which all post-agricultural religions are based.

Debt: Civilization's Conceptual Metaphor

Civilization is the form of human culture unleashed by the intellectual and social forces created during the agricultural revolution. The agricultural revolution changed human cultures from small bands of nomadic hunter-gatherers into much larger populations of sedentary, "civilized" farmers. These larger populations required a new way to guarantee social cohesion. Where trust and autonomy was the way hunter-gatherer bands guaranteed social cohesion, civilization demanded a new cohesive force. Ultimately the creditor/debtor relationship became this new force.

R. I. M. Dunbar has argued that the limitations of the human brain forced this shift. Trust, the social tie of hunter-gatherer bands, meant acting "with that person *in mind,* in the hope that they will do likewise by responding in favorable ways to you."[2] The difficulty was (and is) that the human brain can only keep about 150 people *in mind.* This limitation means that the size of human groups that can use trust as a socially cohesive force is limited.[3] Thus, when agricultural societies became more populous, they needed a new form of social cohesion. The creditor/debtor relationship addressed this fundamental social need for cohesion.

Credit and debt may have emerged in the following way. The agricultural revolution was the first time we thought of food as a commodity. This shift in the way we thought about food had dramatic consequences. For

2. Tim Ingold, "On the social relations of the hunter-gatherer band," *The Cambridge Encyclopedia of Hunters and Gatherers,* ed. Richard B. Ley and Richard Daly (Cambridge: Cambridge University Press, 1999), p. 406.

3. R. I. M. Dunbar, "Coevolution of Neocortical Size, Group Size, and Language in Humans," *Behavioral and Brain Sciences* 16, no 4 (1993): 691.

food to even be a commodity, one person must "own" the food. If owner-ship is not recognized, food can merely be taken. It will not be exchanged. Now the one who "owns" the food has a tremendous advantage over the one who needs food. A man in possession of excess food, for example, can attract more wives and enhance his prestige in other ways as well. Thus certain forms of social stratification emerged when food became a commodity in a small village. Later, the villages would combine under the governance of chiefs — which implies even more hierarchy and social stratification. So far as we can tell from the archaeological record, all ancient empires were preceded by such chiefdoms.[4] Since those without food needed food to survive, they went into the service of those with food, or, one might say, they went into their debt. Creditors and debtors may have been born in this way; for, a person who does not have food might be quite willing to exchange his autonomy (an important social value for hunter-gatherers) or the freedom of his wife or children for food.[5]

Since food is obviously a necessity of life, the one with the "food monopoly" is the powerful one in this relationship. Those in control of food can ask for almost anything in exchange for their food. They can even ask for things that the one in need does not yet have! In a hunter/gatherer band, a person did not ask for what another person did not have (largely because he or she was quite unlikely to receive it). In an agricultural society (modern society is included) it is common to demand from a debtor something he or she does not have.

4. Robert Wright, *Nonzero: The Logic of Human Destiny* (New York: Vintage Books, 2001), p. 79.

5. An example from eleventh-century England serves as an illustration of how a creditor — a person controlling the food supply — might place a debtor — one in need of food — into bondage. "People also surrendered themselves into bondage at times of famine or distress, when they simply could not provide for their families any more. In later centuries there was the poorhouse or the bankruptcy law to help cope with such tragedies, but in the year 1000 the starving man had no other resort but to kneel before his lord or lady and place his head in their hands. No legal document was involved, and the new bondsman would be handed a bill-hook or ox-goad in token of his fresh start in servitude. It was a basic transaction — heads for food. The original old English meaning of lord was 'loaf-giver,' and Gearfleda, a lady of Northumbria, made the transaction explicit in the will she drew up in the 990s: 'for the love of God and for the need of her soul [Gearfleda] has given freedom to Ecceard, the blacksmith, and Aelfstan and his wife and all their off-spring, born and un-born, and Arcil and Cole and Ecgferth and Ealdhun's daughter, and all those people whose heads she took for their food in the evil days.'" In Robert Lacey and Danny Danziger, *The Year 1000: What Life Was Like at the Turn of the First Millennium/ An Englishman's World* (Boston: Little, Brown, 1999), pp. 46, 47.

> The agricultural revolution replaced trust and sharing
> with creditors and debtors as the social "glue" that binds
> the culture and allows a particular culture to persist.

Our laws and social pressure usually favor the creditor in such transactions, and religion often plays a role in maintaining the creditor's favor. Indeed, I have argued that religion as we know it begins when priests granted moral sanction to the arbitrary criteria the owners of food use to determine who merits food and who does not. Eventually this leads to ancient religions sanctifying the creditor/debtor relationship. The politicians and the priests become the creditors. Almost everyone else becomes debtors. Sometimes the politicians *force* the people to pay their debt, tribute, or taxes, but most of the time the religious leaders use myth and ritual to convince the population that debt and credit are divinely created. Failure to repay a creditor may have serious consequences to the fabric of the cosmos itself. Such unquestioned beliefs pacify enough of the population, and the agricultural machinery expands.

It must be duly noted that debt produces a specific morality. It exploits a kind of trust that has nothing to do with the belief in new possibilities in life. Instead, debt appropriates the future of the debtor; for, repaying a debt requires certain specific acts that enable the debtor to repay the debt. Moreover, the creditor must be reasonably certain that the debtor will perform these specific acts — like work — in order to pay his or her bills. The creditor's "trust" that the debtor will do what is necessary to fulfill these obligations is enhanced by political power, which is an external force that stands behind all loans, and by a moral subjectivity that makes a debtor feel guilty if he or she does not repay the debt.[6] Religion establishes these moral consciences. This has been one of religion's important social roles since the agricultural revolution.

Since religions sanctified this divide between creditors and debtors, the religion called Economics emerged with agricultural civilization. Economics reveals its continuing dominance of all religion in the sense that all religions understand salvation in terms of debt, and most people

---

6. Maurizio Lazzarato, *The Making of the Indebted Man*, trans. Joshua David Jordan (Los Angeles: Semiotext[e], 2012), pp. 44-48.

("religious" or not) assume that debts should *always* be paid. Moreover, those who do not pay their debts are usually deemed morally deficient in some profound and fundamental way.[7] These moral assumptions are a consequence of debt's continued function as a "conceptual" metaphor in civilization.

A "conceptual" metaphor is not your ordinary metaphor. An ordinary metaphor describes one thing in terms of another. A conceptual metaphor is much more powerful and life shaping. It gives form and structure to *all* our thoughts and activities that pertain to the metaphor. In introducing their book *Metaphors We Live By,* George Lakoff and Mark Johnson give an excellent example of war as the conceptual metaphor through which we understand each and every argument.

> It is important to see that we don't just *talk* about arguments in terms of war. We can actually win or lose arguments. We see the person we are arguing with as an opponent. We *attack* his positions and we *defend* our own. We *gain and lose ground.* We *plan* and use *strategies.* If we find a position *indefensible,* we can abandon it and take a new line of *attack.* Many of the things we do in arguing are partially structured by the concept of war. Though there is no physical battle, there is verbal battle, and the structure of an argument — attack, defense, counterattack, etc. — reflects this. It is in this sense that the ARGUMENT IS WAR metaphor is one that we live by in this culture; it structures the actions we perform in arguing.[8]

On an even larger scale, debt is a "metaphor we live by." Debt is the conceptual metaphor behind all civilization's religions. To paraphrase Lakoff and Johnson, many things we *do in religion* are given form, structure, and are understood through debt. We worship and sacrifice because we *owe* something to our God, our parents, nature, or our society.

Most modern religions use debt as a conceptual metaphor. Hinduism, Buddhism, and Christianity maintain that we are *born* owing God or the cosmos or perhaps our parents an enormous debt. Islam and Judaism contend that something must be done in this life to avoid debt and/or repay debts incurred in life. Modern religions differ concerning what it

---

7. Graeber, *Debt,* p. 113.

8. George Lakoff and Mark Johnson, *Metaphors We Live By* (Chicago: University of Chicago Press, 1980), p. 4. Emphases mine.

takes to balance our accounts, but all agree that it is important for our accounts to be balanced. Some religions perpetuate themselves because their adherents never get out of debt. At best we only pay the interest. There is little we can do to pay the principal. Our sacrifices only put off the inevitable day when we will have to make a final account or, to use Christian parlance, "pay for our sins." Only a few exceptional people — Jesus or the Buddha — can ever pay the debt in full.

Geoffrey Ingham gives further evidence of debt's continued dominance of both society and religion.

> The ultimate discharge of this fundamental debt is sacrifice of the living to appease and express gratitude to the ancestors and deities of the cosmos. In addition to human sacrifice, "debt payment" also took the form of sacrificial privation. Scarce and valuable materials or food would be given up to a "brotherhood" of priests who mediated between the society and the cosmos. Such hypotheses must remain conjectural, but there is considerable indirect etymological evidence. In all Indo-European languages, words for "debt" are synonymous with those for "sin" or "guilt," illustrating the links between religion, payment, and the mediation of the sacred and profane realms by "money." For example, there is a connection between money (German *Geld*), indemnity or sacrifice (Old English *Geild*), tax (Gothic *Gild*), and of course, guilt.[9]

The idea that all human beings are born with debts we cannot repay is a rather dubious assumption, particularly if debt is understood economically as some sort of contractual obligation. Speaking personally, I do not recall negotiating such a contract with God, the saints, my parents, or my country before agreeing to be born.[10] I am quite sure my parents were not thinking about me when I was conceived, and even though my mother remembers her *three days* of labor with me, I do not actually *owe*

---

9. Geoffrey Ingham, *The Nature of Money* (Cambridge: Polity Press, 2004), p. 90.

10. This would not be an argument made by a Buddhist or Hindu. For them, a person's *karma* might be compared to an accounting ledger that either is your real self or accompanies your real self throughout a near-infinite number of existences. Your current state in life is the consequence of your *karma*, which is like a ledger of what you owe from previous lives. You may not have agreed to be born into your particular life and body, but your particular life and body are just compensation (or punishment) for your previous lives.

her anything for risking her life to give me life (which she in fact did). I do not *owe* her because she provided me a service for which I did not contract. Just as I am under no obligation to pay a construction company that builds an addition to my house without my say-so or knowledge, I do not *owe* my mother for giving me life — which she in fact did. By the same token, I am not in debt to God, nature, my country, or my predecessors because there was never a contract either negotiated or implied. Everything has in fact been given to me, but without my agreement. I may not deserve my life, but I do not owe anyone for it. Whatever debt I have incurred, I have incurred since birth through my legal contractual obligations, which are a product of social convention. I was not born in debt.

Most people think that I am crass or immoral for holding such beliefs (particularly those related to my mother), but their thinking simply reflects the dominance of debt as a conceptual metaphor. The idea that we are not born in debt and are not in debt to God or our parents or the universe, however, precludes neither loving one's parents nor one's God. In fact, living debt free actually makes love possible because, as some have said, love is not love if it is forced, obligatory, or coerced. Most modern religions have understood this in principle, but religious people often have difficulty being just, loving, merciful, or gracious because all of our religions have been unable to jettison debt as the conceptual metaphor that supports religious life and discourse.

Debt: The Conceptual Metaphor behind Modern Religions

All modern religions — Judaism, Buddhism, Christianity, and Islam — began as critiques of ancient, archaic religions. Archaic religions were the religions of great ancient empires like Egypt, Babylonia, Assyria, India, China, and the empires of the Pre-Columbian Americas as well. In archaic religions, the king was believed to be God or at least God's representative on earth. Through rituals and myths, archaic priests made opposition to archaic kings unthinkable. As long as they did their jobs, it would not even cross people's minds to envision an alternative to the ways of the empire. Since God was believed to create these empires, and since the king embodied divine presence, opposing the archaic order was to oppose the God of the universe. It was unthinkable. It did not cross your mind.

Despite the best efforts of archaic priests, however, people were not simply automatons. When the king could not keep the forces of chaos at bay, questions arose. Sometimes famines and other natural disasters undermined the king's rule. Sometimes other empires threatened an empire's demise, but war often settled the issue. If one archaic kingdom was conquered by another, the conquered kingdom would worship the God and king of their conquerors and the same sort of unquestioned obedience might follow under new rule.

For one reason or another (we have argued that the emergence of coins may have helped), modern religions like Buddhism (c. 534 BCE)[11] and Judaism (c. 538 BCE)[12] and the philosophies of Thales and Anaximander (610-546 BCE) in the Greek world and Confucius (531-479 BCE) in the Chinese emerged to criticize their respective archaic civilizations.[13] Each began as a critique, but each was unable to liberate us from our archaic past because, to one degree or another, each critique could not jettison the metaphor of debt.

Hinduism, Buddhism, and Debt

Hinduism and Buddhism have a common framework, which is articulated through the doctrines of *saṃsāra, karma, dharma, mokṣa, and duhkha.*[14] *Saṃsāra,* often called reincarnation, is the process whereby "souls" undergo a nearly endless cycle of birth-death-rebirth-death-rebirth until liberated *(mokṣa)* from the need to be born once more. *Karma* is the reason why a particular "soul" occupies a particular position in life.[15] One's

---

11. I date the beginning of Buddhism to the Buddha's awakening at the age of twenty-nine.

12. I date the founding of Judaism to the first reading of the Torah on the site of Solomon's destroyed Temple upon Israel's return from Babylonian captivity.

13. The distinction between religion and philosophy in this sentence is made for us moderns, who routinely make such distinctions. Ancient religions were far more philosophical than we now think, and ancient philosophies were all quite religious.

14. David E. Cooper, *World Philosophies: An Historical Introduction* (Malden, MA: Blackwell, 1996, 1999), p. 19.

15. This description will permanently leave aside the question of what exactly is transmitted from one living creature to another in the process of *saṃsāra.* Whatever this is maintains an entity's identity through a process where the death of a human being could result in this same entity's being reborn as a god or a cat. This identity that passes from one living entity to another in the process of *saṃsāra* is alternately translated as "soul" or "elemental soul" or "self." Scholars seem to say that all translations are inadequate, so "soul" and "self" will be used despite their inadequacies.

position in this life is the consequence of one's acts in previous lives. Virtuous acts in this life will help a particular soul or self be reborn to a higher station in the next life. By the same token, bad actions in this life mean a lower station in the next. *Karma* is the record of these virtues and vices that accompany a soul throughout the near-eternal process of *saṃsāra*. *Karma is literally an accountant's ledger that records the good and bad acts of a particular soul.* A soul cannot escape the cycle of *saṃsāra* until all its debts are paid. "What makes the 'elemental soul' currently occupying body X the one which previously occupied body Y is precisely the load of karmic effects which it carries as a result of actions performed during the occupancy of Y."[16]

> ### *Karma* functions as an accounting ledger in both Hinduism and Buddhism.

Neither Hinduism nor Buddhism has any arguments to support the existence of *karma*.[17] *Karma* is just taken for granted. This omission makes complete sense if debt is functioning "behind the scenes" as the conceptual metaphor on which these religions are founded. *Karma* is simply the way cosmic accounts are kept and recorded. As long as a "self" persists, it will have some karmic debt to pay.

All Indian religions assert that it is both desirable and possible to attain liberation *(mokṣa)* from *saṃsāra*. It is desirable because life is *duhkha*. *Duhkha* is most often translated as suffering, but sometimes it merely means unsatisfactory. Pleasures are *duhkha* because they do not last. This is hardly painful, but it is unsatisfactory. *Duhkha* is a consequence of the fact that "our existence is conditioned; *saṃsāra* is a prison-house. Cessation of *duhkha* implies an unconditional state of freedom that the Buddhists call *nirvana*."[18] While it may take eons to secure, all Indian religions think liberation *(mokṣa)* is possible. It is *dharma* that makes *mokṣa* (liberation) possible.

Dharma has a number of meanings, but for our purposes, *dharma* teaches *karma*. It says that everything has an explanation, and nothing is

16. Cooper, *World Philosophies*, p. 20.
17. Cooper, *World Philosophies*, p. 20.
18. B. K. Matilal, *Logic and Reality: Indian Philosophy and Contemporary Issues* (Delhi: Motilal Banarsidass, 1985), p. 348.

by chance. The goal of *dharma* is to expel ignorance *(avidyā)*, which is the source of suffering *(duhkha)*. For example, *dharma* tells us that we do not occupy our position in life by luck or by a random act. We occupy our position as the fruit of all choices we have made in previous lives. It also tells us that our desires are the source of the bad choices we have made in previous lives, and overcoming such desires is a step toward our liberation. So, after teaching adherents about *karma*, *dharma* teaches how these desires might be overcome and *mokṣa* (liberation) achieved. Each Hindu and Buddhist school of thought may differ in the content of their *dharma*, yet each school believes *dharma* provides the path of liberation from the prison-house of *saṃsāra*.

Śankara (c. 788-820) is one of Hinduism's most celebrated theologians. His *dharma* teaches that nothing is truly real except *Brahman*, which is unitary, seamless, and ineffable being. *Brahman* is all that exists, but it is not a thing. Since *Brahman* is *all that exists,* and since *Brahman* is *not a thing*, Śankara deduced that no-thing actually exists. Hence, the commonsense reality of our world of things is an illusion. Śankara notes that since everything within the process of *saṃsāra* only involves this normal, everyday commonsense reality, and since everyday reality is an illusion, *saṃsāra*, the process of death-rebirth-death-rebirth, is itself an illusion.

The tightly reasoned paragraph immediately above — a paragraph you might have to read again — is Śankara's *dharma*. It teaches that liberation *(mokṣa)* from *saṃsāra* can be achieved if a person recognizes that every-thing is an illusion.[19] Śankara was one of the intellectual and spiritual giants of India. His intellectual gifts have been compared to Thomas Aquinas (both because of their intellectual powers and their relatively short lives). His thought, therefore, is far more substantial and subtle than what has been presented here, but this sketch of one relatively important feature of his thought — why the world is an illusion — is enough to show that *Śankara was more inclined to jettison the reality of our commonsense, everyday world than he was to reject the accounting ledger called karma.* In this discussion of Economics as the primal or seminal religion, this is an interesting fact. Śankara simply cannot bring himself to reject the accounting mechanism called *karma*, so he rejects the visible, everyday world instead.

Buddhists have the same theological difficulty. They may not reject the commonsense world, but some Buddhists reject the reality of the self. *Saṃsāra* requires at least three things: the accounting mechanism called

---

19. Cooper, *World Philosophies*, p. 34.

karma; one or more universes where *saṃsāra* takes place, and a self or soul that undergoes this nearly endless process. The *dharma* of Tibetan Buddhism is to reject the self. Liberation from *saṃsāra* requires the self to be debt free. If there is no self, then there is no-thing to be freed from karmic debt.

These discussions of Hinduism and Buddhism are hardly meant to be exhaustive. They are, however, meant to illustrate how debt functions as a conceptual metaphor underlying and supporting both Hinduism and Buddhism. Both religions would rather deny things like the reality of our commonsense world or the reality of the self than deny the accounting ledger called *karma.* As a consequence, both Hinduism and Buddhism maintain the conceptual metaphor of debt. Moreover, they do so without even thinking about it. The conceptual metaphor of debt is so integral that it never even remotely occurs to them — because it is an unspoken assumption — to critique *karma.* Buddhism and Hinduism are not the only religions where debt is so fundamental. Christianity is too. Like Buddhism and Hinduism, Christianity also attempts to free its adherents from debt bondage while maintaining this unquestioned conceptual metaphor of debt. This proves theologically challenging, if not logically impossible.

Christianity and Debt

Christianity's most controversial debates are a consequence of its struggle to discuss God's graciousness without abandoning debt as a conceptual metaphor. If grace can be described as "being treated lovingly and in *discontinuity* with one's past," then its opposition to the creditor/debtor relationship becomes clear. Creditor/debtor relationships depend upon *continuity* with the past. A debtor's *past* promise to repay must be binding on the *future* if the creditor/debtor system is to function. The entire creditor/debtor edifice collapses if past promises are not binding on the future.

Unlike debt, grace is not based on past performance. The recipient of grace receives what is needed *despite* the past rather than because of the past. Moreover, the one who acts graciously is not *owed* anything specific in return. In a slightly different context, St. Paul reminds us that the wages of the one who works are not grace but one's due. For an act to be gracious, the recipient of the act cannot have earned what has been received.[20]

20. Romans 4:4, 5.

Since grace is a fundamental Christian concept as well as *discontinuous* with the past, Christianity will never be able to adequately articulate the radical nature of grace if debt remains its conceptual metaphor. Unless this metaphor is jettisoned, God will always be the creditor, and we will always be the debtors. As debtors, we must do something in order to pay our debt to God. (What this "something" is differs, and these differing opinions constitute the different beliefs of Christian denominations.)

Asserting the primacy of grace without abandoning the conceptual metaphor of debt is logically impossible; yet Christian theology has always been engaged in futile attempts to speak of grace while maintaining the metaphor of debt. These attempts received classical expression in the controversy between North African bishop Augustine (354-430) and the British monk Pelagius (c. 390-418). Pelagius argued that a human being can decide for or against God because humans have the free will to do so. In other words, people had the power, by virtue of free will, to do something that would pay the debt owed to God and thereby earn salvation. Augustine, on the other hand, said that human beings lost such freedom through Adam's fall. We do not have the power to earn our salvation. If we are saved, we are saved by God's grace. We are saved despite the fact that nothing we do can repay our debt to God.

> Christianity has always equated salvation with the removal of debts. Even Jesus prayed, "Forgive us our debts" in the Lord's Prayer.

This debate persists throughout the history of the Christian church. In most cases it concerns the issue of how much a person can cooperate with God in matters of his or her salvation. Few still believe in the "extremes" of Augustine and Pelagius in the sense that they think salvation is totally up to God (Augustine) or in the sense that they think salvation is totally our responsibility (Pelagius). Most adopt one of two middle positions. The first contends that God "graciously" initiates the process of salvation (something human beings do not have the power to do), but humans must cooperate with God's grace and complete their salvation largely by their own efforts. This view maintains the primacy of grace in the sense that in discontinuity with one's past, God initiates the entire process of salvation. Technically salvation is not earned because it could not happen without God's initiation, but we must do something to complete the process God started. The second middle position contends that human beings actually initiate the process of salvation. In modern parlance, for example, a person might, without God's help, decide to trust God or accept Jesus as her Savior. Few who hold this view believe human beings have the capacity to bring salvation to completion on their own. For salvation to be complete, God must "graciously" grant salvation to those for whom it is willed.[21] Both middle positions are attempts to speak of God's love and grace without abandoning the conceptual metaphor of debt. We either *owe* it to God to initiate our own salvation or we *owe* it to God to cooperate with the salvation process that God graciously initiated.

Even when Augustine's radical understanding of God's grace is maintained, the metaphor of debt still remains. Some very radical Lutheran reformers insisted that human beings have nothing to do with salvation. They insisted that we can neither initiate the process of salvation nor cooperate with God in the process of salvation. They proclaimed that salvation is accomplished only through God's grace. But even these radical believers in God's absolute grace could not abandon the conceptual metaphor of debt.

Hardly a familiar name today, Matthias Flacius Illyricus (1520-1575) was a leader of this branch of Lutheranism. His thinking has been summarized as follows:

> [People] are called into the divine forum to be judged: God presides, holding in his hands *a book of accounts containing the debts of [humanity] and the treasure of Christ.* Each [person] is accused and threatened with eternal torture; then Christ, the mediator, steps forth to plead for *remission of debt* on the basis of his own merit. God listens carefully to the plea; finally, he agrees to acquit [the accused] by accepting *Christ's credit.* The "sinner" . . . has been declared "righteous" . . . through divine transaction based on the merits of Christ; God is not only gracious, but also just.[22]

21. Anyone remotely familiar with Christianity realizes that these middle positions dominate debate today, but they may not know that these positions have been around for at least a millennium. Medieval theologians called the ability to do good *without* the benefit of grace "the merit of congruity," and they called the effort to do good *with* the benefit of grace "the merit of condignity."

22. Eric Gritsch and Robert Jenson, *Lutheranism: The Theological Movement and Its Confessional Writings* (Philadelphia: Fortress Press, 1976), p. 55. Emphases mine.

Even though this is one of the most radical views of the centrality of grace, the conceptual metaphor of debt remains central. Justice is still synonymous with balancing the accounting ledger. Even though God's grace has the final say, God still appears as an accountant. He still holds the ledger containing the debts of humanity and the credits of Christ. Salvation is conceived as the *forgiveness* of debt. The conceptual metaphor of debt, which supports the creditor/debtor relationship that binds civilization, is never questioned. Abandoning this metaphor is unthinkable. By unthinkable I mean it never crosses our mind.

It must be recalled that making the opposition to the social order "unthinkable" was the tacit goal of ancient religions. Apparently, religions like Hinduism, Buddhism, and Christianity achieved this goal quite well with respect to debt. While these three religions are the best expression of the dominance of the debt metaphor, they are not alone in their uncritical attitude toward the conceptual metaphor of debt. To one degree or another, the debt metaphor undergirds other modern religions as well.

Judaism and Debt

Judaism's use of debt as a conceptual metaphor is evident in the covenant between God and Israel. Sometimes the covenant is described as a contract between God and Israel, but if this is an adequate description, God's covenant with Israel is not your ordinary contract. Ordinary contracts have a certain *quid pro quo*. One party to the contract agrees to perform particular tasks, and the other agrees to certain obligations. Both sides receive a benefit of some kind through the contract. In God's covenant with Israel, however, it is difficult to understand what benefit God could possibly derive from this covenant with Israel *even if* Israel actually keeps its end of the bargain — which it often does not.

Since God fulfills his promises come what may, the covenant between Israel and God dramatically alters the traditional creditor/debtor relationship. Normally the creditor receives much more than the debtor, and the debtor is saddled with crushing future obligations. In Israel's covenant, the stronger party is obligated to the weaker party, and the weaker party's obligation to God is questionable. God promises to make Abraham a great nation. All God wants is for Abraham to trust this promise. Sometimes Abraham and his descendants do, but most of the time they do not. In spite of Israel's failure, God keeps God's promises. Indeed, the biblical story of Israel can be read as God adjusting to Israel's failure to meet its obligations to God. Apparently, the covenant binds God to Israel's destiny despite the fact that Israel breaks it. This is no *quid pro quo* contract. Israel does not fill its end of the bargain, and yet, God's very being is tied to Israel's destiny.[23]

The creditor/debtor relationship remains, but its structure is altered. To be sure, this is a radical alteration, but, like Christianity and Buddhism, the creditor/debtor relationship is not jettisoned. It still remains a conceptual metaphor within Judaism.

This covenant is even more interesting because of the sort of person with whom God covenants. Generally, God makes his covenant with shepherds. In the context of our contention that the agricultural revolution is a watershed moment in human history, shepherds are the ones who try to live apart from agricultural civilization. Shepherds want little to do with the sedentary life of farmers. In a certain sense, they are in rebellion. Jewish philosopher and theologian Yoram Hazony argues that the Cain and Abel story is very significant in this regard. The story's outline is simple. Cain, the farmer, and his brother Abel, the shepherd, offer sacrifices to God. God accepts Abel's sacrifice, but rejects Cain's offering. Cain gets angry and kills his brother. For many, God's actions are unintelligible because there does not appear to be a reason for God to accept Abel's offering and reject Cain's.

Hazony exasperates us further by noting that Cain was actually *obeying* God, and Abel was not! Adam and Eve were Cain and Abel's parents. When Adam disobeyed God and ate the forbidden fruit, God "sent him forth from the garden of Eden, *to till the ground from which he was taken.*"[24] Cain accepted this divinely ordained role and, like his father before him, became a farmer and piously submitted to God's curse on the soil.[25] Abel did otherwise. He did not submit to God's plan and his father's obedience to God's plan.

---

23. This discussion of Judaism has an important and vital limitation. It is pre-Holocaust! The Holocaust marks a turning point in Jewish theology, in which some have even argued that the relationship between the covenant partners has changed dramatically. A radical expression of this is that prior to the Holocaust Israel was the unfaithful party to the covenant. After the Holocaust God is the unfaithful party and the Jews are the faithful ones. See Richard L. Rubenstein, *After Auschwitz* (Baltimore: Johns Hopkins University Press, 1992).

24. Genesis 3:23. Emphasis God's.

25. Genesis 3:17, 18.

Abel resists and becomes a shepherd. He lives a life of personal initiative and dissent. *His aim is to change what God has ordained!* He endeavors to improve upon the life that Adam and Cain believed to be their only possible God-given destiny. When God accepts Abel's offering, God approves of the one who uses his own initiative and tries to improve upon what God has ordained. It is in such initiative that Hazony finds God's criteria for accepting Abel's but refusing Cain's offering. God says to Cain, "Why are you angry, and why is your face fallen? If you improve *(teitiv),* will you not be lifted up?"[26]

In contrast to the idea that God is the creditor who demands payment of debts, Hazony argues that Hebrew Scriptures tell a story about a God who ". . . is not particularly impressed with piety, with sacrifices, with doing what you are told to do and what your fathers did before you. He is not even that impressed with doing what you believe has been decreed by God. All these things, *which Cain has on his side of the ledger,* can be a part of a beast-life, or even of a life of evil. They are worth nothing if they are not placed in service of a life that is directed toward the active pursuit of [humanity's] true good."[27] Hazony extends this contrast between the obedient farmer and the innovative shepherd by reminding us that Abraham, Jacob, Moses, and even King David are all shepherds! They live their lives and form their communities outside the purview of the agricultural empires. They have no conception of debt or obligation to God or the state. It is not so with Greek "patriarchs" like Socrates.

In *The Crito,* Socrates, and perhaps Greek philosophy in general, demonstrates a commitment to debt as a conceptual metaphor that borders on the irrational. To understand the irrational basis of Greek philosophy, however, one must deny the universality of the debt metaphor that Socrates maintains throughout. *The Crito* begins with Socrates in prison where he awaits a death sentence. His students try to convince him to escape. Socrates refuses because he thinks a person *owes everything* to his country and therefore must "patiently submit to any punishment that it imposes. . . ."[28] Socrates' uncritical acceptance of the metaphor of debt is obvious here. Moses, however, presents a sharp contrast.

---

26. Genesis 4:6, 7, trans. Yoram Hazony, *The Philosophy of Hebrew Scripture* (New York: Cambridge University Press, 2012), p. 108.

27. Hazony, *The Philosophy of Hebrew Scripture,* p. 109. Emphasis mine.

28. Plato, *Crito,* 51 b.

If ever there was a child who owed his ruler gratitude, it was this child, who was saved from death by an Egyptian princess and raised in the royal palace of Egypt. Yet Moses kills an Egyptian, violating the laws of the Egyptian state, and then, with the threat of execution over his head, does precisely that which Socrates declares to be the epitome of injustice: Faced with the accusation of a crime that he has *really* committed, Moses will submit to neither trial nor punishment, rejecting outright the state's jurisdiction over him. And much the same can be said of other heroic figures of the Hebrew Scriptures, virtually all of whom are portrayed as being in a condition of acute conflict with the rulers of the nations in which they live, and as disobeying their laws and commands almost as a matter of course.[29]

Moses and other prominent biblical figures like Abraham, Ruth, and David lived outside the farmer's code of debt and obligation. They are difficult to interpret as long as we "live by" the conceptual metaphor of debt — particularly if we place God in the position of creditor and think of human beings in the position of debtors. Judaism reinterprets the creditor/debtor relationship more radically than either Buddhism or Christianity. But despite this radical reinterpretation — a reinterpretation that almost jettisons the metaphor of debt — debt remains an unspoken metaphor behind Israel's covenant with God.

Islam and Debt

Islam's employment of debt as a conceptual metaphor is less obvious. Clearly, Islam disagrees with Buddhism, Hinduism, and Christianity's assumption that human beings are in debt from birth. In Islam, if a person is in debt to God, that person has acquired this debt in his or her lifetime. Islamic law — the straight path — tells us how to stay out of debt, and, because God is merciful, Islam proclaims that God will forgive our debts if we repent and acknowledge God as supreme.

29. Hazony, *The Philosophy of Hebrew Scripture*, p. 132. This quotation demonstrates that Hellenistic philosophy — at least Plato — is subject to the conceptual metaphor of debt. As a matter of fact, Socrates (and Plato) appear incapable of emancipating themselves from debt. Like modern Hindus, Buddhists, and Christians, Socrates believes he is in debt to his state from birth, and that he owes it everything. Moses did not make this error in judgment.

Like Judaism and Buddhism, Islam was formed in opposition to a dominant culture and its religions. The prosperous and powerful people of Mecca generally opposed the Prophet Mohammad (570-632). His monotheistic message did not simply challenge the polytheistic religions of Arabia. It also challenged the economically powerful. Mohammad threatened the economic, social, and political advantages of the rich and defended the rights of the poor. His message denounced false contracts, usury, and the exploitation of widows and orphans. He defended the rights of the poor and oppressed. He preached that the rich had an obligation to the poor.[30] While Islam did not jettison the metaphor of debt, Islam tried to alleviate many of the dire personal and social consequences that often accompany the creditor/debtor relationship.

While Islam rejects the idea that we are in debt from birth, it never ceases to remind us that we are responsible for the debts we incur in our lives. Islamic law provides a way to avoid such debt to God and obtain salvation. God in his mercy provides the law *(sharia)* which is grounded in the following: the Qur'an; the life of the Prophet Mohammad; the consensus of the community; and, when the problem is not directly addressed by these sources, the reasoning of Islamic theologians. The centerpiece of Islamic law is the five pillars of Islam: the Profession of Faith; Prayer *(salat);* Almsgiving *(zakat);* the Ramadan Fast; and the Pilgrimage to Mecca *(Hajj).*[31]

Since it is our current purpose to discuss the relationship between contemporary religions and debt, it is not necessary to go into important elements concerning Islamic law. However, it is quite important to mention that the literal meaning of the word *sharia* (translated as Islamic law) is "the road to the watering hole."[32] This could be the most vital and vibrant image of salvation that a desert people could conceive! It implies two things. It says that a merciful God offers a straight path to life and salvation, and it warns that deviation from that path courts death. Remaining on this path is what we owe God *and ourselves.* Deviation from the path requires repentance, but not all deviation is fatal. For, in the end, God's justice and mercy will prevail if we acknowledge God's oneness and supremacy by following Islamic law.

30. John L. Esposito, *Islam: The Straight Path* (New York: Oxford University Press, 1988), p. 10.

31. Esposito, *Islam,* pp. 75-89.

32. Esposito, *Islam,* p. 79.

In some way all modern religions tried to emancipate themselves from their bondage to Economics' creditor/debtor relationship by trying to demythologize the ancient religions that they challenged. They never completed this task because they never completely jettisoned the conceptual metaphor of debt. Since debt remains the conceptual metaphor behind all the religions of all civilizations, Economics — the creator of debt as a metaphor we live by — is the primal religion behind all of civilization's religions. If modern religions are to continue the demythologizing task they themselves began, their critiques must now extend to the conceptual metaphor of debt itself.

CHAPTER 8

Beyond Our Current Religious Configurations

The first step in any new area of theory development is always antimythic: things and events must be stripped of their previous mythic significance before they can be subjected to what we call "objective" theoretic analysis.

Merlin Donald, *Origins of the Modern Mind*[1]

Many believe that human culture passes through certain stages. Medieval mystic Joachim of Fiore (1135-1202) believed human culture was divided into three epochs he called the Church of the Father (Israel), the Church of the Son (the hierarchical church), and the coming Church of the Holy Spirit. Socialist philosopher Auguste Comte (1798-1857) believed human culture has passed through three stages he called the theological, the metaphysical, and the positive scientific. More recently Merlin Donald has proposed the mimetic, the mythic, and the theoretic as three stages of human culture. Donald's stages are an important introduction to the following discussion.

Humanity itself emerges with the mimetic stage. Here human beings pushed their ability to mimic — an ability our species shares with other primates and with birds like parrots and mocking birds — to another level when we consciously and intentionally used mimicry to communicate. This prelinguistic form of communication may have involved imitating

---

1. Merlin Donald, *Origins of the Modern Mind: Three Stages in the Evolution of Culture and Cognition* (Cambridge, MA: Harvard University Press, 1991), p. 275.

the animal that hunters were hunting in order to communicate its presence and location to others, or mimicry may have been a precursor to rituals that acted out a successful hunt before the actual hunt took place.

The mythic stage evolves with the advent of language. Language allowed us to create myths and other narratives that integrated our knowledge. This ability transformed humanity. In the mimetic stage, human beings probably experienced life as one unrelated event after another. People living within the mimetic stage might see an animal in one place one day and in another place another day. But they would not be able to understand the relationship between these two events. Myths allowed us to synthesize these heretofore disconnected, time-bound snippets of information through a story that connected one event to another.[2] The final stage (so far) Donald calls the theoretic.

The fundamental difference between mythic and theoretic cultures resides in the way information is stored. In mythic culture information is stored in the human mind using stories, poems, and rituals that are practiced and memorized. Homer's *Iliad* and *Odyssey* originated in mythic culture. These were epic poems designed to be memorized, recited, and perhaps enacted. Initially they were not written. They were stored in the minds of human beings. In theoretic culture, knowledge is not stored in human memory.

> Modern religions like Judaism and Buddhism actually began the process of demythologization. This process is essential to the emergence of theoretic culture — the last stage (so far) of human cultural evolution.

Instead, human knowledge is "offloaded" from human memory to writing, art, film, computers, and other media. This cultural change has a tremendous influence on education. Since mythic culture relied on human memory, mythic education concerned memorization. In theoretic culture we normally are not taught to memorize. We are taught to master certain skills like reading, how to access the Internet or use cell phones. Skills such as these enable us to access our "offloaded" information. Something quite new has happened. The difference is in the hardware.

2. Donald, *Origins of the Modern Mind*, p. 275.

"Whereas the first two transitions were dependent upon new *biological* hardware, the third transition was dependent on an equivalent change in *technological* hardware, specifically, on external memory devices."[3]

Since human memory is no longer where the vast majority of information is stored, and since anyone with a code (like the ability to read or to use a computer) can retrieve information, knowledge is now external to the human mind. Accordingly, knowledge is objective rather than subjective. This is very important because one level of potential disagreement — our different subjective memories — is eliminated by the external document. If two people agree to discuss a particular document, for example, they do not have to argue about what is factual. The document is the objective reality they are discussing. To be sure, their interpretations may widely differ, but as long as they discuss the same document, they are dealing with the same object of inquiry.

The objective, external, and somewhat communal knowledge that is fundamental to theoretic culture undermines mythic dependence on memory alone. Since theoretic culture relies on material external to an individual's subjective mind, the way is open to abandon myth as the way we integrate, retrieve, and discuss information. In other words, the cultural evolution from mythic to theoretic involves the *demythologization* of mythic culture. "In fact, the meaning of 'objectivity' is precisely this: a process of demythologization. . . . Nothing illustrates the transition from mythic to theoretic culture better than this agonizing process of demythologization, which is still going on, thousands of years after it began. The switch from a predominantly narrative mode of thought to a predominantly analytic or theoretic mode apparently requires a wrenching cultural transformation."[4] *What everyone forgets is that our modern religions began the "wrenching transformation" of culture known as demy-*

---

3. Donald, *Origins of the Modern Mind*, p. 274. Author's emphases. Robert N. Bellah, *Religion in Human Evolution: From the Paleolithic to the Axial Age* (Cambridge, MA: Belknap Press of Harvard University Press, 2011), relies heavily on Donald's work. Specifically Bellah notes that religion can be divided into the archaic and the axial. Archaic religions are grounded in the mythological stage of human culture. Here alternatives to the dominant religion are unthinkable — that is, alternatives rarely come to mind. In contrast, axial religions are a product of the theoretic stage in human evolution. They are religions of books and written words. As such, they are more objective in the sense that referring to the written word allows a person to question the dominant religious interpretations. A new, demythologizing process begins here — a process we owe to the modern, axial religions like Judaism and Buddhism.

4. Donald, *Origins of the Modern Mind*, p. 275.

thologization.[5] While Judaism, Buddhism, Christianity, and Islam never completely purged themselves of myth, these modern religions in fact inaugurated the process of demythologization so essential to the emergence and progress of theoretic culture.

The fundamental difference between the religions of ancient empires and our modern religions is that the ancient religions were founded on myth. Their foundation narratives are stories about gods and power struggles between the gods that occurred before time began. In the case of the Babylonians, for example, these power struggles culminated when their God, Marduk, killed Tiamat. Victory achieved, Marduk then created the Babylonian peoples and established them at the center of the cosmos to worship and serve Marduk. Thus, Babylon was not established in common time. Common time began when the cosmos was created and the Babylonians were established at its center. Since their existence coincided with the creation of common time, there was never a time when the Babylonians did not exist (at least according to their foundation myth). While modern religions still *contain* myths, their foundation narratives are not myths. *All modern religions are acutely aware of the fact that there was a time in history when they did not exist.* They testify to their historical origins and not their mythological origins.

Buddhism traces its origin in time to a particular historical figure, the Buddha (563-483 BCE). The Jews believe they owe their existence to a historical event called the Exodus. Christians believe that Jesus, a historical figure, rose from the dead in historical time. Islam traces its existence to the Prophet Mohammad (570-632), a particular historical person. Now one might question the historicity of the events that modern religions consider to be foundational. It is clearly possible that Jesus did not rise from the dead or the Exodus did not happen. But, since myths are stories about events that happen before historical time begins, modern religions are not founded on myth. To be sure, modern religions could be founded on false reports, but false reports are not myths.[6]

---

5. Bellah, *Religion and Human Evolution*, pp. 265-82.

6. Today we are inclined to equate a false report with a myth because we wrongly equate the word *myth* with the word *false.* We do this because we think only facts can be true, and we reason that since the myth is not factual, it is false. But truth and facticity are not exactly the same thing. Their equation can be challenged if one asks the question, "Can a work of fiction, like a novel, be true?" Did Tolstoy speak the truth in *War and Peace* or did Mark Twain speak the truth in *Huckleberry Finn*? If you think so, then you think truth encompasses more than mere facticity, and even myths, which are clearly not factual, can, in some sense,

The historical origins of modern religions enabled their early adherents to begin a process of demythologization of ancient religions. In Donald's terms, modern religions may have started the transition from mythic to theoretic culture. Medicine, space exploration, history, physics, etcetera are now all part of the demythologizing process, but these disciplines owe a debt to our modern, "axial" religions that began this demythologization process.

Demythologization persists within all modern religions to this day. In the mid-twentieth century, Christian theologians were engaged in a debate concerning the demythologization of Christianity. Led by Rudolf Bultmann (1885-1976), some Christians thought that Christianity demands to be demythologized for the simple reason that its mythological character *obscures* the meaning of Jesus, his message, and his teaching.[7] In other words, it was Bultmann's belief that demythologization, rather than being a rejection of Christianity, was actually an enhancement of Christianity. Today, some Christian theologians agree. Many do not.

Economics has much less specific talk of demythologization. Economists do not quite believe that Economics contains myths, but, as has been repeatedly stated, this is not exactly true. If myths are stories that happen before common time that explain events inside common time, then the barter myth is one example of Economic myth. This myth is learned by nearly everyone in our society. Even without formal training, nearly everyone (wrongly) believes that the barter myth is an accurate, historical account of the origin of money. Moreover, as money's foundational myth, the barter myth explains many issues related to Economics in an uncritical way. This myth allows us to say that human beings "by nature" engage in exchange despite the fact that there is much historical evidence that contradicts this belief. The barter myth also transmits the belief that private property has always been in existence despite much evidence to the contrary. It permits the dubious assumption that Economic Markets have always existed and governments were a later invention. From this shaky premise, Economists are allowed to assert that government involvement in the market is unnatural and perhaps evil. The barter myth also proposes a nonfactual narration of the origin of money. Since

---

be true. Like novels and poems, myths are a particular sort of narrative. They are not the same as a historical account — which is also a certain sort of narrative. If a historical account — like the Exodus — proves to be inaccurate, this does not make it a myth. It makes it a false report.

7. Rudolf Bultmann et al., *Kerygma and Myth,* trans. Reginald H. Fuller (New York: Harper & Row, 1961), pp. 3ff.

this myth is a lens through which we understand our economic issues, the barter myth is a source of much economic error. It must be demythologized — as was attempted in the account of the origin of money in Chapter 5 — for economics to even begin to study some important topics.

Generally speaking, Economists mistake their myths for scientific fact because they do not even remotely entertain the notion that Economics functions as a religion in our culture. In this respect, the religion called Economics is more like the religions of ancient empires. In great empires like Egypt and Babylon, the religious leaders, through wise use of ritual and myth, made opposition to their religious worldviews unthinkable. This means that alternatives to the dominant order were unlikely to even cross someone's mind. Today, Economic priests — as described in Chapter 3 — fulfill the same archaic function. They too make alternatives to the Economic worldview unthinkable. Through ritual and myth they make Economic pronouncements synonymous with reason itself. At the very least, demythologizing means that if facts (scientific or historical) are discovered that are inconsistent with the narratives that integrate our knowledge, these narratives must be adjusted or abandoned.

Demythologization from a Socialist Perspective: Karl Marx

There have been a few economists who recognized the existence of myth and ideology in their discipline. In fact, Karl Marx may have been the first to expose Economic myth and the Economic ideologies based upon myth (at least in the theories of others). The myth of private property is one myth Marx demythologized. In the process, Marx disclosed some important features of demythologization.

> Karl Marx demonstrates two important features of the process of demythologization. First, recognize myth as myth. Second, construct an alternative narrative based on historical and scientific facts — a narrative that reinterprets the phenomenon in question.

The myth of private property had a number of adherents in Marx's day. As all myths do, it begins before common time when two sorts of people existed. One was diligent, intelligent, and frugal. The other was frivolous, lazy, and undisciplined. The first group accumulated wealth. Their counterparts squandered their resources until they had nothing to sell except their labor. From this group descended the poor working majority. From the descendants of the frugal came the wealthy ones, who, ironically, may have stopped working and saving long ago. Just as Christians believe that the human race must now live with the permanent consequences of Adam and Eve's original sin, the myth of private property asserts that the entire human race is now bound to the decisions of their predecessors. No matter how hard the poor now work, they are unlikely to reverse the curse of their slothful predecessors. Likewise, the rich live off of the good judgment of their predecessors even though they may now be far less intelligent and diligent than the poor with whom they share the planet.

In response to this myth, Karl Marx wrote, "Such insipid childishness is every day preached to us in defense of property. M. Thiers, for example, still repeats it with all the solemnity of a statesman to the French people.... But as soon as the question of property is at stake, it becomes a sacred duty to proclaim the standpoint of the nursery tale as one thing fit for all age-groups and all stages of development."[8]

This myth of private property's origin provides a preconceived and uncritical solution to what might be a rather troubling discovery of the actual origin of private property. This myth allows us to believe that the rich are not responsible for the plight of the poor, and poverty itself is not a consequence of our Economic system in any way. The blame for poverty resides in the bad decisions of the predecessors of the poor. Although their predecessors are long ago dead, the poor still must live with the dire consequences of these primal acts, and there is nothing anyone can do about this sorry state of affairs. As is true of all myths, our uncritical acceptance prevents people from discovering the true nature of private property's origin. Only when myth is recognized to be myth can demythologization begin.

After a myth is recognized to actually be a myth, the next step is to construct an alternative narrative that explains the phenomenon (in this case private property) using and interpreting facts that are available to everyone. This is important because myths, in fact, provide an important function. They provide a way to understand reality. Without an integrative narrative of some sort, reality appears meaningless. In other words,

8. Karl Marx, *Capital: A Critique of Political Economy*, vol. 1, trans. Ben Fowkes (New York: Penguin Group, 1990), pp. 873, 874.

demythologization recognizes that integrative narratives are still necessary, but these narratives should not be about an event occurring outside common time. In part 8 of *Capital* (vol. 1), Karl Marx provides one alternative narrative to the myth of private property, and in the process discloses how an alternative, nonmythological narrative can be developed.

Whereas the myth of private property relied on an unhistorical fantasy world where human beings were divided into the diligent and the lazy, Marx contended that private property is a consequence of the notorious historical *facts* of conquest, enslavement, robbery, and murder. In short, force plays the greatest role in the origin of private property. Marx traces this use of force from the expropriation of agricultural lands, the movements of common lands to private property, the dislocation of peasants that creates beggars, laws against vagrancy that include the death penalty for repeat offenders, the creation of surplus labor, and colonization.[9]

In contrast to a mythological narrative, Marx's alternative narrative is based on history, contemporary facts, and government statistics. He documents certain facts and interprets them. For example, he uses English laws, statistics from government sources, and historical events that had been independently collected and archived. He then uses these facts to develop a narrative that explains private property. Clearly, there are other ways to interpret these facts, but the facts that he discusses come from the world in which he lived. Anyone can see them if they took the time, as Marx did, to look. Marx's understanding of private property is not grounded on a mythological narrative about a time different from our common time. His argument is grounded in a time that is in historical continuity with his present moment.

Demythologization from a Capitalist Perspective: Joseph Schumpeter

A year before his death in 1950, Joseph Schumpeter delivered a presidential address to the American Economic Association (AEA) that, according to one of his biographers, marked the "intellectual and professional climax" to his career.[10] This address was titled "Science and Ideology," and

---

9. Marx, *Capital,* pp. 847-940.

10. Thomas K. McCraw, *Prophet of Innovation: Joseph Schumpeter and Creative Destruction* (Cambridge, MA: Belknap Press of Harvard University Press, 2007), p. 480.

if it is correct to say that many of our ideologies are propositions derived from our myths, this address can be taken to be a bold outline of the task of demythologization from the perspective of a Capitalist economist.[11]

Schumpeter does not discuss ideology in terms of myth *per se*. He discusses ideological bias for truth claims that are a consequence of class or social affiliations. In his view there is an important distinction between the social sciences and the so-called hard sciences. In the hard sciences a proposed truth is never challenged on the basis of the class affiliation or social status of the scientist, but this often happens in the social sciences. A feminist might challenge the finding of a particular social scientist on the basis of ideological biases the social scientist has because he is male. A Communist might challenge a finding of an anthropologist because he is a member of the bourgeoisie. In any case, the ideological bias to which Schumpeter referred in this address concerned how the objectivity of a finding can be undermined by an investigator who unknowingly allows his or her unexamined biases to undermine research findings.[12] But he adds:

> *Ideologies are not simply lies;* they are truthful statements about what a man thinks he sees. Just as a medieval knight saw himself as he wished to see himself and just as the modern bureaucrat does the same and just as both failed to see whatever may be adduced against their seeing themselves as the defenders of the weak and innocent and the sponsors of the Common Good, so every other social group develops a protective ideology which is nothing if not sincere. *Ex hypothesi* we are not aware of our rationalizations — how then is it possible to recognize and to guard against them?[13]

The issue Schumpeter addresses is how it is possible to recognize our ideological biases when, by definition, we are always unaware of these biases. In his subsequent discussion of three famous economists, Adam Smith,

11. Joseph A. Schumpeter, "Science and Ideology," reprinted from *The American Economic Review* (March 1949): 345-59, in *Essays on Entrepreneurs, Innovation, Business Cycles and the Evolution of Capitalism,* ed. Richard V. Clemence (New Brunswick, NJ: Transaction Publishers, 1989, 2008), pp. 272-86.

12. Schumpeter, "Science and Ideology," pp. 274-76.

13. Schumpeter, "Science and Ideology," p. 276, Schumpeter's emphases. From the perspective of several decades after this address, we glimpse Schumpeter's own "male" ideology in this quotation. By definition, Schumpeter was not aware of this ideological bias.

Karl Marx, and John Maynard Keynes, Schumpeter gives his answer — an answer that advances our knowledge of the process of demythologization.

Adam Smith demonstrates that certain ideological biases are relatively harmless. Schumpeter notes that Adam Smith was an academic who became a civil servant. He lived in Scotland and his family was somewhat educated, but his family did not belong to the business class. In Schumpeter's view this allowed Smith to understand economics in a critical manner. As he did not strongly identify with any class, he was an outside observer, and this enabled him to take a critical stance. In fact, he called landowners "slothful" and businesspersons who hire industrious people for subsistence wages a "necessary evil." Adam Smith was biased, to be sure, but his ideology actually prevented him from identifying with the classes he studied. In Schumpeter's view, this put Smith in a position to propose mechanical solutions to economic problems that were devoid of political and social assumptions.[14] Not only was Smith's ideological bias relatively benign, it enabled him to be more objective in his analysis because he had "nothing to lose" if he reached embarrassing conclusions.

Schumpeter credits Karl Marx with the actual discovery of ideology and ideological bias. Marx clearly understood the nature of ideology. But he clearly thought that ideology applied only to *other* people. He was blind to his own biases even though his biases continue to be quite clear to many. Schumpeter believed that Marx's ideological biases were the consequence of the fact that Marx did not understand himself to be an economist until the end of the 1840s. Before his serious analytic work had begun, Marx had already adopted the Hegelian notion of history. Hegel taught that history was a consequence of a struggle between two and only two opposing principles. But whereas Hegel asserted that these principles, popularly known as the thesis and the antithesis, were spiritual or intellectual principles, Marx thought they were material or economic.

For Marx, these two conflicting principles took the form of a class struggle between the haves (bourgeoisie) and the exploited have-nots (proletariat). Schumpeter thought that this belief was not a consequence of economic analysis. Instead, it was the consequence of a preexisting ideological bias into which Marx tried to fit the economic facts he discovered through his economic analysis. Marx's ideology was so "closely linked to the innermost meaning of his message" that it could not be discarded, and, since this bias provided the political impetus for Marx's

14. Schumpeter, "Science and Ideology," p. 280.

economic theories, Marx's followers could never jettison his ideological bias without, at the same time, abandoning Marxism itself.[15] Thus, despite Schumpeter's belief that Marx's economic analysis is unprecedented and his belief that Marx "discovered" ideological bias, Schumpeter maintains that Marxism is a victory of ideology over analysis.[16] While Adam Smith and Karl Marx had their own ideological biases, Smith's biases were more benign while Marx's ideological biases often had priority over the very facts that he expertly uncovered and analyzed.

While Schumpeter may have been the most well-known *living* economist when he addressed the AEA as its President in 1949, he was not the most well-known and influential economist of his generation. John Maynard Keynes, who died in 1946, still holds that honor. In fact, the vast majority of Schumpeter's audience considered themselves Keynesians. This makes Schumpeter's comments about Keynes's ideology quite interesting.

Schumpeter argued that Keynes presupposed a "static" understanding of Capitalism, and that Keynes had ideologically assumed that this static Capitalism had reached a mature, "arteriosclerotic" state. As a consequence, Keynes thought that the role of the economist was to prolong the life of this declining system. This was Keynes's ideological downfall, and it captured all subsequent Keynesians. For Schumpeter, innovation and change were the essence of Capitalism, and business cycles of boom and decline were the consequence of Capitalist innovation. Moreover, these recurring cycles indicate that Capitalism is anything but mature and "arteriosclerotic." These cycles display a dynamism through which rich and poor alike benefit. (Schumpeter is quick to point out, the rich benefit much more than the poor.) While this dynamic system of "creative destruction" always has its victims, the business cycle has, in Schumpeter's view, demonstrably raised the standard of living of everyone under its sway since the sixteenth century.[17]

Keynes's view had triumphed not because of the truth of Keynes's analysis of Capitalism. It triumphed because of the existential fact that

15. For example, the idea that history is composed of two conflicting classes precludes from the start the idea that the division of labor creates a variety of classes, which may or may not be opposed to each other. It also precludes the idea that the interests of the workers and the interests of the owners might, from time to time, be in accord rather than in opposition. These are in some sense facts that Marxism cannot accommodate.

16. Schumpeter, "Science and Ideology," pp. 281, 282.

17. Schumpeter, "Science and Ideology," pp. 282, 283.

the Great Depression of the 1930s was the time when Keynes published his classic *The General Theory of Employment, Interest and Money* (1936). Keynes, like nearly everyone, was captured by the ideology of his time. Just as Adam Smith had more or less used the Market Economy of eighteenth-century England as if it were universal to humanity, and just as Karl Marx thought the nineteenth-century oppression of workers would be a constant of all Capitalist enterprises, so did Keynes think that economic depression might be the norm against which an economist must struggle. Schumpeter countered Keynesian claims with the facts of history, through which Schumpeter believed he could see the dynamics of Capitalist innovation — a dynamic he described as "creative destruction." These dynamics, Schumpeter argued, would over time raise the living standard of everyone in the Capitalist system. For Schumpeter, understanding economic history is an antidote to economic ideologies that assume the current moment is static instead of one moment in the dynamic process of economic history.

> On the one hand, myth and ideology give our lives purpose and meaning. On the other hand, they undermine the growth of factual, scientific knowledge because we substitute our ideological pronouncements for facts.

The conclusion of Schumpeter's address is even more helpful to our understanding of demythologization. Here he notes that since our biases are so difficult to perceive, individuals, classes, and groups will never be able to completely escape them. What then is to be done? To this question Schumpeter gives a unique answer. *Nothing* is to be done. *Nothing* is to be done for two reasons. First, specific ideologies do not last forever. The dynamics of human discourse, in Schumpeter's view, eventually reveals an ideology to be an ideology. Its pre-rational assumptions are exposed. Clearly we have experienced this sort of dynamic in the last part of the twentieth century as feminist thinkers have exposed the ideologies of male-dominated societies, and Latinos, Africans, and American Indians have exposed the ideologies of the dominant American culture.

In recent years, however, Daron Acemoğlu and James Robinson — two proponents of Schumpeter's dynamic understanding of economics — have recognized that demythologization will not simply take care of itself.

Such intellectual dynamics require the continued existence of institutions that promote discussions necessary to eventually expose an ideology.[18] This being so, the "nothing" that Schumpeter proposes to be done probably should be expanded to include the development and maintenance of institutions that create arenas that promote the free discussions necessary to expose ideology and myth.

Finally, and of extreme importance, Schumpeter recognizes that ideology and myths are not an unequivocal evil. "It is pertinent to remember another aspect of the relation between ideology and vision. *That pre-scientific cognitive act which is the source of our ideologies is also the prerequisite of our scientific work. No new departure in any science is possible without it.* Through it we acquire new material for our scientific endeavors and something to formulate, to defend, to attack. Our stock of facts and tools grows and rejuvenates itself in the process. And so — though we proceed slowly because of our ideologies, we might not proceed at all without them."[19]

Economic ideologies are quite often rationalizations of our Economic myths and rituals. Since these rituals and myths are pre-rational, the rationalizations we make from these myths and rituals are not subject to critical reflection, and they are often confused with the mind of God. Schumpeter reveals two things about this state of affairs. On the one hand, our ideological rationalizations have undermined the growth of factual, scientific knowledge because our ideological pronouncements are substitutes for facts. Just as Galileo's (1564-1642) religious opponents famously refused to look through his telescope because their ideology already informed them that everything in the cosmos circled the earth, modern Economists refuse to observe the evidence that money first emerged as credit rather than coin because their barter myth informs them otherwise.

On the other hand, our myths and the ideologies derived from them give our lives coherence, meaning, and in Schumpeter's words, vision. Human history has demonstrated that no "new departure" in culture or science happened without myths because they enable us to envision alternatives to the current moment. For example, the coming Kingdom of God gave Christians an alternative vision of the future, and the Economic belief

---

18. Daron Acemoğlu and James Robinson, *Why Nations Fail: The Origins of Power, Prosperity and Poverty* (New York: Crown Business, 2012).

19. Schumpeter, "Science and Ideology," p. 286. My emphasis.

in progress does the same. Demythologization requires the elimination of myth to be sure, but it does not require the elimination of all narratives that give meaning and coherence to the facts we discover. Karl Marx did this when he created an alternative to the myth of the origin of property, and Schumpeter tried to do the same in his critiques of his predecessors.

Features of Demythologization

- *Recognize myth as myth.* Demythologization requires that a myth first be recognized as myth. This means that we must first know the characteristics of a myth. First, the events narrated by a myth happen outside common historical time, and second, these nonhistorical events explain phenomena that occur inside common time. As long as a myth is not acknowledged as myth, an intelligent conversation about the topics the myth addresses is precluded. Such discussion becomes possible when a myth is finally acknowledged to be a myth.

- *Humbly acknowledge that everyone, including our own individual selves, is subject to myth and ideology and, more often than not, is blissfully unaware of the fact that this is so.* If Schumpeter is correct, you and I will never know the full extent to which our myths and ideologies dominate our thoughts and actions. Moreover, it is quite unlikely that we will become aware of this fact through introspection. Someone else — likely someone from another class, sex, or culture — is far more likely to see our ideological biases than we are ourselves. Karl Marx is just one important example of this. He readily understood the ideological biases of others, but there is little evidence to suggest that he even remotely suspected that he also had such biases.

- The above implies that *demythologization is a cross-cultural, cross-sexual, and cross-class enterprise that demands listening to others — particularly those who are considered "different."* Understood in this way, demythologization requires the virtue of listening. Listening is not just the ability to repeat what was said. And it does not mean obedience. It involves making an adjustment in one's life on the basis of what someone has said. Insofar as myth and ideology are concerned, a person or group must take a challenge to ideological bias very seriously indeed, and do something about it.

- *The central feature of demythologization is that ideology and myth are no longer substitutes for facts, and when undeniable facts are opposed to our ideology, our ideology must be abandoned.*
- *It is the central ideology of our scientific worldview that the view expressed immediately above is all there is to demythologization. This view is incomplete and, in a way, quite dangerous.* Such a limited view of demythologization denies an important fact, namely, that only primitive, prelinguistic, mimetic human beings did not develop myths, and they could not relate one experience to another as a consequence. Myth changed this. Myths allowed human beings to integrate what would otherwise seem to be disjointed or unconnected experience. What is lost on our contemporary world is that myths advanced human knowledge by allowing its integration. One might call this integrative function the *epistemological advantage of myth.* We lose this epistemological advantage if we, as our scientific ideology suggests, live only with the facts that our scientific techniques discover.
- *Demythologization, therefore, must maintain the epistemological advantage of myths even as it abandons myths themselves.* On the one hand, myths undermine the growth of factual "scientific" knowledge because our myths and ideologies are substitutes for facts. On the other hand, myths are, in Schumpeter's words, a prerequisite for innovation and scientific work.[20] The question is, "How can we deny the power of myth to undermine our understanding of reality but keep the vision and imagination our myths provoke?" The work of Karl Marx is helpful here. In his critique of the Myth of Private Property, he discarded the mythological story of property's origin and developed a new narrative. This new narrative was not mythological because it used facts (as they were then available to Marx and anyone else who bothered to look). Using these facts he constructed a new, nonmythological narrative that described the origin of private property. To be sure, the facts Marx uncovered can be interpreted differently. In addition, new pertinent facts can be discovered and different narratives can be developed as a consequence of these new discoveries. Nonetheless, the story Marx told is not based on myth. Yet, Marx's narration of the origin of private property integrates the facts of our common experience and provides a

20. Schumpeter, "Science and Ideology," p. 286.

new vision that inspires further inquiry into the nature of private property.

- *Institutions that promote the sort of criticism necessary to expose myth and ideology and develop alternative narratives must be developed and maintained.* Demythologization is a conscious and dangerous process. Before the Enlightenment, anyone engaged in demythologization — people like Confucius, Buddha, Jeremiah, Socrates, and Jesus — risked life and limb. They could not count on political support because the established powers relied on myths to sanction their power. Daron Acemoğlu and James Robinson have recently argued that the Enlightenment began a process that created and preserved institutions (political, educational, economic, legal, and religious) that challenged ideologies and myths, and created narratives that are an alternative to myths as well. Such institutions can preserve the vision that is essential to scientific development and economic innovation and, at the same time, avoid the substitution of our myths and ideologies for facts. As long as these institutions are a valued part of culture, the process of demythologization will continue, but the entire enterprise will fail in cultures that refuse to give sanctuary to these vital institutions.

- *It is important to recognize that our modern religions (Buddhism and Judaism, Christianity and Islam) and philosophy (Greek and Chinese) actually began this process of demythologization.* Each questioned the mythological assumptions of their respective cultures. We have argued that all of the ancient civilizations used the creditor/debtor paradigm as their conceptual metaphor, and this metaphor received its sanction from the myths, rituals, and ideologies present in each civilization. Under the influence of Judaism, Buddhism, Confucius, and Greek philosophy, large groups of people began to collectively believe that "things need not be the way they are," and envisioned alternatives to their dominant cultures. Since the seventeenth century, the process of demythologization has become more rapid. It has grown to encompass many areas of human inquiry. Chemistry, medicine, geology, physics, astronomy, biology, and geology have largely been demythologized. But demythologization's success in these arenas should not lead to the common mistake we make when we assume that demythologization is a secular, nonreligious process. It remains a religious process to which Economics has much to contribute, particularly if Economics admits that it functions as a religion in our culture.

Summary

We must continue to develop nonmythological narratives that synthesize and interpret our experience. These narratives must be based on the facts as we currently know them. Just as Christianity must adjust itself to the geological fact that the earth is 4 billion years old, Economics must adjust its theories to the fact that the barter myth is a myth. For this to happen, of course, Economics must realize that it functions as a religion. If it does not do so, myth and ideology will dominate Economics in important but unforeseen ways.

The hope is that demythologization will move human culture to a new stage of evolution. But there is danger as well. This danger can be illustrated if we return to Lakoff and Johnson's "Argument as War" metaphor encountered in Chapter 7. War is a conceptual metaphor through which we understand the nature of all arguments. In other words, when we talk about arguments we also talk about war. The following, rather normal statements about arguments are illustrative:

> Your claims are *indefensible.*
> He *attacked every weak point* in my argument.
> His criticisms were *right on target.*
> I *demolished* his argument.
> I've never *won* an argument with him.
> If you use that *strategy,* he'll *wipe you out.*
> He *shot down* all my arguments.[21]

"Argument as War" is a conceptual metaphor because we always think about arguments in terms of war.

Lakoff and Johnson note the possibility of expressing arguments with other metaphors. Arguments could be viewed like a dance instead of a war. Participants could be seen as performing an aesthetically pleasing event where their disagreement moves them to different positions on the dance floor. "In such a culture, people would view arguments differently, experience them differently, carry them out differently, and talk about them differently. But we would probably not view them as arguing at all:

---

21. George Lakoff and Mark Johnson, *Metaphors We Live By* (Chicago: University of Chicago Press, 1980), p. 4. Authors' emphases.

they would simply be doing something different. It would seem strange even to call what they were doing arguing."[22]

Chapter 7 contended that debt is the conceptual metaphor behind all religions. Moreover, since debt first emerges as a way to deal with the transfer of goods and services, debt is fundamental to all post-agricultural economic systems. It is in this way that the religion called Economics has priority over all the religions that have emerged since the agricultural civilizations. Economics provides all other religions with their conceptual metaphor! Every modern religion understands salvation in terms of remission of some sort of debt.

Thus the question before us is, "Would we even recognize something to be a religion if debt did not provide its underpinnings?" Would Buddhism and Hinduism be recognizable without *karma*? Could Christianity be intelligible without our "debts" from which Jesus saves us? Is there Judaism without the covenant? What is the point of Islam if we have no obligations to God? If the metaphor of debt was "demythologized" from our religions, it might be possible to conceive of a God who requires nothing from us. But, practically speaking, would not such a God become superfluous? Would not a religion void of debt be a radical reconfiguration of religions as we now know them?

Reconfigurations produced by demythologization have already happened in modern science. The Christian seven-day creation myth had to be demythologized before geology could be established as a rational discipline. The stars and planets had to be demythologized before astronomy was possible. As long as we thought (as we in fact did think) that these celestial bodies were gods or composed of matter different from terrestrial matter, we would have astrology rather than astronomy. By the same token, alchemy became chemistry only when the ancient ideology that said that earth, air, fire, and water were the fundamental and basic elements of the terrestrial realm was eliminated. As long as we thought earth, air, fire, and water could not be broken down into more fundamental elements, it did not occur to anyone that the air we breathe might contain more basic elements like hydrogen and oxygen. Modern medicine was also a by-product of demythologization. Since it was a taboo to dissect a dead body, our understanding of anatomy was quite limited until the human body was demythologized.[23]

22. Lakoff and Johnson, *Metaphors We Live By*, p. 5. My emphasis.
23. Thomas S. Kuhn, *The Structure of Scientific Revolutions* (Chicago: University

Wherever demythologization has occurred, we now proclaim the result to be beneficial to humanity. The same sort of benefit might await us if we complete the task of demythologization in all religions including Economics. Nonetheless, the question still remains, "Would we recognize Buddhism, Christianity, Islam, Judaism, and even Economics if debt were somehow demythologized?" We might dimly envision an answer if astrology and alchemy can be used as a guide. Demythologization enabled astronomy and chemistry to emerge, but they probably would not have emerged if astrology and alchemy had not already been in existence.

So it may be with religions. The modern religions of Buddhism and Judaism actually began the process of demythologization that has proved so beneficial to human knowledge. The Jewish prophets were among the first to say that the social order that now exists need not be the way it is, because it was established by human beings and not by a god. The Buddha had the same thing to say about Hinduism — particularly its caste system. Buddhist demythologization of the caste system meant people were not locked in to their caste "in this life" as Hinduism thought them to be. The lower castes could actually do something about their station in life by following Buddhist teachings.

In the process of their critiques, these new religions inaugurated a new age that is still unfolding. In many ways, it was a consequence of demythologization and could prove to be as profound a transition as the one from hunter-gatherers to the agricultural revolution. This transition would be to a new social arrangement that does not use debt as a fundamental component of its order. From our perspective — a perspective that cannot even be thought without employing debt as a conceptual metaphor — it is difficult to understand how Economics and other religions would look in this new configuration. But from a perspective beyond debt, our current religions might be understood as the path to a new, more vibrant future — a future perhaps envisioned by the "founders" of all modern religions.

---

of Chicago Press, 1962, 1970), is and will always be the classical expression of these facts of intellectual history. He coins the phrase "paradigm shift" to account for the fact that the origin of modern science is a consequence of a shift in the way we understand the subject matter of a given discipline. In my view, each paradigm shift is a consequence of demythologization.

Bibliography

This lists the publications that are of some importance to this project, but a mere list does not disclose their relative importance. Some indication of relative importance can be gained by noting the number of citations given within the text itself. In that category David Graeber's *Debt: The First 5000 Years* wins hands down. The book introduced me to three important ideas: The Barter Myth, the idea that religions all deal with debt in some way, and, following Geoffrey Ingham's book *The Nature of Money,* the fact that our understanding of money has important social consequences. Robert Nelson's *Economics as Religion: From Samuelson to Chicago and Beyond* was also frequently employed. It provided tremendous insight into the "theological" debates that occur within Economics.

Other influential authors are not cited as often, but provide profound insights that shaped the direction of this study. George Lindbeck's book *The Nature of Doctrine* influences the understanding of religion used here. His cultural/linguistic approach to religious doctrine says that theology and doctrine are derived from the rituals, myths, and everyday practices of a religion. In his book *Personal Knowledge,* Michael Polanyi's insistence that all articulated knowledge depends on a tacit, unspoken dimension — like the unspoken elements or religious ritual that influence theology — also has had a profound epistemological influence on this study, although, like Lindbeck, Polanyi is not cited very much.

Neil Postman's work, particularly *Technopoly,* demonstrates to my satisfaction that technology is never neutral. A given technology is always biased in a particular intellectual, political, social, and institutional manner. Daniel Quinn's many writings drove home the point that the agricultural revolution was a profound technological watershed. After the agricultural revolution things were so different that we cannot use the same words to describe what happened before and what happened later. Quinn's writings set me on a path to discover that things like morality, religion, the creditor/debtor relationship, money, etcetera were a consequence of a path begun when we first turned food into a commodity, or as Quinn says, when we first placed food "under lock and key."

Acemoğlu, Daron, and James A. Robinson, *Why Nations Fail: The Origins of Power, Prosperity and Poverty.* New York: Crown Business, 2012.

Ahlstrom, Sidney E. *A Religious History of the American People.* Vol. 2. Garden City, NY: Image Books, 1975.

Ali, Mir Ahmed. *Prohibition of Usury: Islamic and Jewish Practices.* Denver: Outskirts Press, 2009.

Ames, Roger T., and Henry Rosemont, Jr. "Introduction to the Analects of Confucius." In *The Analects of Confucius.* New York: Random House, 1998.

Associated Press. "Monsanto seed case going to high court." *Washington Post,* October 6, 2012.

Bauman, Zygmunt. *Globalization: The Human Consequences.* New York: Columbia University Press, 1998.

Bellah, Robert N. *Religion in Human Evolution: From the Paleolithic to the Axial Age.* Cambridge, MA: Belknap Press of Harvard University Press, 2011.

Berardi, Franco "Bifo." *The Uprising: On Poetry and Finance.* Los Angeles: Semiotext(e), 2012.

Bernstein, Peter L. *Against the Gods: The Remarkable Story of Risk.* New York: John Wiley & Sons, 1996.

Berry, Wendell. *The Way of Ignorance.* Emeryville, CA: Shoemaker & Hoard, 2005.

Bottomore, T. B. *Karl Marx: Early Writings.* New York: McGraw-Hill, 1964.

Broch, Hermann. *The Sleepwalkers.* Translated by Willa and Edwin Muir. New York: Random House, 1996.

Bultmann, Rudolf (and five critics). *Kerygma and Myth.* New York: Harper & Row, 1961.

Carmichael, Joel. *Karl Marx: The Passionate Logician.* New York: Charles Scribner's Sons, 1967.

Clark, Tony. "Mechanisms of Corporate Rule." In *The Case Against the Global Economy and For a Turn Toward the Local,* ed. Jerry Mander and Edward Goldsmith, pp. 297-309. San Francisco: Sierra Club, 1996.

Cohan, William D. *House of Cards: A Tale of Hubris and Wretched Excess on Wall Street.* New York: Random House, 2009.

Company, Robert F. "Xunzi and Durkheim as Theorists of Ritual Practice." In *Readings in Ritual Studies,* ed. Ronald L. Grimes, pp. 86-103. Upper Saddle River, NJ: Prentice Hall, 1996.

Cooper, David E. *World Philosophies: An Historical Introduction.* Malden, MA: Blackwell, 1999.

Cooper, George. *The Origin of Financial Crises: Central Banks, Credit Bubbles and the Efficient Market Fallacy.* New York: Random House, 2008.

Copleston, Frederick, S.J. *A History of Philosophy, Volume IX: Maine de Biran to Sartre.* New York: Newman Press, 1974.

Cowen, Tyler. *Creative Destruction: How Globalization Is Changing the World's Cultures.* Princeton: Princeton University Press, 2002.

Cox, Harvey. "The Market as God." *The Atlantic Monthly,* March 1, 1999.

Cox, Judy. "An Introduction to Marx's Theory of Alienation." *International Socialism* 79 (July 1998).

Deloria, Vine, Jr. *Custer Died for Your Sins: An Indian Manifesto.* New York: Macmillan, 1969.

Descartes, René. *Discourse on Method and Meditations.* Translated by Laurence J. Lafleur. New York: Library of Liberal Arts, Bobbs-Merrill, 1960.

Donald, Merlin. *Origins of the Modern Mind: Three Stages in the Evolution of Culture and Cognition.* Cambridge, MA: Harvard University Press, 1991.

Douglas, Mary. *Purity and Danger: An Analysis of Concepts of Pollution and Taboo.* New York: Penguin, 1966.

Drinnon, Richard. *Facing West: The Metaphysics of Indian-Hating and Empire-Building.* Norman: University of Oklahoma Press, 1997.

Driver, Tom. "Transformation: The Magic of Ritual." In *Readings in Ritual Studies,* ed. Ronald L. Grimes, pp. 170-87. Upper Saddle River, NJ: Prentice Hall, 1996.

Drover, Cara. "Disney as Religion." 2010. http://religion31812.webs.com.

Dunbar, R. I. M. "Coevolution of Neocortical Size, Group Size, and Language in Humans." *Behavioral and Brain Sciences* 16, no. 4 (1993): 681-735.

Durkheim, Emile. *Les formes élémentaires de la vie religieuse.* In Emile Durkheim, *Selected Writings,* ed. Anthony Giddens, pp. 229-32. New York: Cambridge University Press, 1972.

Dussell, Enrique. *Ethics and Community.* Maryknoll, NY: Orbis Books, 1986.

Eisler, Riane. *The Real Wealth of Nations: Creating a Caring Economics.* San Francisco: Berrett-Koehler Publishers, 2007.

Eliade, Mircea. *The Sacred and the Profane: The Nature of Religion.* Trans. Willard R. Trask. New York: Harcourt, Brace & World, 1959.

Ellul, Jacques. *The Meaning of the City.* Grand Rapids: Eerdmans, 1970.

————. *The Technological Society.* Translated by John Wilkinson. New York: Vintage Books, 1964.

Ely, Richard T. *The Social Aspects of Christianity.* New York: T. Y. Crowell, 1889.

Bibliography

Esposito, John L. *Islam: The Straight Path.* New York: Oxford University Press, 1988.

Evangelical Lutheran Worship: Pew Edition. Minneapolis: Augsburg Fortress Press, 2006.

Fitzpatrick, Sheila. *Stalin's Peasants: Resistance and Survival in the Russian Village After Collectivization.* New York: Oxford University Press, 1995.

Fjellman, Stephen M. *Vinyl Leaves: Walt Disney World and America.* Boulder, CO: Westview Press, 1992.

Fowler, James. "Agenda Toward a Developmental Perspective on Faith." *Religious Education* 69 (March-April 1974): 209-19.

Fretheim, Terence E. *Exodus.* Interpretation: A Bible Commentary for Teaching and Preaching. Louisville: John Knox Press, 1991.

Galbraith, John Kenneth. *The Affluent Society.* Boston: Houghton Mifflin, 1958.

Gardella, Peter. *Domestic Religion: Work, Food, Sex and Other Commitments.* Cleveland: Pilgrim Press, 1998.

Gowdy, John. "Hunter-gatherers and the mythology of the market." In *The Cambridge Encyclopedia of Hunters and Gatherers,* ed. Richard B. Ley and Richard Daly, pp. 391-98. Cambridge: Cambridge University Press, 1999.

Graeber, David. *Debt: The First 5000 Years.* Brooklyn, NY: Melville House Publishing, 2011.

Grimes, Ronald L. *Beginnings in Ritual Studies.* 3rd edition. Waterloo, ON: Ritual Studies, 2010.

Gritsch, Eric W. *ChristianDumb: A Tongue-in-Cheek History of Christianity.* Eugene, OR: Cascade Books, 2013.

————. *A History of Lutheranism.* 2nd edition. Minneapolis: Fortress Press, 2010.

Gritsch, Eric W., and Robert Jenson. *Lutheranism: The Theological Movement and Its Confessional Writings.* Philadelphia: Fortress Press, 1976.

Gustafson, Scott. *Behind Good and Evil: How to Overcome the Death-dealing Character of Morality.* West Conshohocken, PA: Infinity Publishing, 2009.

————. *Biblical Amnesia: A Forgotten Story of Redemption, Resistance and Renewal.* West Conshohocken, PA: Infinity Publishing, 2005.

Hahn, Chris, and Keith Hart. *Economic Anthropology: History, Ethnography, Critique.* Malden, MA: Polity Press, 2011.

Halstead, Ted, and Clifford Cobb. "The Need for a New Measurement of Progress." In *The Case Against the Global Economy and For a Turn Toward the Local,* ed. Jerry Mander and Edward Goldsmith, pp. 197-206. San Francisco: Sierra Club, 1996.

Hartmann, Thom. *Unequal Protection: How Corporations Became "People" — and How You Can Fight Back.* 2nd edition. San Francisco: Berrett-Koehler Publishers, 2010.

Harvey, David. *The Enigma of Capital and the Crises of Capitalism.* New York: Oxford University Press, 2010.

Hayek, F. A. *The Counter-Revolution of Science: Studies on the Abuse of Reason.* Indianapolis: Free Press, 1979.

———. *The Road to Serfdom.* Chicago: University of Chicago Press, 2007.

Hazony, Yoram. *The Philosophy of Hebrew Scripture.* New York: Cambridge University Press, 2012.

Hiaasen, Carl. *Team Rodent: How Disney Devours the World.* New York: Random House, 1998.

Ho, Karen, *Liquidated: An Ethnography of Wall Street.* Durham, NC: Duke University Press, 2009.

Humphrey, Caroline. "Barter and Economic Disintegration." *Man* 20 (1985): 48-72.

Humphrey, Caroline, and Stephen Hugh-Jones, eds. *Barter Exchange and Value: An Anthropological Approach.* Cambridge: Cambridge University Press, 1992.

Ingold, Tim. "On the social relations of the hunter-gatherer band." In *The Cambridge Encyclopedia of Hunters and Gatherers,* ed. Richard B. Ley and Richard Daly, pp. 399-410. Cambridge: Cambridge University Press, 1999.

Ingham, Geoffrey. *The Nature of Money.* Cambridge: Polity Press, 2004.

Jaspers, Karl. *The Origin and Goal of History.* London: Routledge & Kegan Paul, 1953.

Jenson, Robert W. *Visible Words: The Interpretation and Practice of the Sacraments.* Philadelphia: Fortress Press, 1978.

Juergensmeyer, Mark. *Terror in the Mind of God: The Global Rise of Religious Violence.* Berkeley: University of California Press, 2000.

Kebbede, Germa. *The State and Development in Ethiopia.* Englewood, NJ: Humanities Press, 1992.

Key, Wilson Bryan. *Subliminal Seduction.* New York: Signet, 1974.

———. *The Clam-Plate Orgy and Other Subliminal Techniques for Manipulating Your Behavior.* New York: Signet, 1980.

Keynes, John Maynard. *The General Theory of Employment, Interest and Money.* Lexington, KY: BN Publishing, 2008.

Khor, Martin. "Global Economy and the Third World." In *The Case Against the Global Economy and For a Turn Toward the Local,* ed. Jerry Mander and Edward Goldsmith, pp. 47-60. San Francisco: Sierra Club, 1996.

Kindleberger, Charles P., and Robert Aliber. *Manias, Panics and Crashes: A History of Financial Crises.* 5th edition. Hoboken, NJ: John Wiley & Sons, 2005.

Kimbrell, Andrew. "BIOCOLONIZATION: The Patenting of Life and the Global Market in Body Parts." In *The Case Against the Global Economy and For a*

Turn Toward the Local, ed. Jerry Mander and Edward Goldsmith, 131-45. San Francisco: Sierra Club, 1996.

Kohlberg, Lawrence. *Essays on Moral Development.* Vol. 1. New York. Harper & Row, 1981.

Korten, David C. *Agenda for a New Economy.* San Francisco: Berrett-Koehler Publishers, 2009.

———. "The Failures of Bretton Woods." In *The Case Against the Global Economy and For a Turn Toward the Local,* ed. Jerry Mander and Edward Goldsmith, pp. 20-30. San Francisco: Sierra Club, 1996.

———. *When Corporations Rule the World.* 2nd edition. San Francisco: Berrett-Koehler Publishers, 2001.

Kuhn, Thomas S. *The Structure of Scientific Revolutions.* Chicago: University of Chicago Press, 1970.

Kurzweil, Ray. *The Age of Spiritual Machines: When Computers Exceed Human Intelligence.* New York: Penguin Putnam, 1999.

Lacey, Robert, and Danny Danziger. *The Year 1000: What Life Was Like at the Turn of the First Millennium/An Englishman's World.* Boston: Little, Brown, 1999.

Lakoff, George, and Mark Johnson. *Metaphors We Live By.* Chicago: University of Chicago Press, 1980.

Landau, Elizabeth. "How Human Genes Become Patented." *CNN Health,* May 13, 2009. CNN.com.

Lazzarato, Maurizio. *The Making of the Indebted Man.* Translated by Joshua David Jordan. Los Angeles: Semiotext(e), 2012.

Lenin, Vladimir. *The State and Revolution.* 1917. In *Essential Works of Lenin,* ed. Henry M. Christman, pp. 171-364. New York: Bantam, 1987.

———. *What Is to Be Done?* 1902. In *Essential Works of Lenin,* ed. Henry M. Christman, pp. 53-175. New York: Bantam, 1987.

Lewis, Michael. *Flash Boys: A Wall Street Revolt.* New York: W. W. Norton, 2014.

Lindbeck, George A. *The Nature of Doctrine: Religion and Theology in a Postliberal Age.* Philadelphia: Westminster Press, 1984.

Lopez, David S., Jr. *The Story of Buddhism: A Concise Guide to Its History and Teachings.* San Francisco: Harper, 2001.

Loy, David R. *Money, Sex, War, Karma: Notes for a Buddhist Revolution.* Boston: Wisdom Publications, 2008.

———. "Religion and the Market." *The Religious Consultation on Population, Reproductive Health and Ethics.* www.religiousconsultation.org/loy.htm. 1997.

———. *The Great Awakening: A Buddhist Social Theory.* Somerville, MA: Wisdom Publications, 2003.

Luther, Martin. *The Large Catechism.* In *The Book of Concord: The Confessions of the*

Evangelical Lutheran Church, ed. Theodore G. Tappert, pp. 357-462. Philadelphia: Fortress Press, 1958.

Luxemburg, Rosa. "Organizational Questions of Russian Social Democracy." 1905. In *The Rosa Luxemburg Reader,* ed. Peter Hudis and Kevin B. Anderson. New York: Monthly Review Press, 2004.

Marshall, Peter. *Demanding the Impossible: A History of Anarchism.* Oakland, CA: PM Press, 2008.

Marx, Karl. *Capital: A Critique of Political Economy.* Vol. 1. Translated by Ben Fowkes. New York: Penguin Group, 1990.

———. *The Poverty of Philosophy.* 1847. Marxist.org.

Marx, Karl, and Friedrich Engels. *The Communist Manifesto.* New York: Simon & Schuster, 1971.

Matilal, B. K. *Logic and Reality: Indian Philosophy and Contemporary Issues.* Delhi: Motilal Banarsidass, 1985.

Mauer, Bill. "Repressed futures: financial derivatives' theological unconscious." *Economy and Society* 31, no. 1 (2002): 15-36.

———. "The Anthropology of Money." *Annual Review of Anthropology* 35 (2006): 15-36.

McLean, Bethany, and Peter Elkind. *The Smartest Guys in the Room: The Amazing Rise and Scandalous Fall of Enron.* New York: Penguin Group, 2003.

Meyerhoff, Barbara G. "Death in Our Time: Construction of Self and Culture in Ritual Drama." In *Readings in Ritual Studies,* ed. Ronald L. Grimes, pp. 393-411. Upper Saddle River, NJ: Prentice Hall, 1996.

Mill, John Stuart. *On Liberty.* Library of Liberal Arts, ed. Currin V. Shields. New York: Bobbs-Merrill, 1956.

Nader, Ralph, and Lori Wallach. "GATT, NAFTA, and the Subversion of the Democratic Process." In *The Case Against the Global Economy and For a Turn Toward the Local,* ed. Jerry Mander and Edward Goldsmith, pp. 92-107. San Francisco: Sierra Club, 1996.

Nelson, Robert. *Economics as Religion: From Samuelson to Chicago and Beyond.* University Park: Penn State Press, 2001, 2006.

———. *The New Holy Wars: Economic Religion vs. Environmental Religion in Contemporary America.* University Park: Penn State Press, 2010.

Norberg-Hodge, Helena. "The Pressure to Modernize and Globalize." In *The Case Against the Global Economy and For a Turn Toward the Local,* ed. Jerry Mander and Edward Goldsmith, pp. 34-46. San Francisco: Sierra Club, 1996.

Orrell, David. *Economyths: Ten Ways Economics Gets It Wrong.* Toronto: John Wiley & Sons, 2010.

Packard, Vance. *The Hidden Persuaders.* New York: Simon & Schuster, 1972.

Pahl, Jon. *Shopping Malls and Other Sacred Places: Putting God in Place.* Eugene, OR: Wipf & Stock, 2008.

Pastor, I., and Pietro Veronese. "Was There a Nasdaq Bubble in the Late 1990s?" *Journal of Financial Economics* 81, no. 1 (July 2006).

Pierce, Charles. *Idiot America: How Stupidity Became a Virtue in the Land of the Free.* New York: Random House, 2009.

Polanyi, Karl. *The Great Transformation: The Political and Economic Origins of Our Time.* Boston: Beacon Press, 2001.

Polanyi, Michael. *Personal Knowledge: Towards a Post-Critical Philosophy.* Chicago: University of Chicago Press, 1974.

Pollan, Michael. *Omnivore's Dilemma: A Natural History of Four Meals.* New York: Penguin Books, 2007.

Popper, Karl. *Objective Knowledge: An Evolutionary Approach.* Revised edition. Oxford: Oxford University Press, 1979.

Postman, Neil. *The Disappearance of Childhood.* New York: Vintage Books, 1994.

———. *Technopoly: The Surrender of Culture to Technology.* New York: Alfred A. Knopf, 1992.

Quinn, Daniel. *Beyond Civilization: Humanity's Next Great Adventure.* New York: Three Rivers Press, 1999.

———. *Ishmael.* New York: Bantam/Turner, 1992.

———. *My Ishmael.* New York: Bantam, 1997.

———. *The Story of B.* New York: Bantam, 1996.

Rauschenbusch, Walter. *Christianity and the Social Crisis.* New York: Macmillan, 1907.

Ritzer, George. *The McDonaldization of Society: An Investigation into the Changing Character of Contemporary Social Life.* Revised edition. Thousand Oaks, CA: Pine Forge Press, 1996.

Robbins, Richard H. *Global Problems and the Culture of Capitalism.* New York: Pearson Education, 2008.

Rodkin, Dennis. "Lawning of America: Our Quest for a Perfect Patch of Earth Is Harming the Earth." *Chicago Tribune,* July 2, 1995.

Samuelson, Paul A. *Economics.* 4th edition. New York: McGraw-Hill, 1958.

Scheidel, Walter. "The divergent evolution of coinage in eastern and western Eurasia," Version 1.0. *Princeton/Stanford Working Papers in Classics.* www.Princeton.edu/~pswpc/pdfs/scheidel/040603.pdf (2006).

Schor, Juliet. *The Overworked American: The Unexpected Decline of Leisure.* New York: HarperCollins, 1992.

Schumpeter, Joseph A. *Capitalism, Socialism and Democracy.* New York: Harper, 2008.

————. "Science and Ideology." In *Essays: On Entrepreneurs, Innovations, Business Cycles, and the Evolution of Capitalism,* ed. Richard V. Clemence, pp. 272-86. New Brunswick, NJ: Transaction Publishers, 1989, 2008.

Scott, James C. *Seeing Like a State: How Certain Schemes to Improve the Human Condition Have Failed.* New Haven: Yale University Press, 1999.

————. *The Art of Not Being Governed: An Anarchist History of Upland Southeast Asia.* New Haven: Yale University Press, 2009.

Seaford, Richard. *Money and the Early Greek Mind.* Cambridge: Cambridge University Press, 2004.

Sennett, Richard. *The Corrosion of Character: The Personal Consequences of Work in the New Capitalism.* New York: W. W. Norton, 1998.

————. *The Culture of the New Capitalism.* New Haven: Yale University Press, 2006.

Shell, Marc. *The Economy of Literature.* Baltimore: Johns Hopkins University Press, 1978.

Shiva, V. Andina, and Radha Holla-Bhar. "Piracy by Patent: The Case of the Neem Tree." In *The Case Against the Global Economy and For a Turn Toward the Local,* ed. Jerry Mander and Edward Goldstein, pp. 146-59. San Francisco: Sierra Club, 1996.

Simmel, Georg. *The Philosophy of Money.* Translated by David Frisby and Tom Bottomore. London: Routledge, 1978, 2004.

Smith, Adam. *The Wealth of Nations.* New York: Bantam, 2003.

Sorkin, Andrew Ross. *Too Big to Fail: The Inside Story of How Wall Street and Washington Fought to Save the Financial System — and Themselves.* New York: Viking Penguin, 2009.

Stewart, James B. *Den of Thieves.* New York: Simon & Schuster, 1992.

Stiglitz, Joseph E. *Freefall: America, Free Markets, and the Sinking of the World Economy.* New York: W. W. Norton, 2010.

————. *Globalization and Its Discontents.* New York: W. W. Norton, 2003.

Stiglitz, Joseph E., Amartya Sen, and Jean-Paul Fitoussi. *MIS-Measuring Our Lives: Why the GDP Doesn't Add Up. The Report by the Commission on the Measurement of Economic Performance and Social Progress.* New York: New Press, 2010.

Stiglitz, Joseph E., and John Driffill. *Economics.* New York: W. W. Norton, 2000.

Thomas, Elizabeth Marshall. *The Old Way: A Story of the First People.* New York: Picador, 2006.

Virilio, Paul. *The Administration of Fear.* With Bertrand Richard and translated by Ames Hodges. Los Angeles: Semiotext(e), 2012.

Wallendorf, Marlanie, and Eric J. Arnould. "Consumption Rituals of Thanksgiving Day." In *Readings in Ritual Studies,* ed. Ronald L. Grimes, pp. 537-51. Upper Saddle River, NJ: Prentice Hall, 1996.

Bibliography

Wasserman, Harvey. *America Born and Reborn*. New York: Collier Books, 1983.

Weatherford, Jack. *The History of Money: From Sandstone to Cyberspace*. New York: Three Rivers Press, 1997.

Wheelwright, Philip, ed. *The Presocratics*. New York: Odyssey Press, 1966.

Williams, Jay. "Genesis 3." *Interpretation: A Journal of Biblical Theology* 35, no. 3 (1981).

Wilson, Fred. "John Stuart Mill." In *Stanford Encyclopedia of Philosophy*. 2007. http://plato.stanford.edu/entries/mill/.

Winn, Peter. "Legal Ritual." In *Readings in Ritual Studies,* ed. Ronald L. Grimes, pp. 552-65. Upper Saddle River, NJ: Prentice Hall, 1996.

Wolman, David. *The End of Money: Counterfeiters, Preachers, Techies, Dreamers — And the Coming Cashless Society*. Philadelphia: Da Capo Press, 2012.

Wright, Robert. *Nonzero: The Logic of Human Destiny*. New York: Vintage Books, 2001.

Yglesias, Matthew. "How getting rid of paper money could help put an end to recessions." *Washington Post,* December 18, 2011.

Zinsser, William. "Electronic Coup de Grass: The Mowing Ethic." *Life,* August 22, 1969.

Index

Abouhalima, Mahmud, 67
Acemoğlu, Daron, 198, 202
Advertising: depth approach, 17; and ritual, 15-21; subliminal techniques, 17-19; target groups, 19. *See also* Super Bowl Sunday
Agricultural revolution, 4, 112-15, 169-71; and commodification of food, 4, 5, 114, 116; institutional biases of, 113, 114; and origin of creditor/debtor relationship, 170-72; and origin of money, 115-17; and origin of morality, 4-6, 114, 115; as technological revolution, 113-17; values implicit in, 169-72. *See also* Morality; Technological revolutions
Amos (the prophet), 58, 59
Anaximander, 124, 125, 175
Anthony, Susan B., 30
Aristotle, x, 85

Banking and the creation of money, 129, 130
Barter, 34-39, 191-92; and alternative account of money's origin, 112-17; myth of, 34-38, 83, 84; as opposed to credit, 34, 35, 170-72; and undermining of economic doctrines, 37-39, 83, 84; and use by hunter-gatherers,

37. *See also* Graeber, David; Humphrey, Caroline; and Money
Beal, George, 30
Becker, Gary, 67-69
Berardi, Franco, 136
bin Laden, Osama, 67, 87
Boston Tea Party, 93
Bretton Woods, 143, 147
Broch, Hermann, 12
Brown, Hank, 146
Buddha, 173, 190
Buddhism, 121; and debt, 175-78; and demythologization, 188, 205. *See also Dharma; Karma;* and *Saṃsāra*
Bultmann, Rudolf, 191
Bushmen of the Kalahari, 36-37
Business media, 13, 15, 81
Business schools, 80-81; as seminaries, xii, 80-82; curricula of, 82-85
Butz, Earl, 154

Cain and Abel story, 182-83
Capitalism, 52; and capitalist process, 130-32; and critique of socialism, 77, 78; freedom as central value of, 53, 63, 77, 78; and human nature, 37, 39; and money as capital, 130-35; and perpetual poverty, 53-58; as religious denomination, 52, 53, 67-70. *See*

PROPERTY OF
SENECA COLLEGE
LIBRARIES
NEWNHAM CAMPUS